Critical Thinking

Julius Wambua Mbithi

Copyright © 2020 Julius Wambua Mbithi
All rights reserved.

This publication may not be reproduced, in whole or in part, by any means including photocopying or any information storage or retrieval system, without the specific and prior written permission of the publisher.

This book is sold subject to the condition that it shall not, by way of trade or otherwise, be re-sold, hired out, or otherwise circulated without the author's or publisher's prior consent in any form of binding or cover other than that in which it is published and without a similar condition including this condition being imposed on the subsequent purchaser.

First Edition: March, 2020
Published by Nsemia Inc. Publishers (www.nsemia.com)

Editor: Nsemia Inc. Publishers
Cover Design: Linda Kiboma
Layout Design: Bethsheba Nyabuto
Production Consultant: Matunda Nyanchama

Note for Librarians:
A cataloguing record for this book is available from Library and Archives Canada.

ISBN: 978-1-926906-89-8

ACKNOWLEDGEMENTS

I am grateful to Prof. Harvey Siegel, Professor of Philosophy, University of Miami, for his continued patience, support and encouragement. More so, I thank him for taking time to read, suggest corrections, make comments, advice and guide from the word go. In particular, I wish to register my appreciation and many thanks for his generous donations of books on logic and critical thinking that have proved invaluable to my research and to the Machakos University fraternity. Without his enormous support, this project would not have been realized. I will always be grateful and appreciative of his time and recommendations as I advance my scholarly work and interests in being an author. *Asante sana* for your availability!

I would also like to thank Nsemia Inc. Publishers for accepting to publish this book. In particular, I am grateful for the anonymous reviewers for the publisher, whose excellent suggestions have made this work systematic; and Dr. Matunda Nyanchama, for his kindness, efficiency, and patience in the development process of this completed work.

Table of Contents

Acknowledgements - iii

Foreword - vii

Preface - ix

CHAPTER ONE - 1

The Nature of Critical Thinking

CHAPTER TWO - 69

Some Issues Emerging from the Nature of Critical Thinking

CHAPTER THREE - 95

Some Models of Critical Thinking

CHAPTER FOUR - 143

Critical Thinking and Argument Analysis

CHAPTER FIVE - 193

Critical Thinking and Fallacies

CHAPTER SIX - 219

The Relevance of Critical Thinking

CHAPTER SEVEN - 267

Conclusion

SELECTED BIBLIOGRAPHY - 271

INDEX - 275

FOREWORD

It is hard to think of a topic more important, educationally, or richer philosophically, than critical thinking. What is it? What must a critical thinker know, and be able and disposed to do? Why is it important for students to become critical thinkers – and for educators to help them do so – and what does that involve? Answers to these questions raise many contentious philosophical issues, involving several core areas of philosophy. These include logic (what is the relationship between critical thinking and logic, both formal and informal?), epistemology (what is the relationship between critical thinking and fundamental epistemological notions such as truth, justification, rationality, and rational belief?), ethics (what are our duties to children, as far as their education is concerned? What moral constraints govern teaching in general, and teaching for critical thinking in particular?), social and political philosophy (how should educational institutions be organized, and what role should the fostering of critical thinking play in educational activities in democratic societies?), and philosophy of education (what are the legitimate aims of education, and is fostering critical thinking one of them? If so, why? Can we foster critical thinking in a way that eschews indoctrination?). These and other deep philosophical issues in turn raise a host of difficult educational questions concerning the best ways to cultivate students' critical thinking abilities, dispositions, and character. The domain is broad, and the issues are contentious and deep.

Julius Mbithi's **Critical Thinking** ably takes on all this and more. It covers a broad range of educational, logical and philosophical literature, both historical and contemporary. It treats fundamental philosophical issues as well the practical question of how best to teach for critical thinking. It explains the importance of education for critical thinking generally. As such, it is a welcome addition to the literature, serving as both textbook and scholarly monograph.

Foreword

We hope and expect that it will serve as an important tool for students and scholars alike, and welcome the appearance of this important contribution to the theory and practice of education for critical thinking.

Harvey Siegel
Department of Philosophy
University of Miami
Coral Gables, Florida, U.S.A.
January 2020

PREFACE

This book is an outgrowth of an undergraduate course developed by the author and which he has been teaching at Machakos University. The purpose of the book is to familiarize students with the questions regarding the definition, nature and foundations of critical thinking. Furthermore, it will provide them with the necessary tools to cope successfully with graduate level courses and post academic life. In addition, the book contains adequate material for postgraduate studies and research in critical thinking. Readers would appreciate that a great deal of energy has been expended by critical thinking theorists on the debate on the nature of critical thinking and thus generating provocative, interesting and important philosophical perspectives.

Chapter 1 is as an examination of the nature of critical thinking. It defines the meaning, nature, scope, value, and characteristics of a critical thinker and critical thinking. It also examines perspectives of various scholars of critical thinking in details. In this chapter, the material and the choice of topics presented are fundamentally geared to familiarizing readers, whether undergraduate or graduate, with the nature of critical thinking and with the major critical thinking theorists in the field.

Chapter 2 begins with a discussion of the issues or controversies that arise from the nature of critical thinking. These include: the definition of critical thinking; the notion of skills; the relationship between skills/abilities, dispositions and virtues; generalizable or domain-specificity of critical thinking; the role of logic and epistemology; the relationship between rationality and critical thinking; the role of context; the relationship between critical and creative thinking; and critical thinking and related concepts such high-order thinking, inquiry, problem solving and decision making. The chapter captures both the intellectual excitement and the great seriousness that surround the field of critical thinking, demonstrating that such consideration can be worthwhile.

Chapter 3 presents a brief historical overview of some models of critical thinking. It focuses on Critical Thinking Theory that finds its roots in ancient Greek philosophers, to the 16th and 17th centuries, the Age of Enlightenment and the 21st century thinkers.

Chapter 4 examines the relationship between critical thinking and argumentation. It focuses on critical thinking as including studying arguments demonstrating that the quality of argumentation is interrogated by it.

Chapter 5 is discussion of fallacies. The chapters classifies, names, explains, and gives examples of the most common kinds of reasoning mistakes and how they must be avoided.

Chapter 6 demonstrates critical thinking as an ideal in education, religion and democracy.

Chapter 7 summarizes this book indicating the next steps and suggestions.

CHAPTER ONE
THE NATURE OF CRITICAL THINKING

What is the best way to conceptualize critical thinking?[1]

There is, first, the ability to assess reasons properly. Call this the *reason assessment* component. There is, second, the willingness, desire, and the disposition to base one's actions and beliefs on reasons; that is, to *do* reason assessment and be guided by the results of such assessment. This I call *critical attitude* or *critical spirit* component of critical thinking. Both components are, I claim, essential to the proper conceptualization of critical thinking, the possession of which is necessary for the achievement of critical thinking person. They are jointly sufficient as well.[2]

1. Introduction

In this chapter, we explore the nature of critical thinking as understood by the main philosophical theorists most frequently associated with critical thinking who are: Harvey Siegel, Israel Scheffler, Robert Ennis, Mathew Lipman, John McPeck, Sharon Bailin Richard Paul and Linda Elder. In so doing, we will examine their perspectives regarding its definitions, goals, processes, methodology, characteristics, scope and the significant differences among their outlooks. Inevitably, the chapter will demonstrate that their complex views have contributed to bringing the conception of critical thinking as a comprehensive doctrine and are important sources of concepts, issues and arguments that underlie the nature of critical thinking.

1.1 *Normative Conceptualization of Critical Thinking*

The main theoreticians of critical thinking have developed different approaches to defining critical thinking that reflect their respective concerns and providing different perspectives of its nature. In this section, we will examine some of these definitions emerging from the philosophical tradition demonstrating that they emphasize qualities or standards of thought and hence normative conceptualization.

First, it is necessary to explain and elaborate the meaning of philosophical cum normative and psychological definitions of critical thinking. Critical thinking is regarded from a psychological standpoint as descriptive, that is, it describes competence in certain mental procedures. This psychological account entails certain cognitive skills focusing on mental processes. Ideally, they are purely psychological descriptions of mental processes. This descriptive account is contrasted with normative conceptualization of critical thinking.

By connoting that critical thinking is normative, it is essentially to infer that it pertains to thinking that is good: "so understood, critical thinking is a sort of good thinking, so the notion of critical thinking is fundamentally a *normative* one."[3] This point is developed and advocated further by Bailin and Siegel when they assert that:

> Critical thinking is, first and foremost, a variety of *good* thinking. As such, any adequate account of it must explain the sense in which it is good.
>
> To characterize thinking as "critical" is, accordingly, to judge that it meets relevant standards or criteria of acceptability, and thus appropriately thought as "good."[4]

From these quotations, it plausible to infer that critical thinking is connoted as good thinking, underscoring its normative character.

Some Definitions of Critical Thinking

We begin with the perspective of Harvey Siegel who advocates that a critical thinker ought to seek good reasons, that is, "to be a critical thinker is to be appropriately moved by reasons. To be a rational person is to believe and act on basis of reasons."[5] He refers to this account as the *reasons conception*, implying to be "appropriately moved by reason"[6] which entails two important but distinct aspects that contribute to good reasoning. One, to be *appropriately* moved by reason, entails skills/abilities to reason well. Two, to be appropriately *moved* by reason entails the dispositions to be moved by reason, to follow the dictates of reason:

> Critical thinking involves skills and abilities, which facilitate or make possible the appropriate assessment of reasons; it involves dispositions, habits of mind and character traits as well.[7]

We will develop these two aspects in the next section. It suffices here to assert that critical thinking as understood by Siegel is to be *appropriately moved by reason* which emphasis the role of good reasons or thinking hence normative conceptualization.

Robert Ennis in his paper, "A Concept of Critical Thinking," had earlier defined critical thinking as "the correct assessment of statements."[8] This earlier definition implied that critical thinking is a "pure skill" focusing on the skills/abilities. This definition is good but it had problems as Ennis realized in his appraisal that:

> A definition of critical thinking that I at one time endorsed is that critical thinking is the correct assessing of statements (Ennis 1962). If I had not elaborated this definition, it would be as vague as Bloom's taxonomy. But even when elaborate, it suffers from excluding creative aspects of critical thinking such as conceiving of alternatives, formulating hypotheses and definitions and developing plans for experiments. I now think the contemporary conception of critical thinking includes these things, so the "correct assessing" definition is narrower than the standard usage, and thus could interfere with communication among proponents of critical thinking.[9]

In this respect, Ennis redefined critical thinking as "a process, the goal of which is to make reasonable decisions about what to believe and what to do."[10] This implied that critical thinking is reflective and based on rationality whose objective as an event is to arrive at decisions on one's beliefs and actions.

Richard Paul and Linda Elder in their definitional attempts, came up with two levels or degrees namely, "*strong sense and weak sense*"[11] of critical thinking. This is unique to Paul and Elder, and is principal to their theory of critical thinking. Accordingly, critical thinking in the sophistic or weak sense serves the interests of a particular individual or group, to the exclusion of their relevant persons and groups while strong sense critical thinking or fair-minded is disciplined to take into account the interests of diverse persons or groups. With this distinction, it is plausible to infer that there are two degrees or levels to critical thinking according to Richard Paul and Linda Elder.

For John McPeck "the core meaning of critical thinking is the propensity and skill to engage in an activity with reflective skepticism."[12] For him, thinking critically involves predisposition, skills and reflective questioning and doubt.

For Mathew Lipman critical thinking is a "skilful, responsible thinking that facilitates judgements because it relies on criteria, is self-correcting and is sensitive to context."[13]

Sharon Bailin and Mark Battersby introduce a unique definition of critical thinking as critical inquiry. They assert that, "we use the term inquiry to refer to critical inquiry, which is the process of carefully examining an issue in order to come up with a reasoned judgment."[14] The central concept in this definition is the idea of good reasons and thus essentially normative with contextualised focus on issue, careful examination and reasoned judgement as its essential features.

From the above, it is clear that in defining critical thinking, the philosophical theorists reflect the principle idea of their accounts as normative in character. It is therefore plausible to infer that critical thinking connotes good thinking or good reasons. This normative dimension distinguishes what is critical from uncritical thinking. Such an account of critical thinking in normative terms comprises what is most central to it.

Despite differences among the theorists in their approaches to defining critical thinking, they agree that it involves skills/abilities and dispositions. We now turn our attention to skills/abilities and dispositions of critical thinking giving a detailed exposition of the two dimensions, demonstrating their essentiality as core characteristics of critical thinking and critical thinkers. This is informed by Siegel's position that it is important:

> ...to draw attention to the distinction between critical think*ing* and the critical think*er,* and to suggest that a full conception of critical thinking must provide not only criteria for assessing pieces of reasoning, but also a characterization of the attributes of the sort of person who is rightly regarded as a critical thinker.[15]

Clearly, for Siegel, habits of mind, character traits, dispositions or tendencies to think, act or believe in certain ways are not pieces of thinking but properties of rational persons.

Following Siegel, we will examine some philosophical theorists and their understanding of critical thinking as a combination of skills/abilities and dispositions as well as the characteristics of a critical thinker. Therefore, in discussing skills/abilities and dispositions, we will focus on the characteristics of a critical thinker.

1.2 The Skills/Abilities and Dispositions

The various accounts of critical thinking entail the two components, aspects, or dimensions namely: One, skills/abilities and two, dispositions, tendencies, character traits or habits of mind. Siegel captures this when he writes that:

> There are many extant accounts of critical thinking; these accounts differ from one another in a variety of ways. However, most of the main accounts, including those of Ennis, Paul, McPeck and Lipman, agree at least to this extent: critical thinking has (at least) two central components: a reason assessment component, which involves abilities and skills relevant to the proper understanding and assessment of reasons, claims and arguments; and a critical spirit component, which is understood as a complex of dispositions, attitudes, habits of mind and character traits.[16]

Elsewhere, Siegel and Bailin stress this conceptualization and characterisation of critical thinking when they write that:

> On most philosophical accounts of it, critical thinking involves two related, but conceptually distinct, aspects or dimensions: the ability to reason well and the disposition to do so."[17]

In other words, it is not sufficient to have critical thinking skills/abilities to evaluate reasons and arguments but also it is necessary for one to have the disposition to think critically, to be inclined to follow the dictates of reason. These two are central or key components of critical thinking.

In examining these two dimensions or components of critical thinking, we begin with its chief advocate, Harvey Siegel.

Harvey Siegel and the 'Reasons Conception'

One of the major philosophical conceptions or account of critical thinking has been posited by Harvey Siegel which he refers to as the "reasons conception"[18] developed in his book, "*Educating Reason*" and in his other publications clarifying that:

> There is, first, the ability to assess reasons properly. Call this the reason assessment component. There is, second, the willingness, desire, and the disposition to base one's actions and beliefs on reasons; that is, to do reason assessment and be guided by the results of such assessment. This I call critical attitude or critical spirit component of critical thinking. Both components are, I claim, essential to the proper conceptualisation of critical thinking, the possession of which is necessary for the achievement of critical thinking by a person. They are jointly sufficient as well.

Therefore, the Siegelian reasons conception account of critical thinking entails two-component namely: "reason assessment" and "critical attitude or critical spirit component." Accordingly, critical thinking involves skills/abilities as well as dispositions or character traits or habits of mind, which he refers to as reason assessment and critical spirit or attitude components respectively.

In, *reasons conception account of critical thinking*, Siegel cognizes the relationship between critical thinking and rationality when he asserts that "first and foremost, the larger conception is that of rationality: critical thinking is best thought as embodiment of the ideal of rationality."[19] He views critical thinking as not only an element of rationality but also an aspect, which co-exists with it. Critical thinking and rationality are not only correlatives or cognate terms but also intrinsically inseparable notions in the effects that flow from them. This connection between critical thinking, reasons and rationality leads us naturally to examine his reason assessment component account.

The Reason Assessment Component

For Siegel, the reason assessment component of critical thinking entails skills/abilities to evaluate reasons and arguments using logical and epistemological criteria:

> The basic idea here is simple enough: a critical thinker must be able to assess reasons and their ability to warrant beliefs, claims and actions properly. This means that the critical thinker must have a good understanding of, and the ability to utilize, principles governing the assessment of reasons.[20]

By this, he implies that a critical thinker must possess skills/abilities, necessary for evaluating reasons and arguments, that is, one must be "appropriately moved by reasons:"

> A critical thinker is one who has significant skill and ability with respect to the evaluation of reasons and arguments. For to say that one is *appropriately* moved by reasons is to say that one believes, judges and acts in accordance with the probative force with which one's reasons support one's beliefs, judgments and actions. A critical thinker must have, then, both a solid understanding of the principles of reason assessment, and significant ability to utilize that understanding in order to evaluate properly beliefs, actions, judgments, and the reasons which are thought to support them. This dimension of critical thinking may be called the *reason assessment* component of critical thinking.[21]

In addition, one must understand and be able to use the two principles governing the reason assessment component of critical thinking which he classifies as follows:

> There are at least two types of such principles: the subject–specific principles that govern the assessment of particular sorts of reasons in particular contexts; and subject-neutral, general principles which apply across a wide variety of contexts and types of reason.[22]

The implication is that the subject-specific principles are those that apply to specific-subjects or domains. The general, subject-neutral principles are relevant and applicable to various contexts, subject matters, circumstances or claims hence are not restricted to a particular discipline, subject or domain. For example, the principles of logic, both formal and informal; deductive inferences, inductive inferences and recognition of fallacies, critical thinking skills/abilities, the use of statistical and observational evidence are universal and standard principles which are general, subject-neutral skills/abilities of reason assessment applicable to all domains of knowledge or subjects. The mastery of these general, subject-neutral skills/abilities is essential for one to be a critical thinker.

The subject-specific principles are applicable to specific-subject disciplines. The skills/abilities of the reason assessment component are central and guide these specific domains in assessing reasons and their justifying, probative, or evidential force. Competency in the specific knowledge is essential for the utilisation of the specific domain skills/abilities of the reason assessment component. For example, to know the symptoms of malaria, one must be competent in the field of medicine; to know the notions of relativity, laws of motion or quanta, one must be familiar with physics; to comprehend that combustion releases phlogiston substance requires understanding of phlogiston theory of combustion in mechanical engineering; to appreciate electro-magnetic theory, one must be familiar with electrical science; to understand structural issues of buildings, one must be familiar with civil engineering, etc. These domain or subject-specific skills/abilities are not applicable in the domains of merry-go-rounds or in selling of vegetables or in cooking or preaching about African traditional religions for such attempts would amount to penetratingly into murky waters. This is the case because the justifying or evidential force or probative forces of reason are directly divergent.

Understanding and the ability to use the two principles in relation to reason is indispensable to critical thinking for neither is superior to the other. He notes that, "…both subject-specific, non-generalizable, and the subject-neutral skills, principles and information are highly relevant to reason assessment and so to critical thinking."[23] For Siegel, therefore, critical thinking manifests itself in the general, subject-neutral and subject-specific dimensions. He then affirms the indispensability of the two as principles of the reason assessment component without given unnecessary credit to any at the expense of the other. This is the logical character as manifested in reason assessment component.

In addition to its logical character, the Siegelian 'reason assessment component' is necessarily epistemological in the sense that there is the need to comprehend the universality of the nature of reasons, warrants and justifications and how these relate to the subject-specific and subject–neutral principles. Siegel puts it as follows:

> In addition to the ability to assess reasons and their warranting force (and grasp of the related governing principles), critical thinkers need also to have a theoretical grasp of the nature of reasons, warrant and justification, and so some understanding of the way a given putative reason is to be assessed as it is. That is, the reason assessment component involves *epistemology*.[24]

For Siegel, the central place of epistemology in the reason assessment component is important and hence contributes to an adequate characterisation of critical thinking:

> In order to justify a claim about something is a legitimate criterion of reason assessment, one has no choice but to appeal to epistemology–that is, to the general theory of knowledge, truth, reasons, justification and evidence.[25]

Epistemology is the criterion for justifying or evaluating reason assessment component. It provides reasons for accepting the reason assessment component as legitimate. He further writes that:

> ...–the ability to reason well–presupposes an account of the constitution of good reasons upon which the ideal must inevitably rest. How do we determine that a proposed reason for some belief, judgement, or action is a good or forceful one (or not)? What are the guidelines, criteria or principles, in accordance with which the goodness of candidate reasons is to be ascertained? What is the nature of such principles? How are they themselves justified? These questions are epistemological in nature; they call for a general account of the relationship between a putative reason and the belief, judgement, or action for which it is a reason. Such an epistemological account will have to grapple with deep questions concerning the nature of epistemic justification, the relationship between justification and truth (and so the nature of truth), the relativity (or absoluteness) of principles of reason evaluation and so forth.[26]

What in essence Siegel is underlying, is the epistemic nature of the reason assessment component of critical thinking. The reason assessment component is justified and linked to epistemology. He articulates and explains the link between critical thinking and epistemology when he writes that:

> The link is straightforward: the competent assessment of reasons is central to critical thinking; such assessment of reasons is central to critical thinking; such assessment is competent insofar as it meets relevant criteria concerning the strength of candidates reasons; and it falls to epistemology–construed broadly enough to include other loci of relevant criteria such as logic, probability theory, and the like-to

determine the status of such criteria, and thus the strength /weakness of the reasons that fall under purview. Epistemology likewise provides the general account (or meta-account, if you prefer) of all this: what is it to be a reason; the way in which good reasons provide support for the items for which there are reasons; the nature of that support; etc. Here some of the main questions of epistemology enter in: epistemic support is closely related to justification; justification is in turn closely related to rationality; both have contentious connections to truth; the character of the normativity involved in epistemic evaluation stands in need of clarification; etc. So an account of critical thinking must perforce concern itself with the meat and potatoes of epistemology. This is the link between critical thinking and epistemology.[27]

From this long quotation, we infer that since the Siegelian reasons conception entails rationality simpliciter, and in turn, rationality is indispensable to epistemology, then it is clear that critical thinking is linked to epistemology. Therefore, it is plausible to conclude that Siegel stresses on the compatibility of epistemology, and its centrality to critical thinking. This epistemology underlying critical thinking is an important and generalizable component. Further, according to him, rational belief is the essential epistemic aim such that the fostering of the reasons assessment should aim at this goal, of "rational belief,"[28] given the fact of fallibilism. Therefore, critical thinking entails not only the criteria of reason assessment but also the understanding of the nature of reasons, warrant and justifications in general. Hence, the Siegelian 'reason assessment component' is having the intellectual resources necessary for critical thinking as discussed above.

In the light of this discussions, it is clear that the reason assessment component entails skills/abilities as well as the principles of reason assessment and more so the ability to utilise them in determining the reasons that support beliefs, actions and judgments.

Siegel acknowledges that while reason assessment component is a necessary condition for critical thinking, it is not definitely a sufficient one. This is because the acquisition of intellectual resources does not necessarily translate into the using them. He, therefore, sees the need to transcend the reason assessment component, hence introduces the "critical attitude or critical spirit component" of critical thinking.

The Critical Attitude or Critical Spirit Component

According to Siegel, in addition to skills/abilities, subject-specific and the general, subject-neutral principles of reason assessment component, which are logical and epistemological in nature, there is the critical attitude or critical spirit component:

> In order to be a critical thinker, a person must have, in addition to what has been said thus far, certain attitudes, dispositions, habits of mind and character traits which together may be labelled the "critical attitude" or "critical spirit.""[29]

He further writes that:

> The "critical spirit," as I am using the term, refers to a complex of dispositions, attitudes, habits of mind, and character traits. It includes dispositions; for example the dispositions to seek reasons and evidence in making judgments and to evaluate such reasons carefully in accordance with relevant principles of reason assessment; attitude, including a respect for the importance of reasoned judgment and for truth, and a rejection of partiality, arbitrariness, special pleading, wishful thinking, and other obstacles to the proper exercise of reason assessment and reasoned judgment; habits of mind consonant with these dispositions and attitudes, such as habits of reason seeking and evaluating, of engaging in due consideration of principles of reason assessment, of subjecting proffered reasons to critical scrutiny, and of engaging in the fair-minded and non-self-interested considerations of such reasons; and character traits consonant with all this.[30]

For Siegel, critical attitude or critical spirit component entails or comprises of attitudes, dispositions, character traits and habits of mind. Accordingly, a critical thinker or rational person ought to have the disposition to value good reasoning and being inclined to seek good reasons, to assess them, and to govern beliefs, judgements and actions based on such assessment and the disposition or willingness to do so. It is clear that the critical attitude or critical spirit component entails dialoguing with the reason assessment component. It is part of critical thinking itself; it is a step in going from the reason assessment component to evaluating it.

Therefore, it is clear for Siegel that the dispositions or tendencies in addition to the skills/abilities and principles, are necessary and sufficient conditions for critical thinking and for a rational person or a critical thinker. Hence, both are vital and indispensable components of critical thinking. Hence, for Siegel, the sufficient and necessary requirements for critical thinking entail having reason assessment ability as well as the critical attitude or critical spirit, the disposition to use the ability, individually and jointly. Siegel then poses the question:

> Is the critical spirit, so conceived, generalizable? It clearly is. The valuing of good reasoning and the desire and disposition to exercise reasoned judgment is not restricted to any domain or field; nor does it differ in character or substance from field to field.[31]

Just like the skills/abilities, logic and epistemology of the reason assessment component are generalizable so too are dispositions, attitudes, character traits or habits of mind. Therefore, both components of reasons conception account of critical thinking are generalizable. This notion or aspect of generalization of critical thinking will be revisited in chapter two.

So far, we have seen the reasons conception account of critical thinking as understood by Siegel. How does this reflect in a critical thinker? Siegel's account of critical thinking provides the criteria for determining the attributes or standards that characterize a critical thinker. He raises the question: "what abilities, skills, attitudes, and traits does a critical thinker possess?"[32] He perceives a critical thinker as one who evaluates, appreciates, the importance and commanding, putative, evidential or probative force of reasons. Siegel put it as follows:

> A critical thinker is one who recognizes the importance and convicting force, of reasons. When assessing claims, evaluating procedures, or making judgements, the critical thinker seeks reasons on which to base his or her assessment, evaluation, or judgement...a critical thinker is one who can assess claims and make judgement on basis of reason and who understands and conforms to the principles governing the evaluation of the force of those reasons.[33]

A critical thinker must be able to evaluate if the provided reasons are genuine or not; if they support claims, action or judgements, if they support strongly or weakly; essentially be able to evaluate if the given reasons are good. In other words, justification is one of the criterion by which we evaluate forces of reasons, according to Siegel. This, of course, reflects Siegelian conviction that a critical thinker must possess the reason assessment component. He captures this when he asserts that "to be a critical thinker is to be appropriately moved by reasons. To be a rational person is to believe and act on the basis of reasons."[34] To be "appropriately moved by reasons" is to consciously accept and appreciate the importance of having evidential force of reason to justify beliefs, thoughts and actions in various contexts. Therefore, a critical thinker must "generate and seek out good reasons." He asserts that, "when assessing claims, making judgements, evaluating procedures, or contemplating alternative actions, the critical thinker seeks reasons on which to base her assessments, judgements, and actions."[35] He further asserts that:

> Most generally, a critical thinker must not only be *able* to assess reasons properly, in accordance with the reason assessment component, she must be *disposed* to do so as well; that is, a critical thinker must have a well-developed disposition to engage in reason assessment.[36]

There must be a willingness to follow the reason assessment component to its logical conclusion. For Siegel, in addition to the skills/abilities to think and appreciate the forces of reason, a critical thinker must have a critical attitude or critical spirit, which is regarded as the tendency or disposition to think critically. He observes that:

> A critical thinker must have a *willingness* to conform judgement to principle, not simply an ability to so conform. One who possesses critical spirit has a certain character as well as certain skills; a character which is inclined to seek reasons; which rejects partiality and arbitrariness; and which is committed to the objective evaluation of relevant evidence. A critical attitude demands not simply an ability to seek reasons, but a commitment to seek reasons; not simply an ability to judge impartially, but a willingness to so judge, even when impartial judgement is not in one's self interest. A possessor of the critical spirit is inclined to seek reasons and evidence; to demand justification; to query and investigate unsubstantiated claims.[37]

Again, the Siegelian conviction is that a critical thinker not only possesses habits of reason assessment but also has a disposition to do so. He asserts that "...the dispositions to be a critical thinker–that is, the disposition to utilize appropriate criteria in the evaluation of statements and actions, and to value belief and actions guided be reasons-is perhaps the most important "non-skill" component of critical thinking."[38] From the above, it is clear that Siegel identifies a critical thinker as a person who embraces the reason assessment as well as the critical attitude or spirit components of his reasons conception account of critical thinking.

A critical thinker further adheres to certain ethical principles such as impartiality, fairness, truth, open-mindedness, accepts criticism and objectiveness. In his book, *Educating Reason*, Siegel asserts that the person who has critical attitude or critical spirit has the skills/abilities as well as a certain character:

> A character that is inclined to seek, and to base judgment and action upon, reasons; which rejects partiality and arbitrariness; which is committed

to the objective evaluation of relevant evidence; and which values such aspects of critical thinking as intellectual honesty, justice to evidence, sympathetic and impartial considerations of interests, objectivity, and impartiality.[39]

These intellectual virtues must be informed by the reason assessment component, that is, they must be guide by rational abilities as well as the critical attitude or critical spirit.

The Siegelian perspective embraces emotions when it comes to delineating the characteristics of a critical thinker. A critical thinker has and must embrace rational passions or emotions. He confirms this when he observes that:

> The critical thinker has a rich emotional make-up of dispositions, habits of mind, values, character traits, and emotions which may be collectively referred to as the critical attitude. This attitude is a fundamental feature of the critical thinker, and a crucially important component of the reasons conception of critical thinking.[40]

Inevitably, Siegel realizes and sees the need to justify the tendency or dispositions of the critical thinker when he raises the question: *"why should critical thinkers have this tendency?" why should they have these dispositions or traits or habits of the mind?* He writes that:

> The answer, I think, is that critical thinkers should be disposed to think critically, and tend to do so, because (i.e. for the reason that) they recognize the value of critical thinking. This recognition involves the recognition of related values, such as the truth, intellectual honesty, and justice to evidence.[41]

It follows for Siegel that a critical thinker is formed and criticality becomes his identity. This is the case for him, because the combination of reason assessment component and the critical attitude or critical spirit component result to formation of identity, the identity of criticality.

Equally, important characteristic of a critical thinker for Siegel is autonomy. Siegel observes that, "the critical thinker must be autonomous,"[42] that is, free to act and judge independently of external constraint, based on his or her own reasons. An autonomous critical person is an individual who makes his or her own choices by evaluating them critically and rationally.

Therefore, a critical thinker possesses "a certain character as well as certain skills,"[43] and makes reference to "a wide variety of reasoning skills."⁴⁴ This then becomes ideal characteristics of a critical thinker.

In summary, Siegel 'reasons conception' views critical thinking as comprising of two components namely; the reason assessment which has to do with reasons, and the critical attitude or spirit which is the disposition, tendency, motivation, or inclination to implement the former. This, he emphasizes, in his book, *Rationality Redeemed?* By asserting that:

> Thus we should be *appropriately* moved by reasons: we should believe and act on the basis of proper evaluation of the probative force of reasons bearing on the relevant possibilities for belief and action. But we should be appropriately be *moved* by reasons as well: once we have examined the relative strengths and weakness of reasons relevant to possible beliefs and actions, we should believe and act accordingly.⁴⁵

Appropriately moved by reasons calls for embracing of the skills/abilities that is, the reason assessment component of critical thinking while appropriately **moved** by reasons calls for utilisation of the critical attitude or critical spirit component, that is, the dispositions, tendencies or inclination to use it. A critical thinker must conform to the two. In the light of the discussions so far, two key features of reasons conceptions account of critical thinking have emerged, namely; *appropriateness*, entailing the probative or evidential force (reason assessment) and *movement*, entailing the normative (critical spirit or attitude) nature of reason.

Siegel introduces the notion of felt reasons defining it as "…ordinary reasons whose power to move people is made obvious or manifest by the way in which reasons, are portrayed…they are a particular kind of *presentation* of reasons."⁴⁶ Felt reason help in sensitising people on the appropriateness and on the movement of reason.

The above is a substantive discussion of the Siegelian the reasons conception account of critical thinking.

Next, we look at the Israel Scheffler's account.

Israel Scheffler's Account

According to Scheffler, the fundamental concepts of critical thinking are rationality and reasonableness. He states that, "rationality is a central aspect of critical thinking…"⁴⁷ Here what is central to critical thinking as advocated by Israel Scheffler is the concept of rationality. Scheffler's rationality uses specific reasons or evidence as its content, and refers to the capability to involve oneself in a critical and open assessment of rules and principles in all areas of life.[48] In other words, rationality is "the free and critical quest for reasons."[49] Thus, at its core, rationality is the guiding force behind the pursuit of critical thinking. In addition, for him, critical thinking entails dispositions, character traits and habits of mind. He confirms this when he writes that, "...we talk of giving pupils the ability to think critically when what we want is for them to acquire the habits and norms of critical thought."[50] Emotions have been described as impediment to critical thinking, however, he stresses a positive relationship between emotion and reasons assessment. For Scheffler, rational emotions contribute to critical thinking.

We turn to Robert Ennis's conception of critical thinking.

Robert Ennis and the "FRISCO" Account

For Ennis, the conception of critical thinking as *"reasonable and reflective thinking that is focused on deciding what to believe or do,"* entails certain skills/abilities and dispositions, which facilitate thinking critically:

> This includes observing, making judgments, planning experiments, and developing ideas and alternatives. But underlying the development of the abilities to do these things are certain important critical dispositions, which are combinations of attitudes and inclinations. You might also call them virtues.[51]

We first examine his notion of skills/abilities. Critical thinking as *"reasonable and reflective thinking that is focused on deciding what to believe or do,"* involves six elements or skills/abilities namely, focus, reasons, inference, situation, clarity, and overview, which he refers to as *"FRISCO."* He writes that, "in order to provide a reminder of the big ideas, I have developed an acronym *FRISCO*, which stands for *Focus, Reasons, Inference, Situation, Clarity, and Overview*."[52] Ennis states that, "the ideas represented by these letters provide useful checklist, whether you are judging an already stated idea, or trying to develop a new one."[53] This implies that they serve as a guide or tools, which aid a critical thinker. We shall say something about these elements.

Focus, for Ennis is "to figure out the main point, issue, question or problem."[54] A critical thinker must be clear about the issue(s) or problem(s) at hand. Failure to understand and state clearly the issue(s) or problem(s) implies that one cannot proceed to make a reasoned decision. One must ask such questions as "what is the issue(s) or problem(s) or matter? What is this person up to or trying to prove? What is happening here or what is this all about? Such questions help one to know what to focus on.

Reason entails the sufficient grounds to accept or reject a position or to make a decision. He captures this when he writes that, "you must know the reason(s) offered in support of a conclusion and decide whether the reasons are acceptable before you can make a final judgement about an argument."[55] This leads to the drawing of reasonable conclusions, decisions, thinking coherently and logically. One, in essence is persuaded by the prowess of good reason(s), weighing their pro and cons and inevitably, their acceptability.

Inference seeks to justify the ground(s) or reason(s) for supporting or rejecting a conclusion of an argument. Hence, inference refers to the step in going from the reason (s) to the conclusion(s). Ennis observes that:

> Suppose that the reason were true. Would it have been sufficient to establish the conclusion? This is a different question from the question under R, "is the reason acceptable?" The question under the *I* in *FRISCO* is whether the reason, if it is acceptable, would support the conclusion, and how strongly.[56]

A critical thinker must evaluate if the reason(s) are acceptable and if they sufficiently establish or support the conclusion. It is important to note that one must not confuse the meaning of inference in this context. Here it is not used to refer or connote conclusion but as explained above.

"Reasonable and reflective thinking that is focused on deciding what to believe or do," takes place within a context or situation. He writes that:

> The situation includes the people involved and their purposes, histories, allegiances, knowledge, emotions, prejudices, group memberships, and interests. It includes the physical environment and the social environment, which in turn includes families, government, institutions, religions, employment, clubs, and neighbourhoods.[57]

The above stated contexts influence the way people think, act or judge hence significant to critical thinking.

Clarity, for Ennis, calls for preciseness and seeking clarification or proper distinction in order to avoid confusion. He writes that, "when you write and speak, it is important to be clear in what you say. If others are not clear, try to get them to be clear. Make sure you understand what they are saying."[58] This ensures that the point(s) or issue(s) or problem(s) is/are well understood without any confusion. One must ask such questions as; what do you mean? Could you be more specific? Can you clarify what you mean? Can you give an example or case? In essence, *say what you mean and mean what you say*. This is the key aspect of Socrates' philosophy, as we will demonstrate in the subsequent chapters.

Overview entails summing up to see whether all makes sense. Ennis captures this when he writes that, "the sixth element in critical thinking, overview calls for you to check what you have discovered, decided, considered, learned, and inferred."[59] It is an on-going monitoring of one's thinking activity, that is, meta-cognition.

In reference to FRISCO, he concludes by asserting that "this list of interdependent elements is not a sequence of steps; rather, it is a checklist to use to ensure that you have done the major things."[60] These elements work along with the dispositions of critical thinking according to Ennis, which we address next.

Ennis writes that, "a number of people interested in critical thinking have urged that critical thinking ability is not enough, that critical thinking dispositions are needed as well."[61] Accordingly, skills/abilities are necessary for one to be a critical thinker or a rational person but not are sufficient. For Ennis, in addition to the skills/abilities, there are critical thinking dispositions or tendencies. Hence, in deciding what to believe or do, one is helped by the use of a set of critical thinking skills/abilities as well as a set of dispositions. For Ennis therefore, there is a link between critical thinking skills/abilities and dispositions. Ennis identifies three basic dispositions as follows:

> One is the disposition to care about is "getting it right" or, more broadly, to care about coming up with the best, most unbiased answer that you feasibly can in the circumstances. Even if you develop all sorts of high-powered skills and abilities, if you do not care about this, then your prowess will probably be wasted.
>
> Another is the disposition to care to be honest and clear about what is written, thought, and said. If you do not care about getting things clear, then your thinking might well be unfocused and confused, leading nowhere.
>
> A third is the disposition to care about the worth and dignity of every person. If you do not have this care, then you might well be a dangerous person, even if you might otherwise be a good critical thinker.[62]

He then elaborates these critical thinker's dispositions as well as skills/abilities:

"In more detail, ideal critical thinkers are disposed to do the following:

1. Care that their beliefs are true and that their decisions are justified; that is, care to "get it right" to the extent possible, or at least care to do the best they can. This includes the interrelated dispositions to do the following:
   A. Seek alternative (hypotheses, explanations, conclusions, plans, sources), and be open to them.
   B. Endorse a position to the extent that, but only to the extent that, it is justified by the information available.
   C. Be well-informed.
   D. Seriously consider points of view other than their own.
2. Represent a position honestly (theirs as well as others'). This includes the disposition to do the following:
   A. Be clear about the intended meaning of what is said, written, or otherwise communicated, seeking as much precision as the situation requires.
   B. Determine, and maintain focus on, the conclusion or question.
   C. Seek and offer reasons.
   D. Take into account the total situation.
   E. Be reflectively aware of their own basic beliefs.
3. Care about the dignity and worth of every person. This includes the disposition to do the following:
   A. Discover and listen to others' views and reasons.
   B. Take into account others' feeling and level of understanding, avoiding intimidating or confusing others with their critical prowess.
   C. Be concerned about others' welfare."[63]

Robert Ennis's perspective is that a critical person should seek reasons and try to be well informed as well as that she should have a tendency or dispositions to do such things. For Ennis, then a critical person is unbiased, focused and embraces sincerity and clarity. Treating others with respect is a fundamental characteristic of a critical thinker according to Ennis. He summarizes by writing that:

> The above FRISCO elements might all seem like common sense, and in a way they are. In part, they amount to a person's being open to new ideas, caring about getting it right and being careful and well informed, trying to be honest and clear about things, and caring about the worth and dignity of others."[64]

He then asserts that basic critical thinking virtues or dispositions are linked to the six elements, that is *FRISCO*, when he puts it that:

> Actually, these dispositions are embedded in FRISCO, but it sometimes helps to make them more explicit. For example, the disposition to try to be well-informed is needed for the evaluation of the reasons. The disposition to be open-minded and to seriously consider other points of view than one's own is needed for judging the inference. However, a few of the dispositions are explicit in the FRISCO. The disposition to be clear about the meaning of the words is explicitly stated under the C. The disposition to determine and maintain the focus is explicitly stated under the F. In any case, make sure in the overview that you are exemplifying these dispositions.[65]

Ennis account of critical thinking entails skills/abilities and dispositions which are essential for one to be a critical thinker. Therefore, it is plausible to assert that for Ennis, *what to believe and what to do*, is guided by a set of critical thinking skills/abilities and dispositions.

Under FRISCO, Ennis deals with credibility of sources, observation and logic/ argumentation. In this section, we focus on the credibility of sources and observation. In chapter five, we will discuss argument analysis/logic.

Credibility of sources

A critical thinker must have good judgement regarding the credibility of sources. This is under R part of the FRISCO, which deals with determining the acceptability of reasons in judging the credibility of sources. One must judge if the sources are credible, if they are to be believed, if they are mistaken, correct or wrong. Ennis discusses eight basic criteria for credibility:

> These criteria are background experience and knowledge, lack of apparent conflict of interest, agreement with others equally qualified, reputation, established procedures, known risk to reputation, ability to give reasons, and careful habits in similar areas.[66]

A critical thinker or rational person must use skills/abilities and dispositions of critical thinking in judging the credibility of sources. Failure to do so, leads to error in reasoning such as the fallacy of inappropriate appeal to authority. In addition, such a person must distinguish between credibility and acceptability. A premise is credible if it is from a well-informed and reasonable person.

A premise is acceptable if particular person or group believe it. A critical thinker or rational person must evaluate if the given premises are credible and therefore support the conclusion in a credible manner.

Observation

Ennis provides some guidelines, reasons, or criteria for observation. He writes:

> In particular, (to give a summary in advance) they will be justified as observations roughly to the extent that they come from a credible source, are really observations (as opposed to being conclusions), are based on the use of appropriate technology, were made by a competent, careful, unbiased observer under good conditions, are directly reported by the observer, and are based on or corroborated by records of the observation.[67]

Failure to follow such criteria makes the observation suspect. In addition, when making the observation report, one must remain closer to the observation. One must avoid hearsay, gossips or rumours while making the observation report. The records must also be made at the time of observation in order to ensure accuracy. Corroboration is both a necessary and sufficient condition in making records.

The R in FRISCO assists in judging or determining the acceptability of reasons when it comes to the credibility of sources and observations.

In concluding this section, it is vital to note that Siegel criticizes Ennis perspective as wanting asserting that "Ennis list of proficiencies is extremely detailed and elaborate; he himself regards it as "perhaps overwhelming.""[68]

Next, we turn to consider the conception of critical thinking by Richard Paul and Linda Elder.

Richard Paul-Linda Elder Model of Strong Sense Critical Thinking

For Paul and Elder, critical thinking entails intellectual skills, which are classifiable into two: a weak and strong sense critical thinking.[69] Accordingly, the two senses correspond to self-centredness and fair-mindedness ends, which are completely incompatible. Hence, the main task here is to spell in length this distinction.

The weak sense critical thinking is the acquisition or mastery and the use of the skills/abilities for one's selfish gains or interests. This weak sense of critical thinking entails superficial acquisition of skills or proficiencies, which remain external to the character of the person. More specifically, it means the classroom acquired aspects of critical thinking, which are not applicable to the wider context of the society. Accordingly, this weak sense approach to critical thinking is atomistic and selfish construed as critical thinking. Hence, the weak sense critical thinking is referred to as sophistry, the skill of winning arguments.

This is rightly so, for people are more concerned with winning arguments at the expense of the truth or critical thinking in the strong sense.

The end or objective of this use of critical thinking skills/abilities or proficiencies is self-centredness. It is set of lower thinking skills, bad or fallacious thinking, one-sided approach, emotionally loaded, inconsiderate of the viewpoints or views or opinions others, in bad faith or taste, full of mischiefs, trickeries, lacks values and dispositions of critical thinking. It is self-centred critical thinking, lacking fair-mindedness and commonly practiced by preachers, lawyers and politicians.

On the contrary, since weak-sense approach to critical thinking is inadequate, Paul and Elder, advocate for strong sense critical thinking. This in itself reflects a tendency or a disposition or inclination to transcend weak sense critical thinking. It calls for the move from atomistic-sophistry conception, from pure skills/abilities to a tendency or disposition to use them and hence its end is fair-mindedness. A fair-minded thinker is not biased or prejudiced, manipulated by others or manipulates others, or selfish. In addition, a fair-minded person is ethical, responsible, respects other points of view, slow to believe, weighs evidence, regards judgments as probable, has the ability to listen to others, and follows the dictates of reason. Strong sense implies the higher order of thinking. When an individual embraces a strong sense critical thinking, then he or she is not easily manipulated, identifies and exposes weak sense thinkers.

Strong sense critical thinking needs, in addition to, fair-mindedness and higher–order thinking, learning or acquisition of some basic thinking skills/abilities or proficiencies:

The Nature of Critical Thinking

> To think critically in the strong sense requires that we develop fair-mindedness at the same time that we learn basic critical thinking skills, and thus begin to "practice" fair-mindedness in our thinking. If we do, we avoid using our skills to gain unfair advantage over others. We avoid using our thinking to get what we want at the expense of the rights and needs of others. We treat all thinking by the same high standards. We expect good reasoning from those who support us as well as those who oppose us. We subject our own reasoning to the same criteria we apply to reasoning to which we are unsympathetic. We question our own purposes, evidence, conclusions, implications, and points of view with the same vigor that we question those of others.[70]

The implication is that one should develop characteristics of strong sense critical thinker such as ability to use putative and probative forces of reasons in assessing any claims or arguments. In addition, one becomes ethical and responsible for his/her thinking.

In this respect, Paul and Elder in their conception of strong sense critical thinking, develop a framework that has three components namely; elements of thought, universal intellectual standards and the intellectual virtues. These aspects ensure fair-mindedness as opposed to self-centredness goal of critical thinking. Hence, there is an inextricable link between these components and fair-mindedness.

As a recap, fair-mindedness as opposed to self-centredness, entails adherence to intellectual standards such as fairness, clarity, preciseness, accuracy, logicalness, depth, breadth, and respecting others viewpoints, seeking and weighing evidence just but to mention a few. It further calls for rejection and condemnation of selfish goals, desires, interests, or values of friends, relatives, culture, tribe, community, nation or religion. Fair-mindedness abhors biasness and prejudices. To achieve fair-mindedness, one requires intellectual virtues or traits, elements of reasoning and intellectual standards, according to Paul and Elder.

We now explicate these aspects demonstrating how they are essential for strong sense critical thinking as fair-mindedness according to Paul and Elder. Indispensable, we will show how they reflect the skills/abilities and dispositions of critical thinking.

We begin with the intellectual virtues that a fair-minded critical thinker needs.

Intellectual Virtues or Intellectual Traits

According to Paul and Elder, there are nine essential intellectual virtues or intellectual traits. For them, strong sense critical thinking aims at the *development* of intellectual traits or virtues in the thinker, which are; *Intellectual Humility, Intellectual Courage, Intellectual Empathy, Intellectual Autonomy, Intellectual Integrity, Intellectual Perseverance, Confidence in Reason, and Fair-mindedness.* These interdependent traits guide the thinking process and the critical thinker. The opposites of the intellectual virtues are intellectual arrogance, intellectual cowardice, intellectual narrow-mindedness, intellectual conformity, intellectual hypocrisy, intellectual laziness, intellectual distrust of reason and evidence, and intellectual unfairness respectively.

We spell the intellectual virtues that facilitate fair-mindedness and strong sense critical thinking in length.

Intellectual humility entails accepting and acknowledging of the limits of one's knowledge, viewpoints, biasness, prejudices and ignorance. Further, it calls accepting the fact that one should not pretend to know if actually one does not know. This is not the same as being a coward or submissive. The contrary to intellectual humility, is intellectual arrogance, which implies failure to realize one's limits of knowledge or point of view; intellectual pretentiousness, that is, pretending to know, yet they do not know, are biased, prejudiced, boastful or full of pride. In addition, intellectual arrogance entails misconceptions, false beliefs, false knowledge, propaganda, illusions, myths, fallacies, and hasty generalizations construed as the truth. For example, prosecutors, police or teachers are always prejudiced in their line of duty for they tend to be judgmental. Such *status quo* is incompatible with fair-mindedness. Paul and Elder give reasons as why intellectual humility is important for strong sense critical thinking comprising of fair-mindedness and high-order thinking:

> Why is intellectual humility essential to higher-level thinking? In addition to helping us become fair-minded thinkers, knowledge of our ignorance can improve our thinking in a variety of ways. It can enable us to recognize the prejudices, false beliefs, and habits of mind that lead to flawed learning. Consider, for example, our tendency to accept superficial learning. Much human learning is superficial. We learn a little and think we know a lot. We get limited information and generalize hastily from it. We confuse cutesy phrases with deep insights. We uncritically accept much that we hear and read—especially when what we hear or read agrees with our intensely held beliefs or the beliefs of groups to which we belong.

Intellectual courage implies the willingness to question our beliefs, ideas, societal ideals, religion, culture, education, ideologies, belief systems, politics, commonly held truths and viewpoints. One should exercise intellectual courage in the professional as well as personal spheres. Intellectual cowardice is the opposite of intellectual courage which entails the inability to question the status quo hence protecting one's comfort zone or 'sacred' perspectives or 'do not go there' attitude.

Intellectual empathy calls for willingness to put oneself in the place of others and accepting other opposing views. Intellectual self-centredness is the opposite of intellectual empathy.

Intellectual integrity entails holding the same standards to which we hold others, that is, one should not practice or have double standards. Intellectual hypocrisy is the opposite of intellectual integrity, which entails egocentrism, inconsistencies and contradictions. It is a form of injustice or unfairness. It is 'preaching water and taking wine so to speak,' that is, acting in contradictory ways.

Intellectual perseverance is the ability to endure and not to give up due to difficulties, hardships or complexities. A critical thinker must be firm to follow rational principles, be realistic and insightful. Intellectual laziness is the opposite of intellectual perseverance, which is the tendency to give up easily and without trying.

Confidence in reason entails trust or faith in reason and avoidance of emotions or self-centred thinking. It calls for reasoning and rational analysis. Intellectual distrust of reason is the opposite of confidence in reason. According to Paul and Elder, many people live irrational lives following irrational beliefs and behaviours. They follow blind faith guided by:

1. *Faith in charismatic national leaders (think of leaders such as Hitler, able to excite millions of people and manipulate them into supporting genocide of an entire religious group).*
2. *Faith in charismatic cult leaders.*
3. *Faith in the father as the traditional head of the family (as defined by religious or social tradition).*
4. *Faith in institutional authorities (employers, "the company," police, social workers, judges, priests, evangelical preachers, and so forth).*

5. Faith in spiritual powers (such as a "holy spirit," as defined by various religious belief systems).
6. Faith in some social group, official or unofficial (faith in a gang, in the business community, in a church, in a political party, and so on).
7. Faith in a political ideology (such as communism, capitalism, Fascism).
8. Faith in intuition.
9. Faith in one's unanalyzed emotions.
10. Faith in one's gut impulses.
11. Faith in fate (some unnamed force that supposedly guides the destiny of us all).
12. Faith in social institutions (the courts, schools, charities, business communities, governments).
13. Faith in the folkways or mores of a social group or culture.
14. Faith in one's own unanalyzed experience.
15. Faith in people who have social status or position (the rich, the famous, the powerful).

Fair-minded, high-order critical thinkers must only adhere to the dictates of reason.

Intellectual autonomy, as opposed to intellectual conformity, calls for being an independent critical thinker. Such thinkers are rationally independent, question everything, have self-control, have mature and not infantile emotions. They are not passive recipient of information or beliefs; they think through problems or situations, question unjustifiable authorities as well as acknowledge reasonable authorities. Such thinkers weigh evidence, forms of thought or actions and evaluate cultures and traditions. They are open-minded thinkers who weigh the viewpoints of others and theirs. Failure to adhere to this entails intellectual conformity. Factors, which contribute to intellectual conformity due to passive acceptance, include fear of the unknown, politics, economics, religion, culture, society, social institutions, education, and peer pressure among others. Interesting society rewards those who are conformists and punishers independent thinkers such as Socrates, an aspect further developed in chapter three.

Elements of Thought or Reasoning

For Paul and Elder, critical thinking entails parts or structures or elements of thought or reasoning that help guide the reasoning process. These elements are:

> the purpose of the thinking, the question at hand, information and or facts about the question, assumptions made about the question, interpretation or inferences of the facts and data collected, theories and concepts related to the question, inclusion of other points of view and the implications.

According to Paul and Elder, these elements of thought are powerful set of tools for analyzing thinking. The following questions can be raised in relation to the set of parts or elements of thinking: Are we clear about our purpose or goal? about the problem or question at issue? about our point of view or frame of reference? about our assumptions? about the claims we are making? about the reasons or evidence upon which we are basing our claims? about our inferences and line of reasoning? about the implications and consequences that follow from our reasoning? Critical thinkers or rational persons develop skills of identifying and assessing these set of elements in their thinking and in the thinking of others by raising these questions in a clear and distinct way.

Let us elaborate further these elements:

By reasoning having a purpose, implies that thinking or reasoning is always patterned, it tries or aims at accomplish something, it has purpose, a goal, an end and therefore, it is not random about issues or problems or goals, desires, needs, and values. A critical thinker must always be conscious of his/her purpose of thinking. Such a thinker must identify authentic purposes as opposed to inauthentic ones and contradicting goals. The point of view(s) and context(s) influence our purposes, goals, objectives, needs, desires, wants and values. For example, a lecturer will have different perspectives of worldview from those of a hairdresser or a tout.

By reasoning upon some question, issue, or problem, implies the need to answer, problems that need solutions and issues to be resolved. One needs to ask the following questions: "What is the question we need to answer?" or, "What is the problem we need to solve?" or, "What is the issue we need to resolve?"

Thinking is based on set of facts, data, or experiences or information. A critical thinker must establish the credibility of the sources or information been assessed by being analytically critical in order to avoid delusion, biasness, distortion or been misled or accepting falsehoods. Information plays a crucial role in our goals, purposes, desires, aspiration, needs, values, problem solving and decision making. Critical thinkers must seek and question information, be careful with how they use it to derive conclusions. In addition, they cannot ignore information. According to Paul and Elder, critical thinkers must distinguish between inert information, activated ignorance, and activated Knowledge. Inert information implies memorised but not understood knowledge, consequently it becomes verbal rituals. For example, knowledge is power or do not pretend to know if you do not know! Activated ignorance is using false information, false ideas, illusions and misconception as if they were true and hence lacking understanding. For example, false belief that one can drive under influence of alcohol or other substances. Classical example given by Paul and Elder is Rene Descartes ignorance that animals do not feel pain and hence he interpreted their cries as noises as he performed experiments on them. Finally, activated Knowledge implies competence in knowledge. Paul and Elder note that scientific knowledge manifested in scientific methods and principles of mathematics are good examples of activated knowledge and so are:

> The basic principles of critical thinking represent activated knowledge of the parts of thinking, standards by which thinking can be assessed, and ways in which thinking can be improved. These principles can be applied again and again with the consequence that we discover further knowledge on the basis of our present knowledge and disciplined thought about new information.

Critical thinkers must evaluate information distinguishing information and fact, information and verification as well as appreciating the fact that prestige or setting in which information is asserted, or the prestige of the person or group asserting it, do not guarantee clarity, accuracy, relevance, fairness or reliability. A critical thinker must be aware that information or experience usually turns out to be at best incomplete and very often false, misleading, fictitious, and unreliable. According to Paul and Elder, he/she should be skeptical and always asks the following questions:

- *To what extent could I test the truth of this claim by direct experience?*

- *To what extent is believing this consistent with what I know to be true or have justified confidence in?*
- *How does the person who advances this claim support it?*
- *Is there a definite system or procedure for assessing claims of this sort?*
- *Does the acceptance of this information advance the vested interest of the person or group asserting it?*
- *Is the person asserting this information made uncomfortable by having it questioned?*

The attitude of skepticism and these questions are aimed at establishing credibility of sources or verifying information.

Concepts in reasoning imply the general categories or ideas used in interpreting, classifying, or grouping information in reasoning. Concepts influence one's thoughts hence it is important for a critical thinker to be able to master or figure out concepts or words. Such a critical thinker must know which words to use, the proper way to conceptualize an event, activity, situation, or emotions. Concepts can be loaded, carelessly used and therefore misleading and even lead to illegitimate or unjustifiable inferences. One must be able to decode such concepts. Indoctrination, psychological and social conditionings such as stereotypes often contribute improper use of, or distortion of concepts.

Assumption implies whatever we take for granted or presuppose as true in order to figure something else out. One must have good reasons for assumptions in order for them to be justified. Critical thinkers must be aware of the assumptions that underlie their thinking. We always make assumptions about our studies, religions, cultures, shopping, friends, parents, cars, workplace among others, which are either sound or unsound. Hence, critical thinkers must learn to question their assumptions.

By reasoning within a point of view, entails that thinking has some comprehensive focus or orientation such as a point in time (16th, 17th or 18th century), culture and religions (African, Asian, Christian or Islamic) political (Democratic, Marxist, Republican or Socialist), scientific, poetic or philosophical, gender, professional, sexual orientation, academic discipline just but to mention a few. In particular, critical thinkers have a distinctive point of view concerning themselves as champions of critical thinking. They are competent learners, listen more than speaking, are emphatic, dialogue with others, question everything and make less assertions or conclusions. Paul and Elder assert that:

> Critical thinkers share a common core of purposes with other critical thinkers, in keeping with the values of critical thinking. This fact has a variety of implications, one of the most important of which is that critical thinkers perceive explicit command of the thinking process as the key to command of behavior. Applied to the learning process, this entails that they see reading, writing, speaking, and listening as modes of skilled thinking.

By coming to conclusions or making inferences implies *taking something (which we believe we know) and figuring out something else on the basis of it* which can be accurate or inaccurate, logical or illogical, sound or unsound, justified or unjustified especially when done quickly and automatically. For example, we infer that professors are intelligent or priests are holy because of our beliefs. In other words, we make inferences and meanings about what is going on in our lives such; is someone talking to me or with me? Praising or mocking me?

Implications of reasoning, implies that which follows from our thinking either from concrete situations or the words we use or say things or what others say to us. According to Paul and Elder, there are three kinds of implications namely, possible ones, probable ones, and necessary ones. For example, the probable implications or consequences of drinking and driving is that one may cause an accident; a possible implication of beating or insulting one's employer, is that one could lose one's job. A necessary implication of not studying for exams is to fail. Paul and Elder summarize the element of implication as follows:

> In sum, as developing thinkers, we want to realize the important role of implications in human life. When we are thinking through a problem, issue, or question, we want to think through all the significant implications of the decisions we might make. We want to infer only what is being implied in specific situations. When we use language, we want to be aware of what we are implying. When others are speaking to us, either verbally or in writing, we want to figure out what they are logically implying. In every case, we want to interpret precisely the logic of what is actually going on and infer only what is truly implied, no more, no less.

We sum up by observing that as rational persons or critical thinkers concerned with developing our reasoning, we want to begin to notice the questions or issues we raise, the way we handle information and make use of concepts. Further, we should take note of the inferences we are making, the assumptions we are basing those inferences on, and the points of view about the world we are developing, and finally, the important role of implications of our reasoning to our lives. According to Paul and Elder:

> Analysis of the elements of thought is a necessary, but not a sufficient, condition of evaluation. To evaluate requires knowledge of the intellectual standards that highlight the qualities signaling strengths and weaknesses in thinking.

Next, we elaborate on the standards of reasoning as explained and understood by Paul and Elder.

Standards of Reasoning

The intellectual standards determine or assess the quality of reasoning. They include, *"clarity, accuracy, precision, relevance, depth, breadth, logic, significance and fairness."* According to Paul and Elder, a critical thinker must ask the following questions: *Am I being clear? Accurate? Precise? Relevant? Am I thinking logically? Am I dealing with a matter of significance? Is my thinking justifiable in context?* These questions facilitate command of the intellectual standards and lead to better reasoning.

The contrary of these intellectual standards is lack of clarity or being unclear or vague, inaccuracy, too general, irrelevant, superficial, narrow-minded or myopic, illogical, insignificant and unfair respectively. In order to avoid this scenario, Paul and Elder advocate that a critical thinker must raise the following questions based on the intellectual standards:

Clarity: *Could you elaborate further? Could you give me an example? Could you illustrate what you mean?*

Accuracy: *How could we check on that? How could we find out if that is true? How could we verify or test that?*

Precision: *Could you be more specific? Could you give me more details? Could you be more exact?*

Relevance: *How is this idea connected to the question? How does that bear on the issue? How does this idea relate to this other idea? How does your question relate to the issue we are dealing with? How does that relate to the problem? How does that bear on the question? How does that help us with the issue?*

Depth: *What factors make this a difficult problem? What are some of the complexities of this question? What are some of the difficulties we need to deal with?*

Breadth: *Do we need to look at this from another perspective? Do we need to consider another point of view? Do we need to look at this in other ways?*

Logic: *Does all this make sense together? Does your first paragraph fit in with your last? Does what you say follow from the evidence?*

Significance: *Is this the most important problem to consider? Is this the central idea to focus on? Which of these facts are most important?*

Fairness: *Do I have any vested interest in this issue? Am I sympathetically representing the viewpoints of others? Is my thinking justifiable in context? Are my assumptions supported by evidence? Is my purpose fair given the situation? Am I using my concepts in keeping with educated usage or am I distorting them to get what we want?*

These questions facilitate better reasoning and assessment of the eight elements discussed above. A critical thinker must apply these standards to the elements of reasoning. For example, one can ask, "am I clear, precise, accurate about the problem or question or issue? Is the information relevant, adequate, or myopic? Are the assumptions or inferences clear, accurate, precise, fair, and significant?"

In summing up this section, we note that these traits, elements and standards of reasoning are essential for critical thinking, are interdependent as the figure below demonstrates and which captures and summarizes Paul-Elder components of critical thinking:[71]

The Nature of Critical Thinking

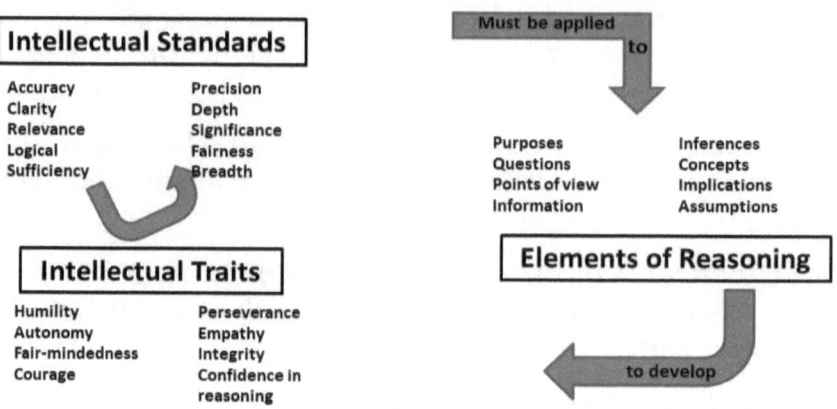

Further, Paul and Elder in their conception of critical thinking develop ideal qualities of a critical thinker. For them, weak sense critical thinkers are those: who use critical thinking skills in a sophistry manner for their vested interests; are not empathic; do not appreciate, listen to others points of view or frames of reference; those who tend to think monologically or do not espouse the values or dispositions of critical thinking.

Contrary, a critical thinker in the "strong" sense is one who is predominantly characterized by the following traits: espouses the values of critical thinking guided the elements, standards and the intellectual virtues; an ability to follow the "Socratic model of critical thinking" that is, the ability to question deeply one's own and others framework of thought; strong sense critical thinkers are not routinely blinded by their own points of view. They know that they have points of view and therefore recognize on the basis of what framework of assumptions and ideas their own thinking is based. They realize the necessity of putting their own assumptions and ideas to the test against the strongest objections that can be levelled against them.

A critical thinker in the "weak sense" means that one has learned the skills and can demonstrate them when asked to do so; a critical thinker in the "strong sense" means that one has incorporated these skills into a way of living in which one's own assumptions are re-examined and questioned as well. Accordingly, a critical thinker in the "strong sense" has a passionate drive for "clarity, accuracy, and fair-mindedness." In summary, Paul and Elder derived a list of the characteristics of a critical thinker as one who:

> Raises vital questions and problems, formulating them clearly and precisely; gathers and assesses relevant information, using abstract ideas to interpret it effectively; comes to well-reasoned conclusions and solutions, testing them against relevant criteria and standards; thinks open-mindedly within alternative systems of thought, recognizing and assessing as need be, their assumptions, implications, and practical consequences; communicates effectively with others in figuring out solutions to complex problems.[72]

It is clear that Paul and Elder emphasize the tendencies or dispositions in addition to skills/abilities in their conception of critical thinking. In essence, being a critical thinker is a matter of degree.

Next, we discuss Mathew Lipman's account of the nature critical thinking.

Mathew Lipman and the Tripartite View

We pointed out that Mathew Lipman, defines critical thinking as *"skilful, responsible thinking that facilitates judgements because it relies on criteria, is self-correcting and is sensitive to context."* Hence critical thinking entails skills, judgement, criteria, self-correcting and is sensitive to context as it characteristics. We analyze these five features of this definition.

By **judgement**, Lipman explicates that critical thinking is an applied thinking and its essential product is judgement. His articulation of judgement connotes that critical thinking relies on criteria, self-correcting and sensitiveness to context as standard of good reasoning.

He further argues that critical thinking relies on **criteria**. According to him, the meaning of criterion "is a rule or principle utilized in the making of judgement."[73] For him, critical thinking uses and is judged using criteria. He asserts that, "the fact that critical thinking relies upon criteria suggests that it is well founded, and reinforced thinking, as opposed to uncritical thinking which is amorphous, haphazard and unstructured."[74] Criteria are one of the standards in accordance with which judgements must be measured and therefore it is important to appreciate criterion-based determinations. This amounts to reasonable judgement.

Reason, for Lipman, is the basic criteria for critical thinking.

By **self-correcting** in critical thinking, he implies that it seeks to expose its own weaknesses and address what is at fault in its processes.

He asserts that critical thinkers should appreciate the **contextual**, uniqueness and particularity of thought process. Hence, the Lipmanian point of view advocates that individuals should recognize that critical thinking processes occur in a given context(s).

Lipman further presents critical thinking as the *community of inquiry*. The *community of inquiry* ensures that its members are aware of their own thinking and more so it warrants self-correcting for oneself and the others. Lipman's *community of inquiry* process is guided by the principle 'letting the argument lead,' which is engaging with critical, creative and caring as the criteria.

Finally, Lipman concludes that critical thinking is skilful thinking, making it clear that criteria are an essential aspect of critical thinking:

> Lastly, a word about the employment of criteria in critical thinking that facilitates good judgment. Critical thinking, as we know, is skillful thinking, and skills are proficient performances that satisfy relevant criteria. When we think critically, we are required to orchestrate a vast variety of cognitive skills, grouped in families such as reasoning skills, concept formation skills, inquiry skills and translation skills. Without these skills, we would be unable to draw meaning from a written text or from a conversation. Nor could we impart meaning to a conversation or to what we write. But just as, in an orchestra, there are such families as the woodwinds, the brasses and the strings, so there are these different families of cognitive skills. And just as, within each orchestral family, there are individual instruments--oboes and violas and French horns, each with its own standards of proficient performance, so there are individual cognitive skills, like deductive inference or classification, that represent particular kinds of proficient performances in accordance with relevant criteria. We are all familiar with the fact that an otherwise splendid musical performance can be ruined if so much as a single instrumentalist performs below acceptable standards. Likewise, the mobilization and perfection of the cognitive skills that go to make up critical thinking cannot neglect any of these skills without jeopardizing the process as a whole.[75]

He points out that critical thinking skills should not work in isolation but it should be 'orchestrated with other cognitive skills such as reasoning skills to derive meaning from judgement. He uses the orchestra in metaphoric sense, that is, just as there are families of instruments that are needed to produce a splendid performance, so there are families of thinking skills such as reasoning skills, deductive skills and other skills such as reading and communication skills, which make up 'good' critical thinking.

For Lipman, being a critical thinker must possess both the skills/abilities and dispositions. The latter is manifested when a critical thinker exercises the process of self-correcting and making judgment. We conclude by asserting that for him, critical thinking involves skills/abilities and dispositions. Accordingly, critical thinking is an activity of conceptual analysis and promotes dispositions.

We now explore John McPeck's conception of critical thinking as domain–specific.

John McPeck and the Domain-Specific view

John McPeck in his book, *Critical Thinking and Education,* addresses the nature of critical thinking. He affirms and embraces the view that critical thinking entails skills/abilities and dispositions when he writes that the *"core meaning of critical thinking is the propensity and skill to engage in an activity with reflective skepticism."*

McPeck then introduces and grapples with the issue, i.e. to what extent are critical thinking skills/abilities and dispositions domain-specific? He argues that general critical thinking skills/abilities that transcend specific subjects do not exist. Accordingly, critical thinking skills/abilities can only be taught in the context of a specific domain or subject. He puts it that critical thinking:

In isolation from a particular subject, the phrase "critical thinking" neither refers to nor denotes any particular skill. It follows from this that it makes no sense to talk about critical thinking as a distinct subject and that it therefore cannot profitably be taught as such. To the extent that critical thinking is not about a specific subject X, it is both conceptually and practically empty. The statement 'I teach critical thinking', simpliciter, is vacuous because there is no generalized skill properly called critical thinking.[76]

For him, critical thinking as a taught subject on its own does not exist and there are no generalizable thinking skills. In this regard, critical thinking cannot be learned in isolation from a subject or discipline or domain. Accordingly, critical thinking can and must be explained by, or reduced to, specialized knowledge or domain-specific skills, which is not generalized.

In addition, McPeck affirms that critical thinking dispositions are domain-specific *simpliciter* when he observes that:

> Since critical thinking is always "critical thinking about X," it follows that critical thinking is intimately connected with other fields of knowledge. Thus the criteria for the judicious use of skepticism are supplied by the norms and standards of the field under consideration.[77]

The characterisation of critical thinking with norms and standards implies the tendencies or dispositions to think critically which are not generalizable. McPeck writes that:

> Let X stand for any problem or activity requiring some mental effort. Let E stand for the available evidence from the pertinent field or problem area. Let P stand for some proposition or action within X.
> Then we can say of a given student (S) that he is a critical thinker in area X if (S) has the disposition and skill to do X in such a way that E, or some subset of E, is suspected as being sufficient to establish the truth or viability of P.[78]

In spite of the circular reasoning manifested in this passage, McPeck's nature of critical thinking entails skills/abilities and dispositions. Essentially, a critical thinker is characterized by the use of skills/abilities and the dispositions to do so. McPeck asserts that, "it is sufficient for our purposes to recognize that training in particular critical thinking skills is not sufficient to produce a critical thinker. One must develop the disposition to use those skills."[79] In essence, though problematic, critical thinking entails skills/abilities as well as dispositions according to McPeck.

He then defines critical thinking as *"a propensity and skill to engage in an activity with reflective skepticism."* For him then critical thinking is reflective skepticism, that is, thinking critically involves questioning and doubting. Scepticism is a vital characteristic of critical thinking, which entails not to accept anything without questioning. For McPeck, this reflective skepticism must be subject-domain or content–specific.

In addition, McPeck emphasizes panoply of epistemologies and the inevitable failure of logic in critical thinking by asserting that his objective is:

> ...to show why courses in logic fail to accomplish the goal of developing critical thinkers and how the epistemology of various subjects would be the most reasonable route to that end...[80]

Clearly, his attempts are to confirm that there is both a conceptual and a pedagogical link between arrays of epistemologies and critical thinking devoid of logic. Therefore, a panoply of epistemologies, and not logic, for McPeck is vital for critical thinking. It is right to confirm that epistemology is both a necessary and a sufficient condition for critical thinking. Up to this point, McPeck is correct. However, an issue arises when there is a change of meaning of the term and of the nature of epistemology as understood by McPeck contrary to its universal standard conceptualization. His characterisation of epistemology *"as epistemology of various subjects"* is a complete deviation from the meaning and the nature of epistemology. For him, critical thinking entails epistemology which is subject- or domain- or content- or field-specific and which is uncalled for. As much as we accept the value of epistemology in critical thinking, this conceptualization is problematic for we end up with many epistemologies.

His attempt *"...to show why courses in logic fail to accomplish the goal of developing critical thinkers..."* is perplexing since logic–formal and informal–is crucial for the development of critical thinking skills/abilities by a rational person or critical thinker. Further, McPeck holds contradicting positions when it comes to the value of logic, whether formal or informal. He asserts that attempts to teach logic have been futile or unsuccessful in fostering critical thinking skills/abilities and dispositions. His perspective is that the subject–domain or content–specific approach cannot benefit from logical knowledge for there is no linkage between critical thinking and logic. He then contradicts himself when he asserts that:

> The standard approach for developing critical thinking ...has been to teach logic and various kinds of general reasoning skills. Presumably, the rationale for this approach is that since logic plays a role in every subject, and logic is intimately related to reasoning, the study of logic should improve one's ability to assess arguments and statements in any subject area.[81]

He again contradicts himself when he connotes this link between logic and reason, as a 'presumption' yet the two are inseparable. Reasoning, rationality, or appropriation of reasons is the fundamental objective of logic. In addition, logic entails reasoning skills/abilities, which are the core features of critical thinking, and therefore his thesis is not sustainable for the two are inseparable.

McPeck contradicts himself further when he writes that to value logic as fundamental for critical thinking, "...can be sustained only by seriously underestimating the complexity of the different kinds of information used in arguments and by overestimating the role of logic in these statements."[82] For, McPeck then, logic plays a role in critical thinking in particular or specialized discipline knowledge. Particular discipline knowledge is the basis of evaluating good reasons, which is epistemological and not logical in character. This is partly true and partly incorrect for if we accept the reasons assessment component, then the subject-specific as well subject-neutral perspectives are basis for assessment of good reasons. The point is that one has to accept the two as vital for critical thinking contrary to McPeck's position. In addition, we can infer that at least he values logic as relevant for critical thinking. What essentially obscures this ideal is his constant *'grinding of the subject-specific axe'* to use Siegel words.

Provocatively and contentiously, McPeck asserts that, "while critical thinking is perfectly compatible with rationality, and with reasoning generally, we should not regard the terms as equivalent."[83] This is not correct for critical thinking is rationality simpliciter.

Harvey Siegel and Richard Paul have been the major critics of the positions of McPeck's account of critical thinking. Siegel questions the notion of critical thinking as domain–, or subject–specific. For Siegel, "critical thinking is widely regarded as a generalized skill or ability (or a set of such skills and abilities), which can be utilized or applied across a variety of situations and circumstances."[84] With this in mind, Siegel questions McPeck's notion that "thinking...is logically connected to an x." This is matter of confusing the general notion of thinking with particular acts of thinking according to Siegel. The particular acts of thinking do not imply the non-existence of independent general acts of thinking. Siegel further, criicizes McPeck's view that critical thinking cannot be taught as a distinct subject on its own. Using the analogy of cycling, Siegel compares teaching critical thinking skills/abilities and dispositions in a general manner to teaching a person how to cycle. One needs the general knowledge of cycling and then can advance to certain techniques like mountain climbing and so forth. Siegel notes that, "as we can teach cycling, so critical thinking might be taught."[85] The McPeckian thesis that teaching critical thinking *simpliciter* is conceptually impossible collapses according to Siegel for if when can teach one cycling so we can teach critical thinking. Teaching critical thinking *simpliciter* facilitates acquisition of skills/abilities and dispositions that are general and applicable to all domains or disciplines. Contra to McPeck, logic provides skills/abilities or principles or reasoning skills that are not domain-, or discipline-, content-specific but are universal. As discussed earlier, rationality is *simpliciter* critical thinking, that is, the two are cognate terms. Hence, the McPeckian view on rationality and critical thinking is not tenable according to Siegel.

Richard Paul labels McPeck's thesis as *"McPeck's Mistakes,"* and regarding McPeck's book, *"Critical Thinking and Education,"* Paul laments that:

> Unfortunately, because of serious flaws in its theoretical underpinnings, the book doubtless will lead some of McPeck's readers down a variety of blind alleys, create unnecessary obstacles to some important programs being developed, and encourage some-not many, I hope-to dismiss the work of some central figures in the field (Scriven, D'Angelo, and Ennis most obviously). At the root of the problem is McPeck's (unwitting?) commitment to a rarefied form of logical (epistemological) atomism, a commitment which is essential if he is to rule out, as he passionately wants to, all general skills of thought and so to give himself a priori grounds to oppose every and all programs that try to develop or enhance such skills.[86]

Like Siegel, Paul has distaste with the notion of critical thinking as domain-specific. McPeck in "Paul's *Critique of Critical Thinking and Education*" responds to Richard Paul, and generally to his critics, asserting that, "I find less evidence of 'mistakes' and 'serious flaws' than of misunderstanding of my position and perhaps genuine disagreement."[87]

It is appreciable that McPeck contributes to the nature of critical thinking but not without major flaws/mistakes. Some of the emerging issues/flaws from the McPeckian account of critical thinking are the non-generalizability of critical thinking; the role of logic, rationality, epistemology, and information. These aspects arising from McPeck's conception deserve more attention than addressed here. In these respect, we will address them in chapter two.

Bailin and Battersby's Critical Inquiry and Spirit of Inquiry

Bailin and Battersby in their book, *Reason in the Balance*, develop an account of critical thinking they refer to as the *"Inquiry Approach to Critical Thinking."* Their account of critical thinking entails two-components namely: critical inquiry and the spirit of inquiry. We explore these two components below.

I. **Critical Inquiry**

Bailin and Battersby assert that, "we use the term inquiry to refer to critical inquiry, which is the process of carefully examining an issue in order to come to a reasoned judgment."[88] Let us look at this definition closely: It calls for *"focusing on an issue"* occasioned by disputes, challenges, controversies or differences in opinions. These range from decision making or problem solving to political controversies, philosophical problems such as 'what is justice'? What is the truth or good or bad? To religious issues such as 'what is role of language in religion', just but to mention a few.

The next aspect of the definition is *"careful examination of the issue."* This entails questioning everything, from hearsay, to rumours, to what we hear or watch from the mass media or internet, and to what we read or are taught. As such, research, investigation, insights, understanding, establish credibility of sources, pursuit of knowledge and seeking evidence is inevitable.

The final aspect of the definition involves *"inferring or arriving at a reasoned judgment"* on the issue, which requires critical evaluation, and taking into account criteria. Critical evaluation involves being reflective, critical, determining validity or invalidity, cogency or uncogency of reasons and arguments aimed at coming to a reasoned judgment. Criteria is used to identify the relevant considerations that provide the matrix for deriving a judgment such as background knowledge, experience and competence or expertise of sources, evidence provided, the putative and probative forces of reasons. The criteria must be publicly available for all to consider. Some, however, are specific to particular areas, and devoid of personal preference if considerations are in public domain. The important general criteria are the evaluation of the given reasons for a conclusion or reasoned judgment. The reasons must be free of fallacies and based on evidence. In addition, critical evaluation calls for focusing on the main issue, ascertaining the credibility of sources, identifying biasness, assumptions, seeking for clarity of words, providing counterexamples, evaluation of claims and arguments. We have compressively developed these aspects of critical evaluation in chapter four.

Accordingly, critical inquiry is an attempt to answer or solve an issue or problem in order to derive a reasoned judgement.

Occasions for Inquiry

For Bailin and Battersby, critical thinking "inquiries may take place in many areas, including science, social science, history, philosophy, ethics, interdisciplinary areas, and everyday life."[89] Besides scientific and academic disciplines, inquiry takes place in social and practical situations or contexts such as in decision making, problem solving, perplexities, dialogue or conversations, dilemmas, debates, disagreements or evaluations. Accordingly, inquiry takes place in many contexts or situations taking different forms aimed at deriving a reasoned judgment.

The Nature of Inquiry

The nature of inquiry involves evaluation of claims, arguments and reasons factoring in different points of views. One must know if the reason(s) provided support the conclusion and determine if they acceptable in making a reasoned judgment.

It entails critically focusing on the main issue in depth, breadth, precisely, logically and with clarity. As noted earlier, the nature of inquiry takes place with a certain context(s) such as decision making, problem solving, dialogue or conversations, dilemmas, debates, disagreements or evaluations.

Historical understanding of an issue(s) or problem(s) is important knowledge in coming to a reasoned judgment. It is important to understand the background and history of an issue(s) or problem(s) in order to identify relevant aspects, which will facilitate in making a reasoned judgment.

The nature of inquiry entails the recognition of the fact that knowledge is not static but is constantly changing or evolving. It undergoes revision, testing, and even rejection. For example, Aristotle rejected much of Plato's philosophy; later scientists rejected the Ptolemy laws and geocentricism theories; Albert Einstein constantly revised his theory of relativity just but to give some examples. Inquiry is the event through which one acquires knowledge and through which it changes.

In this respect, we can only come up with provisional judgments because of the fact that truth changes and knowledge evolves. In addition to this, one must accept the fact of fallibilism, that is, one must recognize ability to err, to make mistakes in his/her reasoning or judgment(s). In spite of fallibility of knowledge, one must also recognize the degree of certainty, which can be obtained with respect to various issues.

In a summary, the nature of inquiry entails fallibilism, appreciation of the fact that we can make mistakes and that knowledge is constantly changing. It also calls for the appreciation that there are many sides or points of view(s), historicality, criteria or situation of an issue (s), and that the degree of certainty varies from one given issue(s) to another. In this respect, critical evaluation comes in handy. Importantly:

> Inquiry is an enterprise which involves creativity and imagination as much as it does logic and reasoning; the two aspects are, in fact very closely intertwined. Inquiry involves the evaluation of information, reasons, and judgement but it also involves thinking of alternatives and objections, imagining counterexamples, and constructing one's own view. Inquiry is the means by which knowledge advances.[90]

Clearly, this reflects the reasons assessment component of critical thinking in the nature of critical thinking as critical inquiry aimed at reasoned judgement. Reasoned judgement seeks good reasons for any actions or beliefs. The link between critical thinking and creativity is manifested in the inquiry approach to critical thinking. We explore this link in the next section.

Inquiry and Dialogue

Inquiry involves dialogue or conversations between person(s) with different perspective(s). This can be in real-life dialogues or one-self dialogue. Hence, dialogues are good matrix for inquiry aimed at coming to a reasoned judgment. It is important to note that not all dialogues meet the standards of inquiry such as gossips, chats, etc.

The Value of Inquiry

Bailin and Battersby, offer five reasons for valuing inquiry as follows:

The first fundamental value of inquiry is justification, that is, it helps in coming up with good reason(s) in support of a position(s) or view(s) or judgment(s). Justification provides reasons for believing something as opposed to blind acceptance or appeal to authority.

Second, inquiry serves as a method of attaining the truth according to this account of critical thinking.

Third, inquiry facilitates understanding of the world.

Fourth, inquiry ensures that one becomes autonomous and self-directed. Hence, one becomes a reflective thinker, one who cannot be manipulated by advertisements, language, and rhetoric of politicians or preachers. In respect, one becomes an independent, responsible person capable of thinking and making decision(s) and judgment(s) on the basis of reason about complex matters.

Fifth, dialogue civilises discourse because it focuses on reasoning, is respectful, takes views of others with seriousness and with due consideration they deserve. Inquiry brings civility and respect among participants even when there is/are disagreement(s). It is important to treat each other with respect in any dialogue and to accept that it one's freedom to hold his or her beliefs in any democratic society.

Next, we explore the second component of inquiry, that is, the spirit of inquiry.

II. **Spirit of Inquiry**

Bailin and Battersby stresses the value of critical thinking attitudes arguing that the mastery of intellectual resources is insufficient if an individual does not have a basic commitment to rational inquiry which disposes her to deploy the resources and the attitudes or habits of mind which characterize critical thinking. They point out that:

> Because of this, inquiry requires of its participants a certain orientation or attitude which we shall refer to as the **spirit of inquiry**. At the most general level, the spirit of inquiry involves a commitment to base one's beliefs and action on inquiry."[91]

The spirit of inquiry comprises an acknowledgment of reason and a commitment to base our beliefs and actions on inquiry. The spirit of inquiry entails open-mindedness and fair-mindedness attitudes:

> The spirit of inquiry is demonstrated in certain attitudes. The first is **open-mindedness**. Because we realize that we are fallible, we must genuinely be open to views which oppose our own as well as to challenges to our views and to evidence which runs against our views. The spirit of inquiry, in fact, requires that we seek out any possible objections or contrary evidence. And we should be willing to revise our views if better arguments are presented and conceded to the most defensible position. Another dimension of the spirit of inquiry centres on **fair-mindedness**. Fair-mindedness means that we are willing not only to consider opposing views but also to make unbiased and impartial judgments about these views. This requires that we be fair in our portrayal of views which we disagree and not mischaracterize them in order to make them easier targets for our criticisms.[92]

Accordingly, the value of these two aspects which embody critical inquiry is worthy recognizing as ideals for conducting inquiry.

In addition to these two attitudes, there is the third one, namely respectfulness:

> A final and central aspect of the spirit of inquiry involves respectful treatment of other participants in the inquiry. This means avoiding insults and manipulations, and it means taking the views of others seriously.[93]

This implies treating others with respect, taking their views seriously and not engaging in manipulations, insults or arrogance is vital in any meaningful inquiry.

The above clearly is in line with the distinction between pieces of critical thinking from the dispositions of a critical thinker. The nature and value of inquiry is to arrive at reasoned judgement and inevitably embraces the spirit of inquiry. The spirit of inquiry is *"certain orientation or attitude"* which facilitates reasoned judgement which include open-mindedness, fair-mindedness and respectfulness. Accordingly, critical thinking is characterized by both critical inquiry, that is, the intellectual resources and the critical spirit, the disposition or orientation towards the implementation of critical inquiry. A critical thinker must have both critical inquiry and spirit of inquiry. A critical thinker must embrace:

> The respect for reason which is one of the defining characteristics of inquiry shows itself in several ways, including curiosity, a concern for truth and accuracy, an admiration of what human beings have achieved through their reason, a willingness to follow arguments and reasoning wherever they lead, a desire to act on the basis of reason, and an acceptance of the uncertainty which is part of inquiry.[94]

In addition, a critical thinker must embrace the spirit of inquiry, that is, dispositions or attitude of mind such as open-mindedness, fair-mindedness, and respectfulness.

Specific Guidelines or Questions for Inquiry

According to Bailin and Battersby, there are specific guidelines or questions for inquiry that should be followed in any process that seeks reasoned judgment through a careful examination of an issue. These "guiding questions"[95] are:

- What is the issue?
- What kinds of claims or judgments are at issue?
- What are the relevant reasons and arguments on various sides of the issue?
- What is the context of the issue?

- How do we comparatively evaluate the various reasons and arguments to reach a reasoned judgment?

These questions serve as a guide to critical inquiry. We analyze them as follows: the question on *Issue* entails identifying what is at stake or issue or problem or question; on *claims or judgements* seeks to understand the various types of judgements; the next question calls for skilfully identifying relevant reasons and arguments on various sides of the issue; this is only possible within *context* such as state of practice, historical, intellectual, social, economic surrounding of an issue for nothing occurs in vacuum; and the final question deals with weighing or comparing the pros and cons of an issue in order to arrive at a reasoned judgment. These guidelines are vital for critical inquiry. In summing up, critical inquiry focuses on an issue, evaluates reason(s), argument(s) and evidence, is contextual in nature and embraces understanding or intellectual resources in order to come up with a reasoned judgment.

In concluding this section, we assert that all the theorists discussed acknowledge and emphasize the importance of the disposition to use skills/abilities or proficiencies, to do critical thinking, in a full conception of critical thinking. Clearly, this tendency or disposition is an important component of full conception of critical thinking. In addition, following the various theorists, in particular, Siegel's perspective, we demonstrated the distinction between characteristics of critical thinking and attributes of the critical thinker or rational person.

Again, three terms emerged, that is skills/abilities, dispositions and intellectual virtues. What is the relationship between the three terms? More so, what is the relationship between critical thinking and the intellectual virtues? These issues have been addressed in the next chapter.

In the next section, we explore the complex relationship between critical thinking and creative thinking.

1.3 The Relationship between Critical and Creative Thinking

In this section, we shall examine the relationship and interaction created by the combination of critical and creative thinking guided by some of the philosophical theorists. A starting point is Siegel's remark that "another time-honored distinction which needs to be exploded is that between critical and creative thinking..."[96] It is against this brief background that we explore the link between critical and creative thinking.

The Opposition View and the Complimentary View

Some philosophical theorists argue out that, though the two terms are not interchangeable, they are strongly linked, bringing complementary dimensions to thinking. Another argument is that there is a considerable difference between critical and creative thinking. The issue concerning the relationship between critical and creative thinking is thus twofold: (a) that is philosophical theorists have either argued that the two, are distinct but complimentary while for others, (b) they are opposed to each other. Bailin captures these dualistic perspectives when she writes that:

> The complementarity view usually entails efforts to teach critical thinking skills on their own or integrated into curricular materials plus techniques to encourage flexibility, spontaneity, divergent thinking, etc. The opposition view usually involves the abandonment of some aspects of critical thinking and disciplinary skills in favour of such creativity techniques, on the grounds that the former are inhibiting to the latter.[97]

It is notable that there are the complementary and opposition views of critical and creative thinking. According to the opposition view, there is a radical and fundamental difference between critical and creative thinking. She points out that:

> This radical separation of critical and creative thinking has its source in a specific picture of thinking and knowledge, namely that ordinary thinking is convergent, analytic, and takes place within rigid frameworks, and that creative thinking requires imaginative leaps to transcend the frameworks.[98]

Further, this radical and dualistic separation is noted by Siegel and Bailin. They write:

> An issue frequently raised in discussions of critical thinking concerns the relationship between critical and creative thinking. The assumption is generally made that they are two different and distinct kinds of thinking.[99]

Hence critical and creative thinking are assumed to be fundamentally different and opposed to each other. On the contrary, some philosophical theorists view that both critical and creative thinking skills are valuable and neither is superior. The perceived dichotomy is neither here nor there, and that they are not mutually exclusive categories.

Bailin notes that "I believe that there are serious conceptual and educational problems in this radical dichotomy between critical and creative thinking."[100] In this section, we will address the serious conceptual problem, and in chapter six we will focus on the educational problem of the radical dichotomy between critical and creative thinking. We will begin with the Siegelian perspective on the relationship between critical and creative thinking.

Siegel addresses the issue of the dualistic conception of critical and creative thinking noting that the opposition view is misplaced and misleading. Siegel captures this when he writes that, "the distinction between boring, automatic critical thinking and wild, unconstrained, undisciplined creative thinking is untenable, and assumes an indefensible conception of creativity."[101] Accordingly, there is no distinction between critical and creative thinking. He further writes that:

> The relationship between critical thinking and creativity is a complex one, but it is not one of mutual exclusion. The critical thinker, for example, needs to be creative in developing reasons, arguments, examples, etc., as well as critical in assessing those creations…I would suggest that critical thinking involves creativity, and that creative thinking involves criticality.[102]

In spite of the complex link between critical and creative thinking, they are two sides of the same coin. They are intertwined that one cannot exist without the other. Siegel's reasons conception account of critical thinking does not foster any sharp split or opposition between critical and creative thinking. He confirms this when he asserts that:

I want to emphasize that nothing about the reasons conception of critical thinking forces a sharp split between critical and creative thinking, or the view that creativity, properly conceived, is not part of the repertoire of the critical thinker.[103]

It is plausible to infer that according to Siegel critical and creative thinking involve each other.

For Bailin, the difference, opposition or radical dichotomy between critical and creative thinking is misplaced due to serious conceptual problems. According to her, the conceptualization of the nature of critical and creative thinking facilitates the sharp separation or radical dichotomy:

> Critical thinking involves arriving at assessments within specific frameworks. It is the means for making reasoned judgments within these frameworks based on the standards of judgment inherent in the framework. It is thus essentially analytic, evaluative, selective, and highly

rule-bound. Given the necessary information from within the framework and the appropriate techniques of reasoning, arriving at judgments is almost algorithmic. In thinking critically one is, however, confined to the specific framework. Because it is circumscribed by the logic of the framework, critical thinking cannot provide the means to transcend the framework itself nor to question its assumptions.[104]

Critical thinking is conceptualized as analytic, evaluative, selective, and highly rule-bound. It follows the logic of its framework. This is contrary to the conceptualization of the nature of creative thinking:

Creative thinking, on the other hand, is precisely the type of thinking which can transcend frameworks. It is inventive, imaginative, and involves the generation of new ideas. Because it involves breaking out of old frameworks, creative thinking is thought to exhibit characteristics which are precisely the opposite of critical thinking. It is essentially generative, spontaneous, and non-evaluative. It involves divergent thinking, rule breaking, the suspension of judgment, and leaps of imagination. And, instead of being characterized by logic or appeal to reasons, it relies heavily on intuition, and unconscious processes.[105]

From the above quotation, we can sum up that creative thinking is conceptualized as inventive, imaginative, generative, spontaneous, rule breaking, entails suspension of judgment, involves the generation of new ideas, and is non-evaluative divergent thinking. In addition, creative thinking appeals to intuition, and unconscious processes over against appealing to reasons or logic. Clearly, for her, the sharp separation or radical dichotomy has to do with conceptualization of the nature of critical and creative thinking.

In addition, for Bailin, another factor that contributes to this "false dichotomy" or sharp separation as she likes to put it, is the notion of framework:

One reason for this dichotomized view of thinking into the critical and the creative might be connected with the notion of frameworks. According to this view, ordinary thinking takes place within rigidly bounded and highly rule-governed frameworks, disciplinary particularly true within disciplinary areas and especially technical ones. Within these frameworks, all necessary information is given, and the mode of thinking required is analytic and evaluative, involving judgments made almost mechanically according to the logic of the framework.[106]

Critical thinking operates within specific frameworks. These frameworks entail their own logic that is analytic, evaluative and all information is given. Such a framework view portrays the picture that critical and creative thinking are opposed to each other.

The framework view conceptualization sees creative thinking as radically different:

> Given this picture of frameworks, it would seem to follow that a radically different type of thinking is required to transcend frameworks, a type of thinking which suspends the criteria of judgment of the framework, breaks rules, which makes irrational leaps, and which generates novelty.[107]

The framework view provides a mode of inquiry for critical and creative thinking which a directly opposed. However, knowledge is not static but dynamic which then negates the rigid framework view. She notes that these two misconceptualizations of critical and creative thinking resulting to the radical dichotomy are mistaken, misplacement and at best misleading. The two dimensions of thinking do not entail sharp separation, neither are they dichotomized, radically different nor unconnected. Bailin asserts that:

> It can be shown that thinking critically plays a crucial role in innovation. Innovation must be viewed in terms of creating products which are not simply novel but also of value, and critical judgment is crucially involved in such creative achievement.[108]

It is plausible to infer that, for Bailin, certain amount of criticality is necessary for creative thought or production. Further, creative thinking is not entirely about breaking rules but it adheres to reason. For her, certain amount of creativity is necessary for critical thought. This is confirmed when she observes that:

> I think that it can also be demonstrated that critical thinking is not merely analytic, selective, and confined to frameworks, but has imaginative, inventive, constructive aspects.[109]

This is to imply that critical thinking skills/abilities promote creativity. She then gives a description of the attitude which she feels is most conducive to creativity as:

> Taking previous thought products seriously implies recognizing the importance of knowledge and skills, of judgment, of in-depth understanding, and of criticism and reasons in creative production. Unwillingness to accept such products as final entails an understanding of the dynamic, lively, evolutionary nature of knowledge and the creative nature of criticism.[110]

Bailin then concludes that:

> I would contend, then, that critical thinking and creative thinking are not separate and distinct modes of thinking which operate within different

The Nature of Critical Thinking

contexts and to different ends. Rather, they are intimately connected and are both integrally involved in thinking well in any area.[111]

Bailin and Siegel assert that:

> It is our view that the dichotomy between critical thinking and creative thinking is ill-founded. There are evaluative, analytical, logical aspects to creating new ideas or products and an imaginative, constructive dimension to their assessment. A conceptualization in terms of two distinct types of thinking critical and creative, is seriously problematic.[112]

It is plausible to infer that the position taken by Bailin and Siegel is that there is an indispensable link between critical and creative thinking.

In their book, *Reason in the Balance*, Bailin and Battersby assert that: "inquiry is an enterprise which involves creativity and imagination as much as it does logic and reasoning; the two aspects are, in fact, very closely intertwined."[113] This implies that critical thinking needs imagination and invention which are essential characteristics of creative thinking.

Finally, it is important to note that Bailin and Siegel define creative thinking as "...strictly generative, the kind of thinking that allows for breaking of rules, the transcending of frameworks, and the creation of new products."[114]

Richard Paul and Linda Elder assert that there is a misconception and misunderstanding that critical and creative thinking are opposed. They write that:

> To the untutored, creative and critical thinking often seem to be opposite forms of thought: the first based on irrational or unconscious forces, the second on rational and conscious processes; the first undirectable and unteachable, the second directable and teachable.[115]

Paul and Elder are very assertive on the inseparability of critical and creative thinking. They point out that, the very definition of the word "creative" implies a critical component.

When we understand critical and creative thought truly and deeply, we recognize them as inseparable, integrated, and unitary.[116] For them, both creativity and critical thinking are aspects of "good," purposeful thinking. As such, critical thinking and creativity are two sides of the same coin. Good thinking requires the ability to generate intellectual products, which is associated with creativity. However, good thinking also requires the individual to be aware, strategic, and critical about the quality of those intellectual products. As the authors note, "*critical thinking without creativity* reduces to mere skepticism and negativity, and creativity without critical thought reduces to mere novelty". It is clear that for Paul and Elder, the two concepts are inextricably linked and develop in parallel.

Lipman weighs in on the relationship between critical and creative thinking. He shows us that creativity is important in thinking and is central to the process of inquiry. For Lipman creative thinking should not be uncritical or irrational and that:

> There is no creative thinking that is not shot with critical judgments, just as there is no critical judgment that is not shot through with creative judgments. We can, of course, construct abstract ideal types in which pure forms of thinking are delineated, but in actuality admixture is the rule.[117]

Accordingly, the idea of letting the argument lead the discussion in his community of inquiry ideal, is in fact a critical and creative process. The dialogue in the inquiry relies on the inventiveness and creativity of the participants to shape the arguments and hence the dialogue itself, we assert that the inquiry rests on engagement in critical and creative thinking. Lipman recognizes, appreciates and argues that these two forms of thinking provide a basis for the philosophical *Community of Inquiry*. Therefore, both critical and creative thinking are fundamental for Lipman.

Robert Ennis also contributes on the relationship between critical and creative thinking. For Ennis, *critical thinking is a process, the goal of which is to make reasonable decisions about what to believe and what to do* and hence, "these decisions call for some creativity in our critical thinking."[118] He advocates for a relationship between the two. They are inextricably connected and reinforce each to improve the process of arriving at reasonable decisions.

1.4 Synthesis on the Relationship between Critical and Creative Thinking

We sum up the views of the above philosophical theorists as follows:

First, creative thinking is generative thinking which in turn is evaluated by critical thinking. This generation or creation of new ideas or products is as a result critical thinking and assessment. If critical thinking evaluates or judges something as wanting, the implication is that creative thinking must generate further information. This implies that it is impossible to pinpoint an evaluative phase of thinking that does not have a generative dimension.

Second, the products of creative thinking must be evaluated in order to determine their worthiness or unworthiness as pertains to their effectiveness or even destructiveness. Thus creative thinking provides materials for critical thinking.

Third, creative thinking proposes alternatives and in turn critical thinking points out the strengths and weaknesses settling for the best option by justification. Therefore, critical thinking does not only find faults in a product of thought, but also provides alternatives to improve it, therefore, it is creative. Succinctly put:

> Thinking that is directed primarily toward the evaluation or criticism of ideas or products is not algorithmic but has a generative, imaginative component. The application of criteria is not a mechanical process but involves both some interpretation of circumstances and to whether the criteria have been met. Similarly, inventing hypotheses, generating counterexamples, constructing counterarguments, and envisioning potential problems are all important aspects of critical thinking that have a generative dimension.[119]

The alternating relationship of activity between critical and creative thinking is important in intellectuals concerns where excellence is the objective. Creative thinking provides the material for critical thinking. Critical thinking in turn polishes the products of creativity. This implies that:

> There is a creative dimension in all critical thinking, and in some cases, critical deliberation leads to the questioning of assumptions, the breaking of rules, the rearrangement of elements-thus results in products that exhibit considerable novelty.[120]

The issue of the relationship between critical and creative thinking from the above proceedings leads to the fact that one cannot with precision distinguish the two. The two dimensions of the thinking activity are interwoven and that both must be interrogated together. Further critical and creative thinking can be encouraged concurrently through activities that assimilate reason, logic, on one hand and imagination and innovation on the other hand.

Fourth, creative thinking entails the generation of products or ideas that manifest improvements or innovations. This process is assessed and critiqued by critical thinking which is necessary and indispensable. That is to say that:

> The very process of generating ideas involves evaluation since it is constrained by various criteria related to the problem situation and to what would constitute an effective and innovative solution. If this were not the case, the result would be chaos rather than creation. Nor is it

possible to identify an evaluative phase of thinking that lacks a generative dimension. The terms "critical thinking" and "creative thinking" can be used to refer to the generative and to the evaluative aspects of thinking for the purposes of analysis and discussion, but it is important to be clear that these are not really two different kinds of thinking that can be engaged in separately.[121]

Finally, critical and creative thinking are processes that develop both flexibility and precision as integral to each of the thinking dimensions. Therefore, the interrogation of critical and creative thinking is an extensive and complex activity. My take and suggestion is that criticality involves creativity, and that creativity involves criticality. However, such a link remains contentious hence we will revisit these two aspects in the next chapter arguing the need for further research.

Finally, what are the implications of the sharp separation or radical dichotomy of critical and creative thinking should it uphold? What are the serious educational problems of radical dichotomy between critical and creative thinking? More specifically, what is the place of critical and creative thinking in education? We will address these questions in Chapter Six, demonstrating that efforts should be made in fostering critical and creative thinking to students.

1.5   Critical Thinking and other Related Terms

Other relationships which need to be examined are those between critical thinking and some terms which connote forms of thinking such as **inquiry, high order thinking, problem solving and decision making**. The fundamental question or issue is the complex relationship between these terms and critical thinking. Critical thinking is sometimes contrasted with problem solving, decision making, high order thinking and inquiry implying that it is one form of thought among others. It is against this brief background that we seek to demonstrate the relationship between critical thinking and these terms, guided by some of the critical thinking theorists.

Higher order thinking is a dimension associated with critical thinking. Bailin and Siegel point out that "the term higher-order thinking refers to advanced or complex thinking in contrast to simpler, less sophisticated, forms of thinking."[122] Richard Paul and Linda Elder, Judd, Bloom (Bloom's taxonomy) among others embraces this hierarchical categorisation of thinking.

Bailin and Battersby contribute to notion of critical thinking as Inquiry and as we have shown, it entails attempts to answer an inquiry, issue or question critically. They assert that "using critical inquiry to inform our decision making greatly reduces the likelihood of being misled by our natural tendencies and biases."[123] Reasoned decision making is informed by critical inquiry as well as critical spirit which ensure that prejudices or biases are eliminated.

In particular, Bailin argues that critical thinking is inseparable when it comes to problem solving: "It involves, as well, improved thinking skills in dealing with real life problems-in assessing information and arguments in social contexts and making life decisions."[124] Hence for her, there is a fundamental link between critical thinking and problem solving.

She asserts that:

> In any creative solution to a problem, the initial recognition that there is a problem to be solved, the identification of the nature of the problem, and the determination of how to proceed all involve critical assessment. Initially, the realization that there is a problem to be solved, that there are phenomena in need of explanation or exploration involves judgment. The recognition that a new direction or approach is required is an evaluation based on knowledge and an understanding of the problem situation. And there is judgment involved in determining the general range and form of possible solutions to problems or next moves in creating, the ideas and directions that might be fruitful, and even the ideas that will count as solutions or achieve the completion of a work. Thus the idea that creative thinking is not dependent upon critical thinking will not hold up under scrutiny.[125]

Critical assessment facilitates creative solutions to problems by recognizing, identifying and determining on how to deal with the problems. Hence there is fundamental link between critical thinking and problem solving. She further points out that:

Creativity is not merely a question of generating new solutions to problems, but of generating better solutions, and is thus not a matter of arbitrary novelty or random invention, but involves change which is effective, useful, and significant. Such change is connected with high-level skills and in-depth knowledge in an area, with a profound understanding of the problem situation and with attempts to solve these problems in ever better ways. This implies highly developed critical judgment. Critical thinking is, thus, intimately involved in creative production.[126]

From these quotations, it is clear that carrying out these tasks typically requires one to make a number of judgments, and thinking that leads to these judgments must fulfil relevant standards of good thinking.

Bailin observes that these activities have been viewed in terms of procedures or steps or frameworks aimed at a solution and in so doing, the normative nature of critical thinking is side lined. On the contrary these aspects can be addressed through critical thinking. Bailin suspects that this definite and fixed procedures or methods especially in education are extended to problem solving:

> I also suspect that this dichotomized view of thinking and this picture of knowledge as definite and fixed which is created by the traditional school curriculum extends, as well, into thinking in non-disciplinary areas and is one reason why it is so difficult to enhance the critical thinking skills of students. They are accustomed to seeking the right answer according to authority and to expecting algorithmic solutions to problems and this is their mode of proceeding with respect to life problems as well.[127]

On the contrary, she observes that "it is vital that they understand that thinking well in any area is based on knowledge, but is questioning and critical according to sound reasons and that creativity is an extension of thinking really well about problems."[128]

In his book, *Critical Thinking and Education*, McPeck observes that critical thinking "does not merely refer to the assessment of statements but includes the thought processes involved in problem solving and active engagement in certain activities."[129] That is, the scope of critical thinking involves problem solving not just limited to "the assessment of statements." Critical thinking for him contributes to problem solving.

We now turn attention to the relationship between critical thinking and decision making.

Richard Paul and Elder Linda, provide an elaborate link between strong sense critical thinking and *"The Art of Making Intelligent Decisions."* They observe that human persons live, act and constantly make rational or irrational decisions in various domains. When on makes irrational decisions, then one lives irrational life. On the other hand, if one makes rational decisions, then one lives a rational life. In order to make rational decisions and to live a rational life, strong sense critical thinking is important and indispensable. Consequently, strong sense critical thinking facilitates rational decision making and inevitably, rational living. They write that:

> Critical thinking, when applied to decision-making, enhances the rationality of decisions made by raising the pattern of decision-making to the level of conscious and deliberate choice.

However, they advocate for steps or patterns or dimensions for decision making. As noted in the conclusion there are no clear patterns or steps established for decision making which can be mastered. One needs to a critical thinker and apply critical thinking skills/abilities and dispositions in order to make rational decisions.

Robert Ennis observes that critical thinking skills/abilities and dispositions can benefit the area of decision making. He writes that:

> Critical thinking is a process, the goal of which is to make reasonable decisions about what to believe and what to do. Because we all are continually making decisions, critical thinking is important to us in personal and vocational, as well as civic, aspects of our lives. Some of these decisions are about whether to believe someone else, or to act in accord with that person's recommendations.[130]

From his definition of critical thinking as *"reasonable and reflective thinking focused on deciding what to believe or do"* clearly appreciates critical thinking as indispensable in 'deciding what to believe or do.' This implies that critical thinking aids in the process of decision making:

How can you decide what to believe and what to do?

> Should you believe everything you hear and read? Should you even believe everything you read in your local newspaper? Obviously not. Which of the things that you hear and read should you believe? Do you have a guess, or a theory, or an idea about something? Should you believe it? How can you investigate to find out? In short, how can you decide what to believe? Suppose you are trying to decide how to vote, what kind of orange juice to buy (if at all), whether to see a doctor, or whether to take a class. How can you decide what to do?[131]

In decision making which can either be easy or difficulty, one needs to rely on credible sources or reliable information, good ideas, ask questions, gather information, dialogue with others and possess proper understanding of the matter at hand in order to make a reasoned judgment. Further, decision making permeates all domains of our lives:

> These decisions call for some creativity in our critical thinking, but other decisions can call for more creativity. For example, we might want to decide what path to follow at some crucial point in our lives, when the paths are not laid out. Then we must at least, to some extent, develop the possibilities as well as choose among. Not all decisions are so significant,

but if they matter at all, and we want to make the best decision, then critical thinking is important.[132]

Ennis sees a good applicability of critical thinking in decision making in the realm of civic decisions or civic matters particularly in democratic way of life. He asserts that:

> Critical thinking is also important to the survival of a democratic way of life. If the people in a democracy do not make reasonable decisions in voting and the conduct of their everyday public lives, then the democracy in which they live is threaten...We have a public responsibility to try to make reasonable civic decisions- that is, to try, to think critically in civic matters, and to help others do so as well.[133]

Such decisions are easy or difficulty to make and hence critical thinking, according to Ennis, helps or provides guidelines in deciding in a reasonable manner what to believe or do.

In particular, the six elements under *FRISCO*, are good guidelines that facilitate or can be applied in the process of decision making for Ennis. FRISCO is important "in approaching decision, considering it, judging it, and the support you have for and against it, gathering more evidence, stepping back and reflecting, and applying your insights in oral presentations and discussions."[134] It is essential to apply these elements of FRISCO or aspects of critical thinking in decision-making. In making a decision about what to believe or do entails asking: what am I trying to decide about? What are the reasons for and against the decision? Is the inference step to the decisions justifiable? What is the situation in which I am about to make a decision? Am I clear of the meaning of the terms involved in decision making? How have I utilised each of the elements of FRISCO? These questions under FRISCO respectively, serve as guidelines in the process of decision making. A critical thinker invents, checks the quality of his or her activity, reformulates, evaluates, and becomes creative in applying these set of interdependent elements in making a decision. He, therefore, regards these elements of critical thinking as important and indispensable in decision making. It is important to note that the guidelines do not guarantee or automatically produce answers according to Ennis.

Bailin and Battersby contribute to the notion of critical thinking and decision making. Accordingly, the Inquiry approach, which focuses on an issue and the inference quality of argument aimed at arriving at reasoned judgment, is vital for decision making.

Inquiry approach to critical thinking evaluates if the given premises establish good prima facie support for the conclusion. They observe that "sometimes we just think in simple-minded dichotomies (sometimes called "black-and white-thinking"), which often leads to very bad decision making."[135] Fallacious reasoning contributes to poor decision making. Persuasions which are not logical considerations tend to influence the processing of making decisions according to Bailin and Battersby.

In concluding this section, it is important to understand that these terms refer to different contexts in which critical thinking take place. In addition, the terms high order thinking, inquiry, problem solving and decision making designate general kinds of thinking tasks which are either solved in a critical or an uncritical manner. So, inquiry, high order thinking, problem solving and decision making are best seen as arenas or contexts in which critical thinking should take place rather than as other kinds of thinking to be contrasted with critical thinking.

In these stated dimensions of thinking, one is helped by the employment of a set of critical thinking skills/abilities and the habits of mind or tendencies or dispositions. This exposition captures the core relationship between critical thinking and higher-order thinking, inquiry, problem solving and decision making.

Finally, one needs the Socratic wisdom and dictum, that is, "know thyself "in applying in critical thinking skills/abilities and dispositions in all these dimensions.

1.6 Obstacles to Critical Thinking

This section focuses on the obstacles (also known as impediments or hindrances) that impair a person's ability to thinking critically. Some of the critical thinking theorists have exposed various obstacles which in essence amount to fallacious reasoning, that prevent critical thinking and have also provided fundamental solutions. We embark on their views on this topic.

Siegel enumerates some of the obstacles to his reasons conception account of critical thinking such as "...partiality, arbitrariness, special pleading, wishful thinking, and other obstacles to the proper exercise of reason assessment and reasoned judgment;"[136] Accordingly, a critical thinker must embrace skills/abilities and dispositions which will facilitate overcoming of these obstacles.

According to Richard Paul and Linda Elder, *"the critical thinker is aware of the full variety of ways in which thinking can become distorted, misleading, prejudiced, superficial, unfair, or otherwise defective."* Paul and Elder identify weak sense critical thinking which is self-centred, personal egocentric and sociocentric habits as obstacles to critical thinking. They assert that there is the need overcome these obstacles via the strong sense critical thinking by developing reasoning skills precisely in those areas where one is most likely to have egocentric and sociocentric biases such as vested interests and world views. Besides these egocentric and sociocentric biases, Paul and Elder identify mental framework or mentality or human mind as another source of obstacles to critical thinking. According to them, there are deep seated tendencies in the human mind to reason in order to ignore other point of views and what is not in our interests. The egocentric, sociocentric and the "deep seated tendencies in the human mind" are, according to Paul and Elder, hindrances, biases or vices which must be eradicated by the use of strong sense critical thinking.

Lipman identifies stereotyping, bias and prejudice as core hindrances to critical and creative thinking. As such these obstacles should be understood and prevented from negatively affecting judgments.

Bailin and Battersby discuss various aspects which are obstacles to critical inquiry. They observe that "although we may all aspire to be open-minded and fair-minded, there are certain common and natural tendencies of an emotional, social, or cognitive nature that tend to bias our thinking and present barriers to achieving these attitudes."[137] A critical thinker must be aware and familiar with the many obstacles or biases which may hinder critical thinking. They write that the *"obstacles to the Spirit of Inquiry"* are:

"Fallacious reasoning

Biases

  I. Emotional and psychological Biases
- Ideological fixity
- Myside bias
- The need to be right
- The desire for certainty
- Identification with our beliefs
- Defensiveness
- Rushing to response

II. Social Biases
- Group think
- Inside-the-box-bias

III. Cognitive biases
- Representative bias
- Availability bias
- Vividness bias
- Overconfidence or poor calibration
- Confirmation bias"[138]

Bailin and Battersby give detailed guidelines for "overcoming the obstacles to inquiry" ... [and provide] ... *"guiding questions for achieving the spirit of inquiry:"*

1. "Know your initial views and biases:
   - What position on the issue I am starting with?
   - What perspective am I bringing to the evaluation of this issue?
   - Am I bringing any personal experiences to this issue that might colour my judgement?

2. Monitor your process of inquiry and dialogue
   - Are my preconceptions and initial perspectives biasing how we evaluate various arguments? Am I really listening to and seriously considering all views and arguments?
   - Am I fairly representing other positions?
   - Am I being open to criticism?
   - Are my responses measured and appropriate?
   - Am I being unduly influenced by the views of the group?
   - Am I identifying with being a reasonable person rather than with a particular point of view?
   - Am I avoiding the use of fallacious reasoning?

3. Evaluate your own view:
   - What are the weaknesses in the view I favour?
   - What are likely criticism and objections to this view?
   - What alternative arguments are there to this view?
   - What evidence or arguments would count against the view I favour?
   - What would make me change my mind about the issue?"[139]

From the above, Bailin and Battersby identify various strategies to overcome obstacles to critical inquiry and each with several guiding questions. In summary, one should embrace the spirit of inquiry with its attitudes of open-mindedness, fair-mindedness and responsibility to accept one's own prejudices, appreciate criticism and to be objective and tactical.

In conclusion we argue that the only proper way to overcome the obstacles or hindrances is to embrace critical thinking skills/abilities and dispositions.

1.7 Conclusion

This chapter has focused on discussing substantively the various accounts of critical thinking as understood by the main theoreticians of critical thinking.

The first topic was on definition of critical thinking where we demonstrated that it is normative in nature, that is, it pertains to good reasoning or thinking as opposed to psychological definitions which are descriptive in nature.

We then demonstrated that critical thinking conceptions involve two notions, that is skills/abilities and dispositions or tendencies or habits of mind. These are related but theoretically or conceptually distinct aspects. The skills/abilities of critical thinking, is thinking in such a way as to fulfil relevant standards. This is to imply that skills/abilities of critical thinking are at the core of intellectual activity or rigour that involves recognizing an argument, use evidence in support of that argument, draw reasoned conclusions, recognizing fallacious reasoning, evaluating credibility of sources and use information to solve problems and make decisions. Examples of thinking skills are reasoning, questioning, analyzing, interpreting, evaluating, explaining, sequencing, comparing, inferring, hypothesising, appraising, testing and generalizing. Further, the skills/abilities view of critical thinking, is determined by the standards of good thinking such as impartiality, objectivity, rationality, clarity, precision, relevance among others that provide the criteria for determining what attributes are imperative for it. Hence the discussed theorists embrace the reason assessment component of critical thinking as advocated by Siegel.

Further, we pointed out that critical thinking goes beyond these set of rules or standards or the use of good reason to certain dispositions, commitments, attitudes or habits of mind that dispose or incline an individual to use these intellectual tools to fulfil relevant standards and principles of good thinking.

What is clear is that all the discussed theorists namely Siegel, Scheffler, Ennis, Paul and Elder, Lipman, McPeck and Bailin et al characterize critical thinking as a skills/abilities and dispositions and hence affirm affinity the Siegelian account. The Siegelian *Reasons Conception* account of critical thinking captures what the above theorists deem as the nature of critical thinking. Their perspectives are in line with the nature of critical thinking as enshrined in the *Reasons Conception* as entailing; One, *Reasons Assessment Component*, *"a set off cognitive skills or criteria of assessment,"* and two, the critical attitude or spirit, i.e. *"tendencies, dispositions, character traits and habits of mind."* Essentially the Siegelian account of critical thinking extends beyond use of reason to the dispositions to use it which Siegel notes as "...perhaps the most important "non-skill" component of critical thinking."[140] Siegel sums up by asserting that "to recognize this is to recognize the depth of the concept of critical thinking, and the importance of character, values, and other moral dimensions of the concept."[141] Such an exposition led to the examination of the characteristics of a critical thinker or of a rational person.

The chapter also discussed the relationship between critical thinking and creative thinking asserting that the two are complement each other. In particular, we emphasized that indispensability or inseparability of critical and creative thinking. In essence, they are two sides of the same coin.

In addition, we discussed the link between critical thinking and other related terms such as high order thinking, problem solving, decision making and inquiry pointing out that these are contexts within which critical thinking takes place.

We also made an examination of the obstacles to critical thinking. We pointed out that a critical thinker or rational person must be aware of the impediments or obstacles to criticality and how to overcome them.

This substantive discussion has shed light on the nature of critical thinking. From the proceedings so far, quite a number of issues have emerged such; the panoply of definitions; notion of skills; the relationship between skills/abilities and dispositions and virtues; generalization or nor generalization of critical thinking; the role of logic, epistemology; the relation between rationality and critical thinking; the role of context; the relationship between critical and creative thinking; critical thinking and related concepts such inquiry, problem solving and decision making. It is against this background that provides the rationale and content or subject matter for the next chapter.

1.8   End Notes

1. Harvey Siegel, *Rationality Redeemed? Further Dialogues on an Educational Ideal* (New York: Routledge, 1997), 65.
2. Harvey Siegel, *Educating Reason: Rationality, Critical Thinking and Education,* (Routledge, 1988), 23.
3. Harvey Siegel, *Education's Epistemology: Rationality, Diversity and Critical Thinking.* (New York: Oxford University Press, 2017), 5.
4. Sharon Bailin and Harvey Siegel, *Critical Thinking in Blackwell Guide to the Philosophy of Education,* (Eds) Nigel Blake et al., (Blackwell publishing, 2003), 181.
5. Harvey Siegel, *Educating Reason: Rationality, Critical Thinking and Education,* op. cit., 32.
6. Ibid., 23.
7. Harvey Siegel, *Rationality Redeemed? Further Dialogues on an Educational Ideal,* op. cit., 2.
8. Robert H. Ennis, *A Concept of Critical Thinking,* Harvard Educational Review, 32, no. 1, 1962, 83.
9. Robert H. Ennis**,** *Critical Thinking Assessment, Theory into Practice/ Summer* 1993, 179-180.
10. Robert H. Ennis, *Critical Thinking* (Prentice–hall, Inc, 1996), xvii.
11. Cf. Paul, R. & Elder, L. *Critical Thinking: Tools for Taking Charge of Your Learning and Your Life.* (Pearson/Prentice Hall, 2008), 17ff
12. John E. McPeck., *Critical Thinking and Education,* (Oxford: Martin Robertson, 1981), 8.
13. Mathew Lipman, *Thinking in Education,* (New York Cambridge University Press, 2003), 212
14. Sharon Bailin & Mark Battersby, *Reason in the Balance: An Inquiry Approach to Critical Thinking* (Cambridge: Hackett publishing Company, Inc. 2016), 6
15. Harvey Siegel, *Educating Reason: Rationality, Critical Thinking and Education,* op. cit., 9.
16. Harvey Siegel, *Rationality Redeemed? Further Dialogues on an Educational Ideal,* op. cit., 2.

17. Sharon Bailin and Harvey Siegel, *Critical Thinking in Blackwell Guide to the Philosophy of Education* op. cit., 182.
18. Harvey Siegel, *Educating Reason: Rationality, Critical Thinking and Education*, op. cit., 23 and 42.
19. Harvey Siegel, *Critical Thinking as an Educational Ideal.* The Educational Forum, 1980; 8, November.
20. Harvey Siegel, **E**ducating Reason: Rationality, Critical Thinking and Education, op. cit., 34.
21. Harvey Siegel, *Rationality Redeemed? Further Dialogues on an Educational Ideal,* op. cit., 2.
22. Harvey Siegel, *Educating Reason: Rationality, Critical Thinking and Education,* op. cit., 34.
23. Ibid., 38.
24. Ibid., 35
25. Harvey Siegel, *Rationality Redeemed? Further Dialogues on an Educational Ideal,* op. cit., 16.
26. Harvey Siegel, *Education's Epistemology: Rationality, Diversity and Critical Thinking.* op. cit., 4.
27. Ibid., 173-174.
28. Ibid., 125.
29. Harvey Siegel, *Educating Reason: Rationality, Critical Thinking and Education,* op. cit., 39.
30. Harvey Siegel, *Rationality Redeemed? Further Dialogues on an Educational Ideal,* op.cit., 35-36.
31. Ibid., 36.
32. Harvey Siegel, *Critical Thinking as an Educational Ideal.* The Educational Forum, op. cit., 8.
33. Ibid.
34. Harvey Siegel, *Educating Reason: Rationality, Critical Thinking and Education,* op. cit., 32.
35. Ibid., 33.
36. Ibid., 39.
37. Harvey Siegel, *Critical Thinking as an Educational Ideal,* op. cit., 9.
38. Harvey Siegel, *Educating Reason: Rationality, Critical Thinking and Education,* op. cit., 7
39. Ibid., 39.
40. Ibid., 41.
41. Ibid., 9.
42. Ibid., 54.

43. Ibid., 39.
44. Ibid., 41.
45. Harvey Siegel, *Rationality Redeemed? Further Dialogues on an Educational Ideal,* op. cit., 49-50.
46. Ibid., 52.
47. Israel Scheffler, *Reason and Teaching* (London: Routledge, 1973), 62.
48. Ibid.
49. Ibid., 63.
50. Israel Scheffler, *The Language of Education,* (Springfield, III.: Charles C. Thomas, 1960), 98-9.
51. Robert H. Ennis, *Critical Thinking* (Prentice–hall, Inc, 1996), xviii.
52. Ibid., xx.
53. Ibid.
54. Ibid., 4.
55. Ibid., 5.
56. Ibid., 6.
57. Ibid., 7.
58. Ibid.
59. Ibid., 8.
60. Ibid., 13.
61. Robert H. Ennis, *Critical Thinking Dispositions: Their Nature and Assessability,* Informal Logic Vol. 18, Nos. 2 & 3 (1996), 165.
62. Robert H. Ennis, *Critical Thinking,* op. cit., xviii.
63. Ibid., 9.
64. Ibid., 365.
65. Ibid., 9-10.
66. Ibid., 69.
67. Ibid., 73.
68. Harvey Siegel, *Educating Reason: Rationality, Critical Thinking and Education,* op cit., 7.
69. Cf. Paul, R. & Elder, L. *Critical Thinking: Tools for Taking Charge of Your Learning and Your Life.* op.cit., 17ff.
70. Ibid., 16.
71. Paul, R. and Elder, L., *The Miniature Guide to Critical Thinking Concepts and Tools.* Dillon Beach: Foundation for Critical Thinking, 2010, 19.

72. Paul, R. & Elder, L. *Critical thinking: Tools for Taking Charge of Your Learning and Your Life.* op.cit., xxiii.
73. Mathew Lipman, *Thinking in Education,* op. cit., 213.
74. Ibid,
75. Ibid., 217.
76. John. E. McPeck., *Critical Thinking and Education,* op. cit., 5.
77. Ibid., 7- 8.
78. Ibid., 9.
79. Ibid.,19.
80. Ibid., 22.
81. Ibid., 23
82. Ibid.
83. Ibid., 12.
84. Harvey Siegel, *Educating Reason: Rationality, Critical Thinking and Education,* op. cit., 18.
85. Ibid., 19.
86. Richard W. Paul, *McPeck's Mistakes Informal Logic VII.1*, Winter 1985, 35-36.
87. John McPeck, *Paul's Critique of Critical Thinking and Education, Informal Logic VI1.1*, Winter 1985, 45.
88. Sharon Bailin & Mark Battersby, *Reason in the Balance: An Inquiry Approach to Critical Thinking* (Cambridge: Hackett publishing Company, Inc. 2016), 6
89. Ibid., 47.
90. Ibid., 17.
91. Ibid., 19.
92. Ibid., 19-20.
93. Ibid., 20.
94. Ibid.
95. Ibid., 26.
96. Siegel, Harvey, *Educating Reason: Rationality, Critical Thinking, and Education,* op. cit., 152.
97. Sharon Bailin, *Critical and Creative Thinking, Informal Logic Vol. IX.1*, Winter 1987, 23- 24.
98. Ibid., 27.
99. Sharon Bailin and Harvey Siegel, *Critical Thinking in Blackwell Guide to the Philosophy of Education,* op. cit., 186.

100. Sharon Bailin, *Critical and Creative Thinking,* Informal Logic, op. cit., 24.
101. Harvey Siegel, *Educating Reason: Rationality, Critical Thinking, and Education,* op. cit., 152.
102. Ibid.
103. Ibid.
104. Sharon Bailin, *Critical and Creative Thinking,* Informal Logic, op. cit., 24.
105. Ibid.
106. Ibid. 26.
107. Ibid.,
108. Ibid., 25.
109. Ibid.,
110. Ibid.
111. Ibid., 27.
112. Sharon Bailin and Harvey Siegel, *Critical Thinking in Blackwell Guide to the Philosophy of Education,* op. cit., 186.
113. Sharon Bailin & Mark Battersby, *Reason in the Balance: An Inquiry Approach to Critical Thinking,* op. cit., 17.
114. Sharon Bailin and Harvey Siegel, *Critical Thinking in Blackwell Guide to the Philosophy of Education,* op. cit., 186.
115. Paul, R. & Elder, L. *Critical Thinking: The Nature of Critical and Creative Thought in Journal of Developmental Education* Volume 30, Issue 2 Winter 2006, 34.
116. Cf. Paul, R. & Elder, L. *Critical Thinking: Tools for Taking Charge of Your Learning and Your Life.* op. cit., 2008,
117. Mathew Lipman, *Thinking in Education,* op. cit., 194.
118. Robert H. Ennis, *Critical Thinking,* op.cit., xvii.
119. Sharon Bailin and Harvey Siegel, *Critical Thinking in Blackwell Guide to the Philosophy of Education,* op. cit., 187.
120. Ibid.,
121. Ibid.,186.
122. Ibid., 188.
123. Sharon Bailin & Mark Battersby, *Reason in the Balance: An Inquiry Approach to Critical Thinking* op. cit., 273.
124. Sharon Bailin, *Critical and Creative Thinking,* Informal Logic, op.cit., 23.
125. Ibid., 25.

126. Ibid.
127. Ibid., 28
128. Ibid.
129. John E. McPeck., *Critical Thinking and Education,* op.cit., 36.
130. Robert H. Ennis, *Critical Thinking,* op. cit., xvii.
131. Ibid., 1.
132. Ibid. xvii.
133. Ibid.,
134. bid., 364.
135. Sharon Bailin & Mark Battersby, *Reason in the Balance: An Inquiry Approach to Critical Thinking,* op. cit., 100.
136. Harvey Siegel, *Rationality Redeemed? Further Dialogues on an Educational Ideal,* op. cit., 35-36.
137. Sharon Bailin & Mark Battersby, *Reason in the Balance: An Inquiry Approach to Critical Thinking,* op. cit., 20.
138. Ibid., 273.
139. Ibid., 276.
140. Harvey Siegel, *Educating Reason: Rationality, Critical Thinking and Education,* op. cit., 7
141. Ibid., 10.

CHAPTER TWO
SOME ISSUES EMERGING FROM THE NATURE OF CRITICAL THINKING

2 *Introduction*

Critical thinking has a reified position in the world of academia as illustrated in chapter one, but this is not without controversies, questions or issues. It is notable that many ideas or aspects of critical thinking have been subjected to criticisms. This current chapter addresses such controversies, criticisms and issues that have emerged from the proceedings in chapter one. These include: the definition of critical thinking; notion of skills; the relationship between skills/abilities and dispositions and virtues; generalizable or domain-specificity of critical thinking; the role of logic and epistemology; the relation between rationality and critical thinking; the role of context; the relationship between critical and creative thinking; critical thinking and related concepts such high order thinking, inquiry, problem solving and decision making. In addition, how to teach critical thinking has occasioned controversy. Our aim will be to show that these issues extend the discussions of critical thinking in new directions. Further, the objective in what follows is to clarify some of the issues that seem to anchor the topic of critical thinking and demonstrating that there is need for further research.

2.1 *Definitional issues*

One of the major issues is the definition of critical thinking. It is notable that there are numerous attempts to define, interrogate and understand the term critical thinking from philosophical and psychological perspectives. Siegel observes that "as already noted, while philosophers generally understand it normatively, psychologists and others often understand it descriptively,"[1] as illustrated in the previous chapter. This means that there is no one single definition of critical thinking. These philosophical and psychological attempts have developed different approaches to defining critical thinking that reflect their respective concerns. Hence, it is evident that there are many different definitions of critical thinking which have been derived providing different perspectives of its nature.

The nature of critical thinking, or its definition, remains a valid concern given the plethora of philosophical and psychological interpretations. While we concede that defining critical thinking is an elusive and convoluted notion, there is the need to explore and consider more fully these approaches to critical thinking that have occasioned controversies and contentions, even if only as way of putting the problem into proper perspective.

2.2   Critical Thinking as Skills

A dominant perspective among theoreticians of critical thinking is the notion of skills which is tainted with difficulties or controversies resulting to criticisms. Notably, Sharon Bailin has a strong aversion for the notion of "skills." According to her, the philosophical theorists discussed have their conceptions of critical thinking framed in terms of "skills", which is problematic. For her, one of the sources of the problem is that the term "skill" is ambiguous. It can have various meanings when used in adjectival form (e.g., a skilled reasoner) and the adverbial form (e.g., she reasons skilfully) or as a noun to refer to some inner entity or ability. She argues out that principles, reasons and arguments are very different from "skills" which are inner while the former are abilities and public entities.

Siegel writes that "...such skill talk acceptable as long as it is taken as referring to thinking that is skilled in the sense that it meets relevant criteria. In this sense the critical thinker is rightly conceived as a thinker who has both the skills/abilities, and the dispositions..."[2] as elaborated in chapter one.

Bailin et al., on the other hand, maintain that the principles, reasons and arguments are to be applied to specific domains while for her, the talk of "skills" leads to the problem of generalization which is addressed below.

It is notable that a proper conceptualization of the notion of skills is inevitable. Another issue closely related to this, is the skills view account of critical thinking.

2.3 The skills View Only Account of Critical Thinking

So far, we have demonstrated that critical thinking entails two components; the reason assessment as well as the critical attitude or critical spirit component. We pointed out that to be *appropriately* moved by reasons is to adhere to the tenets of reason assessment and to be appropriately *moved* by reasons is an inclination or propensity to act or belief which reflects the reasons assessment component. The main theoreticians of critical thinking namely; Harvey Siegel, Israel Scheffler, Robert H. Ennis, Richard Paul, Linda Elder, John McPeck, Mathew Lipman and Sharon Bailin accounts of critical thinking reflect this view.

However, some theorists have criticized this account of critical thinking arguing that it is only viable to talk of a "skills view only account of critical thinking." It has been argued that the dualistic or two components, that is, *appropriately* moved by reasons (reason assessment) and appropriately *moved* by reasons (critical spirit or critical attitude) or the normative impact of reasons account of critical held by these theoreticians is badly flawed.

The major representative of the skills view account is Connie Missimer in her article *"Perhaps by Skill Alone."*[3] Accordingly, the skills view of critical thinking is thinking in such a way as to fulfil relevant standards. This is to imply that skills view only account of critical thinking is at the core of intellectual activity or rigour that involves recognizing an argument, use evidence in support of that argument, draw reasoned conclusions, recognizing fallacious reasoning, evaluating credibility of sources and use information to solve problems and make decisions.

It follows that the skills-plus-dispositions view or 'character view' as she connotes it, which goes beyond these set of rules or standards or the use of good reason to certain dispositions, commitments, attitudes or habits of mind that dispose an individual to use these intellectual tools to fulfil relevant standards and principles of good thinking is badly flawed or mistaken. For her, such character view or dispositions or traits of mind or habits of mind, in short, the critical attitude or critical spirit component is questionable if not defective. She raises the following issues regarding the critical attitude or critical spirit component, which she baptises as the character view:

> Versions of this theory (hereafter called the Character View) have been advanced without much analysis. The impression is that these traits or virtues are obvious accompaniments to critical thinking, yet such is not the case. Versions of the Character View are inconsistent; even within one version unlikely scenarios arise. Furthermore, historical evidence can be brought against this view. Most people assume that the greatest contributors to intellectual progress would be critical thinkers. Yet a number of intellectual giants, including Marx, Rousseau, Bacon, Freud, Russell, Newton, and Feynmann lacked many of the traits which the Character View holds to be necessary for critical thinking. This

> discrepancy calls into question the connection between having certain dispositions or virtues and the ability to think critically. Rather than concluding that these and other great thinkers cannot have been critical thinkers, one can subscribe to an alternative view which makes no claims about character, namely that critical thinking is a skill or set of skills (hereafter, the Skill View). According to this view, a critical thinker is someone who practices the skills of critical thinking frequently, just as a mathematician is a person who does mathematics frequently. Critical thinking is here defined as the consideration of alternative theories in light of their evidence, a definition which we believe encompasses the skill criteria of Ennis and Paul. [4]

She then argues out that these discrepancies challenge the connection between possession of certain dispositions or attitudes and the skills/abilities of critical thinking. She points out that the "character view" of critical thinking as encompassing critical attitude or critical spirit is overtly boring and must be replaced with the skills view. This discrepancies according to her, call for the replacement of the character view with the skill view of critical thinking as a skill or set of skills. Accordingly, the Skill View is more exciting than the skills plus dispositions or character view of critical thinking.

The issues she raises have some positive criticism as well as misleading ideas. We agree that dispositions or character traits have not been adequately specified, there is no proper account of how they relate with each other and even if they are, the repertoire is overwhelming. Two, the theorists differ in their conception of character traits or dispositions. This however does not call for the rejection of the critical attitude or spirit component. She is wrong when she points out that great thinkers are uncritical due to their character. By the fact that they are great thinkers implies that they are critical thinkers. In addition, critical thinking is critical about everything including the ethical or dispositions or the character traits and more so, there is sufficient analysis of the nature of critical thinking as skills/abilities or dispositions. We have demonstrated to this effect following the theoreticians of critical thinking in chapter one. The notion of excitement has to do with the manner of teaching which fosters critical thinking skills by looking at historicality of thought and thinkers but not with the issue of the nature of critical thinking itself. Siegel, in his book, *Rationality Redeemed? Further Dialogues on an Educational Ideal,* offers a comprehensive analysis of the issues raised and gives a detailed response to Connie Missimer than treated here.

We conclude by pointing out that this dispute calls for further philosophical engagement on the relationship between reason assessment and critical attitude or critical spirit components, the relationship between *appropriately* moved by reason and the appropriately *moved* by reason.

2.4 The Generalist versus the Specifist View

A central question we now wish to address is whether or not critical thinking skills/abilities and dispositions are generalizable or domain-specific. The contention centres on the question; to what extent can critical thinking skills/abilities and dispositions be taught in the context of specific subject domain or are they generalizable across subjects? In order to put the issue into perspective, it is necessary here to clearly understand the meaning of generalization and the domain-specific views of critical thinking. There are two diametrically opposed positions or perspectives namely; the *generalist* and the *specifist*. *Generalist* view hold there are generalizable critical thinking skills/abilities and dispositions, in the sense that these can be utilised or applied across a broad range of contexts and circumstances. The *specifist* view hold the contrary, that such skills/abilities and dispositions, are domain, discipline-, or content-specific. In this respect, the theorists discussed on critical thinking are divided along these two perspectives. Some perceive and argue that critical thinking skills/abilities and dispositions can be generalized across different contexts and domains and can thus be taught in a generic way while others are opposed. This means that within the critical thinking discourse, it is essentially observed by some theorists that critical thinking skills/abilities and dispositions are generic, that is, they apply across all domains or subjects. The positions of Siegel, Ennis, Lipman, Paul and Elder, attest to the generic nature of critical thinking. However, it is notable that some theorists namely; John McPeck and Bailin Sharon have argued that critical thinking skills/abilities and dispositions cannot be generalized but are domain, discipline-, or content-specific. It is against this background that the two perspectives can be analyzed more meaningfully and fruitfully.

McPeck and Bailin, advocate for the subject, -domain-specific critical thinking skills/abilities and dispositions. They argue that general critical thinking skills that transcend specific subjects do not exist. Accordingly, critical thinking skills can only be taught in the context of a subject, -discipline, -specific domain.

Robert Ennis[5] challenges the *specifist* view by raising the issue of ambiguity and vagueness of the term subject, topic, domain, and field. These terms need to be clarified within the debate of generalization or non-generalization of skills/abilities and dispositions. This is powerful challenge against the advocates of subject-specific view of critical thinking. This vagueness or ambiguity, for Ennis, poses a major challenge to the idea that critical thinking must take place within a particular subject, discipline, field or domain. The *generalist* and the *specifist* dichotomy of critical thinking is also addressed by Siegel when he asserts that:

> "Epistemological subject specificity"–the idea that different fields utilize different, incompatible criteria for the determination of the goodness of reasons, so that what counts as a good reason in one field does not count in another, and therefore that principles and skills of reason assessment must differ from field to field and so be taught in the context of the subject matter of each field–fails because of the vagueness of "field."[6]

Accordingly, reasons conception account of critical thinking is not domain or field specific but it is applicable generally and the thesis of epistemological subject specificity fails because of the ambiguity or vagueness of "field." He further observes that:

> The fact that there are (at least) two general types of principles of reasons assessment–subject–specific and subject–neutral–suggests that much recent debate between various members of the movement are right; both subject-specific and, non-generalizable skills, and subject-neutral, generalizable skills, principles and information are highly relevant to reason assessment and so to critical thinking.[7]

The subject–specific principle of reasons assessment non generalizable skills/abilities are applicable to specific subjects or domains such as physics, chemistry, mechanical, electrical or telecommunication engineering among others while subject-neutral, generalizable skills applicable across board. For Siegel, neither can be ignored or affirmed as better than the other for they are all central to reason assessment component of critical thinking. Further, it is to be noted that there are general skills, which are applicable as general activity of thinking in as much as some acts of thinking are particular activity. In addition, the domain, discipline-, or content-specific as advocated, is essential knowledge for critical thinking but it does not undercut generalist view. In essence, the generalist view provides the space unto which the specifist view of critical thinking operates. It is clear therefore, that the Siegelian *reasons conception* comprising of the reason assessment component and the critical attitude or critical spirit component addresses and resolves the issue of generalizability of critical thinking.

The reason assessment component as well as the critical attitude or critical spirit are generalizable and applicable to particular "fields." Hence, the advocates of the generalist view are correct in asserting that the reason assessment component is generalizable and not domain-specific. The specifists are correct to assert the essentiality of subject-specific knowledge in critical thinking and also the role of reason assessment component in domain-specific or subject specific. The issues of generalization and the transferability of skills/abilities and dispositions for Siegel are to be put to rest when one conceptualizes properly the *reasons conception* of critical thinking. Siegel, in this regard, is both sympathetic to the generalist and the specifist views of critical thinking. This captures the issue but not adequately hence room for further dialogue.

2.5 The Dispositions and Intellectual Virtues

In chapter one, we discussed the account of critical thinking demonstrating that it has two components namely; 1) the skills/abilities and 2) dispositions pointing out the difference between the two. In the analysis, we also demonstrated that the theoreticians of critical thinking embrace intellectual virtues. From this exposition, the questions or issues which arise include: what are dispositions? Are the virtues the same as skills/abilities and dispositions? The issue is whether there is fundamental difference between the three terms namely; skills/abilities, dispositions and intellectual virtues. This section seeks to spell out these issues at length.

A starting point which would help us in understanding the issues of the skills/abilities and dispositions is Siegel's remark that:

> If inadequate learning results in part from failures of dispositions rather than of abilities or skills, instructional remediation efforts will have to be redirected to some extent from the latter toward the former. More generally, the question of how best to foster desirable dispositions takes on practical and research importance once the relevance of dispositions to thinking performance is granted.[8]

For Siegel, dispositions are important and relevant to educational activities but should their existence be taken for granted? He puts this point as follows:

> But should the "reality" of thinking dispositions, and so their relevance to education, be granted? The answer to these questions depends upon the satisfactory quieting of legitimate doubts concerning the character, the explanatory force, and, more fundamentally, the very existence of thinking dispositions. It is the purpose of this paper to quiet such doubts.[9]

For Siegel there is the need to investigate the nature, character and fundamentally the existence of thinking dispositions. In essence, Siegel seeks to comprehensively and satisfactorily quiet the legitimate doubts and concerns on "...*the question of the reality of thinking dispositions and how best to foster desirable dispositions....*"

In order to address these issues, we will revisit the Siegelian reasons conception account of critical thinking. Siegel provides a clear distinction between skills/abilities and dispositions. As a recap, reason assessment component comprises of the skills/abilities, *the ability to reason well*, that is, to be *appropriately* moved by reason. The critical attitude or critical spirit component entails the *inclination, tendencies or dispositions to reason well and be guided by reason*, that is, to be appropriately *moved* by reason. Hence, the two are distinct but intertwined.

In the exposition of the nature of critical thinking, the notions or theme of intellectual virtues arose. Various theorists advocated for intellectual virtues such as impartiality, honesty, integrity, courage, autonomy, perseverance, empathy, respectfulness, justice or fair-mindedness, open-mindedness among others as core characteristics of critical thinkers. From this understanding, the matter arising is the relationship between the skills/abilities, dispositions and intellectual virtues.

Again, Siegel in his *reasons conception* account of critical thinking addresses this issue of the relationship between critical thinking, dispositions and intellectual virtues. There is a relationship between the three but they are not conceptually the same. This tripartite distinction between skills/abilities, dispositions and intellectual virtues is manifested in the reasons conception account of critical thinking. We have shown the conceptual difference between skills/abilities and the dispositions. Intellectual virtues are not the same as skills/abilities or dispositions. However, it is important to note that dispositions and virtues overlap in many ways but both necessarily and sufficiently require the guidance of reason assessment of the *reasons conception* account of critical thinking, hence rational virtues. This overlap is not to be construed to imply virtues as understood by Plato, Aristotle or St. Thomas Aquinas.

My take and recommendations is that there is the need for further dialogue and philosophical research on these matters.

2.6 *Logic, Rationality, Epistemology and Context*

Within the discussions on the nature of critical thinking, the following concepts emerged; logic, reasons, rationality, epistemology and context. We wish to discuss them further here.

Logic

One of the major disputes or controversies is the relationship between critical thinking and logic. In addressing this issue, perhaps a starting point would be on the nature of logic. Logic is systematic study of arguments or reasoning. It evaluates, analyzes, constructs and seeks to understand arguments. Logic ensures that good argumentation takes place by emphasising on drawing deductive and inductive inferences; determining validity and invalidity, sound and unsound, strong and weak, cogent and uncogent arguments; evaluating causal claims, estimating probabilities and evaluating inferences drawn by others. Further, the nature of logic entails the provision of clear and good reasons.

For example, Siegel emphasizes that the reason assessment component focuses on proper assessing of good reasons and a grasp of the principles governing such assessment. This was termed as the subject-neutral principles which are essential characteristics of formal and informal logic. Therefore, it is plausible to infer that reason assessment component, and critical thinking in general entails logic.

This necessarily leads to the fact that there is a fundamental relationship between logic (formal and informal) and critical thinking. Logic is relevant to critical thinking *simpliciter*. This is to imply that critical thinking is logical in character. Accordingly, there is conceptual and a pedagogical link between the two. This is supported by the view that critical thinking entails reason assessment component which has to do with logic *simpliciter*. Thus, logic and logical knowledge is relevant to critical thinking in so far as the latter is viewed as incorporating reason assessment component. The inseparability of logic from critical thinking, therefore, is a matter of necessity and not a matter of accident.

In this respect, logic (both formal and informal) is relevant to critical thinking. Having this in mind, we have developed a full analysis of formal and informal logic demonstrating their relevance in critical thinking in chapter four. It would suffice here to assert that logical knowledge is indispensable to critical thinking.

Too much or excessive Epistemology?

Another contentious issue that emerged in chapter one, is the relationship between critical thinking and epistemology. Siegel puts it that:

> Without having some epistemological understanding of notions such as reason, rationality, knowledge, truth, evidence, warrant, justification, and so on, the critical thinking student has at best a superficial grasp of her subject. It is central to critical thinking education that students develop some understanding of the epistemology underlying critical thinking.[10]

Such a quest will facilitate a comprehensive grasp of critical thinking subject matter. However, this has not been unproblematic in the attempts of understanding the nature of critical thinking:

> Our trail has led thus far to the conclusion that sound critical thinking pedagogy requires attention to the epistemology underlying critical thinking. So what is that epistemology? What epistemology are we committed to when we favour the ideal of critical thinking; when we think it good to be a critical thinker and encourage our students to become critical thinkers?[11]

Therefore, a comprehensive understanding of epistemology underlying critical thinking is fundamental and indispensable which entails the grasping of the nature of former and its relationship to the latter. Hence, here we wish to explicate this relationship and in so doing, it will become clear that epistemological reflections on critical thinking promise important philosophical insights, both for epistemology, critical thinking and scholarly research.

Epistemology is a branch of philosophy conceived as inquiry or focusing on the study or nature of reasons, warrant and justification for beliefs and actions. It will suffice here to focus on Harvey Siegel who just as he weighed in matters of logic has also considered the notion of epistemology in critical thinking. However, he cautions that:

> While I don't pretend to have anything like a full conception of the epistemology underlying critical thinking to offer, I do think that a commitment to critical thinking requires that we take particular stands on some contentious epistemological issues.[12]

Some of the contentious epistemological issues that Siegel addresses include; McPeckian thesis, Alvin Goldman's *Veritistic*

Social Epistemology, the theory of *Epistemic Dependence* and his response to Emma William *concerns of too much epistemology or "in excess of epistemology."*

In particular, one of the contentious issues that Siegel addresses is the relationship between rational justification and truth:

> The first concerns the nature of rational justification, and the relation between such justification and truth. We saw earlier that for *r* to count as a reason for *q*, *r* must be justified. What about *q* itself? Must *q* be true if belief in *q* is to be rational? The answer required by a commitment to critical thinking, is negative: it can be rational to believe that *q* even if *q* is false. The rationality of believing *q* is independent of *q*'s truth.[13]

For Siegel, rational justification is independent of truth. All beliefs must be rationally justified. He gives the examples of once beliefs held true but now are false. They include; Newtonian physics, the weight of air, belief that the earth was flat, that the sun moves and not the earth. All these beliefs turned out to be false though there were good reasons or evidence in their support then. He also argues that there can be good reasons or powerful evidence, which points against what is true. One can believe what is true or what is false. Hence, truth and rational justification are independent:

> In short, the lesson here is that truth is independent of rational justification; we can be justified in believing that *q* even though *q* is false; and we can be justified in rejecting *q* as false even though it is true.[14]

In chapter one, we argued out, following Siegel, that epistemology is no longer a discipline aimed only at *Justification of True Belief*, as Goldman argued, but *rational belief or rational justification*. This is not to say that Siegel rejects the notion of *true belief* but he is opposed to the idea that it is the only sole end of epistemology. In this respect, Siegel advocates for *true belief* as well as rational *belief*. Goldman views critical thinking as an instrumental value and not as an end in itself in the epistemic endeavour. Siegel challenges this and stresses the value of critical thinking as *rational belief* or *rational justification* and hence an epistemic end in itself. Epistemic dependence, according to Siegel, is an inadequate account of epistemology since one must embrace critical scrutiny of what is given. Hence, he calls for the embracement of *rational belief* or *rational justification*.

He writes that "critical thinking, we have been suggesting, fundamentally involves believing and acting on the basis of reasons; it involves, that is, rational justification."[15] Critical thinking entails believing, judging, and acting rationally, that is, on the basis of reasons, which are properly evaluated. The view that truth is independent of rational justification is a philosophically and epistemological contentious issue:

> The idea that truth and rational justification are independent is contentious philosophically: it contradicts Dewey's view of truth as "warranted assertibility," and it is rejected by contemporary philosophers like Hillary Putnam,...who rejects a "radically nonepistemic" conception of truth and argues that truth should be understood as " ideal rational acceptability," and Michael Dummett (1980) who denies that truth can be coherently conceived of as independent of all possible verification.[16]

In spite of their position, Siegel asserts that truth and rational justification are independent.

Another issue that Siegel addresses is the relationship between critical thinking and relativity asserting that relativism of reasons is incompatible with critical thinking education:

> In such education our aim is to help students develop the ability to evaluate arguments and the probative force which putative reasons have, and to encourage students to believe and act on the basis of reason– *to be appropriately moved by reasons.*[17]

Such a conception entails proper evaluation of reasons and hence incompatible with relativism. He writes that "so critical thinking is incompatible with, and must defeat relativism."[18] This is because relativism undermines and it is an obstacle to the fostering of critical thinking skills/abilities and dispositions.

Siegel goes on to point out that, clearly the pre-eminent aim of critical thinking cannot be the identification of truths *simpliciter*, given fallibilism; it must rather be the identification of what is true at a given time. Given fallibilism and the need for justification, and due to lack of easy accessibility of truth, critical thinking skills/abilities and dispositions are central to the lives of truth-seeking epistemic agents:

> In other words, we have no immediate or privileged access to the truth; we "get at" the truth by assessing warrant. We take justification to be a sign of truth. Truth thus functions for us, as Kant might say, as a regulative *ideal*: the upshot of justification is prima facie case for truth.[19]

This is informed by the fact that knowledge is fallible and there is limited access to the truth. Siegelian view of epistemic aim is that it should strive to foster, not knowledge or justified true belief, but rather the skills/abilities and dispositions constitutive of, and sustained by critical thinking. Accordingly, critical thinking is not only an epistemic end in itself but also independent from it. This is to imply that critical thinking justifies truth. This notwithstanding, critical thinking is epistemically valuable "independently of its instrumental tie to truth."[20] Consequently, critical thinking, and the pursuit of epistemology as incorporated in reasons conception account of critical thinking is a crucial skill that should be developed in students to help them attain *rational belief* or *rational justification*. The prime goal of epistemology is not only *justified true belief*, but also rather the development of the skills/abilities and dispositions to judge or estimate the truth skilfully and well, and this is a matter of critical thinking. Hence, the goal of critical thinking is the development of the ability to assess *truth* status skilfully and accurately. For Siegel, critical thinking should facilitate *justified rational belief*. Critical thinking and justification have a fundamental epistemic value. *Truth* is by way of justification on the basis of reasons and evidence. As an elaboration, Siegel asserts that "it is not truth which is critical to critical thinking, but rather justification."[21] Truth is independent of justification but the both are related "for claims which are rationally justified are claims which have reasons to regard as true."[22] In the light of these discussions, Siegel asserts that "this is the route to true as well as justified belief."[23] In addition, for Siegel, critical thinking as an epistemic dimension calls for reflections about beliefs, fostering dispositions and autonomy.

Siegel then delineates five reasons why there is need to "motivate critical thinking students with epistemology." These are; it motivates students; gives critical thinking weight; facilitates understanding of what is taught; and leads to the appreciation that critical thinking is a philosophical and in particular, an epistemological discipline, finally and most importantly, it facilitates thinking about critical thinking. He further asserts that:

> Moreover, when we help students to become critical thinkers– by helping them to understand and apply appropriate criteria of reason assessment, and by encouraging them to seek reasons by which to justify candidates beliefs and actions–we in effect invite them to demand reasons for accepting as legitimate the criteria of reason assessment we are teaching them. In encouraging students to become critical thinkers, then, we encourage them to pursue epistemological questions concerning reason assessment and critical thinking for themselves. That is, we encourage them to be critical thinkers about critical thinking itself.[24]

Students should be encouraged to think critically about critical thinking itself and more specifically, the justification of the reason assessment component. This is the rationale of incorporating epistemology into critical thinking.

Up to this point, we have exposed that for Siegel, *rational belief* and *rational justification* are more serious epistemological concerns than the traditional approach of epistemology as pure desire for justification of truth or true belief. For Siegel, those epistemological reflections and critical thinking deserve more attention than given within the critical thinking debate. Questions such as; should epistemology remain the classical discipline of acquiring truth? What is place of truth, true belief, relativism, justification, fallibilism in critical thinking? Is education an epistemic endeavour? These are desiderata as it were for further research. Finally, it is clear that Siegelian perspective is an important philosophical insight, for his discussions are important contributions to our broad theoretical understanding of the epistemology and critical thinking. What follows from this is that:

> Once it is seen how critical thinking and its instruction presuppose contentious epistemological stances, how epistemology is basic to the theory of critical thinking, and how it contributes (both motivationally and intellectually) to educational efforts aimed at enhancing critical thinking, epistemology's centrality to critical thinking, and place in educational efforts aimed at promoting it, is clear.[25]

We conclude by asserting that further work on these issues has enormous promise for the enhancement of the relationship between the two.

Rationality and Critical Thinking

The notions of rationality and reason are philosophically problematic as evidenced by Siegel when he writes that:

> Being a critical thinker requires basing one's belief and actions on reason; it involves committing oneself to the dictates of rationality. The notions of "reason" and "rationality," however, are philosophically problematic. Just what is reason? How do we know that some consideration constitutes a reason for believing or doing something? How do we evaluate the strength or merits of reasons? What is it for a belief or action to be justified? What is the relationship between justification and truth? Why is rationality to be valued?[26]

These central questions to epistemology are basic to critical thinking as far as it is thought to involve reasons and rationality and they are essential in facilitating the understanding of its subject matter.

The abstract, complex nature of reason and rationality and their determination, merits, strengths, justifications are some of the thorny issues. In other words, how should rationality and reason be understood?

Let us begin by examining the formalistic conception of rationality, which is the common market-place view of rationality. This perspective entails that rationality is "formal" abstract notion, which focuses on logical relationships between sentences or statements and arguments. Siegel observes that "while it is true that "rationality" can be construed as denoting a formal relationship between sentences or positions, such a formalistic conception is epistemologically and educationally inadequate."[27] This formalistic view is of course noble but a limited conception of rationality. We have discussed the epistemological positioning of rationality above and here we wish to focus on the formalistic conception of rationality, which is contrasted by the substantive view discussed and endorsed in this book. The substantive view of rationality/critical thinking entails skills/abilities (formal conception of rationality) as well as dispositions or habits of mind or character traits (critical attitude and critical spirit).

According to Siegel:

> ...rationality is substantive at least in the sense that it involves epistemic or evidential relations between sentences or propositions, and therefore propositional contents as well as formal relationships. Moreover, in so far as rationality is regarded as an educational ideal, it must be understood as involving properties of persons, in particular their attitudes, dispositions, habits of mind and character traits. Only such a conception as this would be thick enough to allow us plausibly to regard rationality as a fundamental educational ideal.[28]

This is a wider conception of rationality than the formalistic view and we will look at the educational ramifications of it in chapter six. Here, we wish to recap this favoured conception of rationality by the theoreticians of critical thinking discussed in chapter one in order to clearly address the question: how should rationality be understood? In so doing, we will be able to highlight and discuss other issues arising from the notion of rationality besides its formalistic conception. In this respect, it is important to briefly look at the relationship or connection between reason, rationality and critical thinking. Such a task will facilitate better a comprehension of those reasons, which not only make rationality and critical thinking inseparable at least in their prime objectives but also, together and reciprocally reinforce each other in the consolidation of those principles and dispositions, which ultimately make critical thinking an ideal.

Rationality is *simpliciter* coextensive with critical thinking. This implies that rationality is impeccably compatible with critical thinking and necessarily the terms are equivalent. Rationality and critical thinking are neither distinct nor incompatible. Therefore, it is impossible to talk of one without necessarily inferring the other. This inseparability of critical thinking and rationality is espoused by Israel Scheffler, Harvey Siegel, Richard Paul, Linda Elder, Robert Ennis and Sharon Bailin.

These named theoreticians hold that rationality is essential for critical thinking. However, McPeck present a misleading and definitely a misconception of the relationship between rationality and critical thinking. Perhaps what rankles many according to Siegel, is McPeck's view that rationality is not *simpliciter* with critical thinking. McPeck contentiously asserts that, "while critical thinking is perfectly compatible with rationality, and with reasoning generally, we should not regard the terms as equivalent."[29] For him, rationality is a particular aspect of critical thinking. Rationality, according to him, is broader than critical thinking. This McPeck's distinction between critical thinking and rationality is unwarranted. Siegel observes that rationality is *simpliciter* for critical thinking when he writes that:

> In so far as rationality consists of believing and acting on the basis of good reasons, and in so far as we accept McPeck's epistemological approach-or any approach which makes reasons assessment central-we must perforce regard critical thinking not as a dimension of rationality, but as its equivalent or educational cognate.[30]

Now pursuing this point to its logical conclusion, rationality is *conditio sine qua non* for critical thinking. Hence, rationality and critical thinking are connected not as matter of accident but as a matter of necessity, they are in *simpliciter* coextensive.

Hence, there is an inseparability of rationality and critical thinking but this is not without its attendant problems. Siegel summarizes these problems when he writes that:

> I have noted several problems in the theory of rationality which are directly relevant to the theory of critical thinking: the inadequacy of the means–ends conception of rationality and the need to develop a more adequate conception; the need for a full development of an epistemology of reasons; the problem of the justification of the commitment to rationality;

the delineation of the limits of rationality; and the problematic nature of the alterability of principles of reason assessment.[31]

We examine these problems briefly below.

As earlier discussed, one of the problems discussed by Siegel is the philosophical market-place conception of rationality or the formalistic conception: "for example, by far the most prevalent conception of rationality in the philosophical market-place is that of the rational person as a means-end reasoner, a maximizer of expected utility or of subjective preference."[32] This utilitarianism use of rationality becomes or serves as a subjective means of preference to an end irrespective of whether such means are rational or moral. In addition, this utilitarian means-end use of rationality does not have rational evaluation of the end. Such a means-end utilisation of rationality is contrary to the ideal of the critical attitude or critical spirit component in which values or character traits or habits of mind that connote a critical thinker are not fostered. This is a limited conceptualization of the "end" within the means-end view of rationality since their many other ends and not just one. In this respect, Siegel points out that:

> We need an account of rationality which recognizes various sorts of reasons, and which provides insight into the nature and epistemic forces of reasons, and which affords that possibility of the rational scrutiny of ends. We need, in short, a deeper conception of rationality than the means-end conception, and an epistemology of reasons alongside it.[33]

These shortcomings contribute to *"the inadequacy of the means–ends conception of rationality and the need to develop a more adequate conception,"* for facilitation of a better account of rationality or theory of critical thinking according to Siegel. Such new conception must overcome the means-end conception of rationality with its limitations by fostering both the skills/abilities and dispositions.

Two; *"The problem of the justification of the commitment to rationality"* concerns the justification of rationality itself. The dispute has been raised on the basis of inconsistency, begging the question and circular reasoning by Riggs, O'Hear and Popper.[34] Therefore, the main rational discontent is that the justification of rationality is irrational, a bogus demand and at best, illegitimate due to fact that in seeking justification one uses the very notion of rationality for its justification. As an elaboration, this rational discontent is based on the fact that if you set out to justify rationality, you will be faced with the inevitable, namely that, you would also be required to use rationality itself to explain rationality. Such a task implies assuming knowledge of what you are in effect required to explain. The explanation of rationality will inevitably entail been rational about rational or rationality. There is yet another complication of essential attributes or qualities in relation to rationality. In justifying rationality, it is essential to look for those things akin to it in order to detect the common characteristics or dissimilarities on the basis of which a comparison can be made in respect to genus and specific difference. However, is this situation applicable if you are addressing rationality? Obviously not; because it will be begging the question, that is, using rationality to explain rationality. In essence, it implies one unique thing that has no genera from which it is possible to deduce common characteristics. Notwithstanding what has been raised above, this is addressed by the use of "self-reflexive justification of rationality,"[35] as argued out by Siegel and Nicholas Rescher.[36] Siegel asserts that:

> Critical thinkers must be critical about critical thinking itself. The quest for reasons and justification which is central to critical thinking must be respected even when that quest self-reflexively involves reasons for engaging in critical thinking. "Why should I (or anyone) engage in critical thinking?" and "Why should I value critical thinking?" are questions which must be respected, and seen as legitimate, by proponents of critical thinking. Since those proponents conceive of their commitment to critical thinking as itself justified, they are bound to strive to provide reasons which justify that commitment. If they don't or can't, their commitment to critical thinking is inconsistent with their own ideal of having their commitments accord with reasons which justify them.[37]

That is, using reasons to justify reasons is acceptable since there is no other source of validation except by the use of reason and therefore legitimate to seek to justify rationality.

Three; "the delineation of the limits of rationality" is yet another issue arising. Siegel notes that:

> Yet another question which is basic to the theory of rationality and which has ramifications for the theory of critical thinking concerns the bounds, or limits, of rationality. Do reasons settle every question? Are we ever justified in "setting reason aside"?[38]

The answer is positive since there are other powerful reasons which can override reasons such as emotions or felt reasons. For example, "if making love will benefit in quality and intensity by "shutting my mind off,""[39] then reason or mind must be shut off, of course for a good reason! Ideally being critical about critical.

The fourth problem entails "the alterability of principles of reason assessment." The charge here is that knowledge or rational traditions evolves and so too are the principles of reason assessment. In spite of the changes, rationality remains the same.

In the light of these discussions, it is clear that the development, an understanding of the theory of rationality, it refinement, it links with critical thinking and other attendant issues need to be researched further. Siegel recommends that: "consequently, the development of a deeper understanding of the notion of rationality is a task which confronts virtually the whole of philosophy; a general theory of rationality is fundamental to philosophy."[40] These problems are relevant to critical thinking and qualify as philosophical problems that need to be resolved.

We conclude this section by quoting Nicholas Rescher's answer to the question; why be rational? "One should be rational because that is the rational thing to do"[41]

Context and Critical Thinking

Another contentious issue is the relationship between critical thinking and context. The theoreticians of critical thinking view it substantively as incorporating the skills/abilities as well as character traits or habits or dispositions. In addition, argue that critical thinking must be viewed contextually.

Thus the accounts of Siegel, Scheffler, Ennis, McPeck, Paul-Elder, Lipman, Bailin et al., link critical thinking with contexts. However, this is not without some problems as Siegel captures it:

> But some writes who favour educational ideals associated with "reason" argue that this ideal must be understood not only substantively but also contextually. The suggestion here is not only that contextual consideration are highly relevant to determining what, in a given context, it is rational to believe, judge and do–with this I agree–but also that what rationality is, the very substance of this notion, is itself contextually determined, so that rationality itself–as concept, and, therefore as an educational ideal–is contextually bound, and alters from context to context.[42]

Clearly, consideration of context and critical thinking is important for the latter does not occur in vacuum and more so we think different in different contexts. One can identify a myriad of contexts in which critical thinking takes place. For example, Siegel stresses education as the proper context of critical thinking; Bailin et al, critical thinking occurs in response to a particular issue, task, question, problematic situation or challenge such as problem solving, decision making in conducting inquiries, and in hermeneutics. It is clear these challenges occur in particular contexts.

However it is contentious to assert that rationality/critical thinking itself is "contextually bound" implying that its nature varies from context to context, that is, "...rationality itself is determined by context, in the sense that what "rationality" means, and whether and why it is to be valued, themselves are determined by context."[43] Critical thinking may be practised in a particular context or culture, but to find it defined in a different way in another culture does raise the question about its true nature.

Nicholas C. Burbules is the major advocate of the contextually bound conception of rationality/critical thinking. For him, "thinking in terms of substantive rationality, or reasonableness, compels us to inquire deeply into how we foster such a set of virtues; into the contexts that support or encourage them; into the barriers that impede them."[44] Contexts are helpful in critical thinking, however problems arise when Burbules asserts that rationality/reasonableness is dependent and incorporate the notions of context, social relations or persons or virtues.[45] This is incompatible with the substantive notion of rationality/critical thinking as entailing skills/abilities and dispositions.

The substantive understanding of critical thinking as encompassing skills/abilities and dispositions or character traits or values is not dependent on any particular culture, persons, personal characteristics, social relations for it is a universal non contextualised perspective. In addressing these issues, the employment of the reason assessment and the critical attitude or critical spirit is a universal activity applicable to different contexts but stand above such contexts.

2.7 Critical Thinking and other Related Terms Connoting Thinking

The relationship between critical thinking and other related terms such a creative thinking, high order thinking, problem solving, decision making and inquiry are equally contentious and therefore subject to debate. The issue of relationship between critical and creative thinking has been raised, the contention been that they are distinct, different and opposed. As we argued, the two terms are not distinct, different and opposed. We also pointed out that high order thinking, inquiry, problem solving and decision making are instance in which critical thinking take place. However, these controversies and challenges call for further examination of the proper relationships of these terms.

2.8 Rationalistic Foundations of Critical Thinking

Another controversial issue is "that critical thinking privileges rational, linear, deductive thought over intuition."[46] The issue centres on the rationalistic foundations of critical thinking. Embracing this rationalistic foundation of critical thinking leads to the view that critical thinking undermines other modes of thinking and understanding such emotions or intuitions. This also implies that the voices of the others including minority groups are sidelined. Inevitably, this is tantamount to prejudices and biases in critical thinking practice and theory. This in turn makes critical thinking be class or culture biased or relativistic in nature. In addition, critical thinking is perceived to side line the role of emotion. However, this is not the case because leading scholars like Siegel, Scheffler, Paul and Elder relate critical thinking to emotions.

From a feminism perspective, the discussed prime authors in critical thinking are predominantly male. The most visible figures in the debates between these traditions have been men.

Therefore, it is arguable that the field of critical thinking has been a male dominated activity. Feminist's philosophical theorist namely; Sharon Bailin, Connie Missimer, Emma Williams and Linda Elder among others have recently contributed to critical thinking debate. This does not address the charge per se and hence the need to encourage and motivate more women to research and write on this subject and in philosophy in general.

Categorically, critical thinking is criticized as favouring values and practices of the dominant groups in society and marginalising others. Such a position excludes the voices of others.

The above criticisms allude to the fact that claims of universalism are especially suspect in a world of increasingly self-conscious diversity. Inevitably, this leads to a moral/ethical concern since any exclusion violates the respect of others as argued by Mark Weinstein.[47] However, it is notable that critical thinking standards are universal and embedded in the traditions of thought or rationality.

We conclude this section by quoting Siegel when he writes that:

> ...many philosophers and philosophers of education today accept the argument that these scholarly fields have been in fact practised in an exclusionary way, that such exclusion is bad, and therefore that these areas of scholarship ought to open themselves up to hitherto excluded voices.[48]

In *What Price Inclusion*, Siegel advocates the need for inclusion. However, the charge that critical thinking is "privileged" on the basis of its rationalistic nature, promotes and endorses various frames of exclusion, merits further attention since it questions the very foundation of critical thinking.

2.9 *Philosophy and Critical Thinking*

According to Siegel, the proceedings so far bring to bear two charges: First, the theory of critical thinking is rather not a detailed philosophical endeavour. Second, it does not address philosophical issues or questions and if it does, it has limited itself to education.[49] As we have demonstrated, the first charge points to the fact that critical thinking theorists have focused on conceptualizing its nature. Consequently, and inevitably critical thinking approach remains dishevelled in questions regarding it nature. The second charge points to the fact that the approach to critical thinking must transcend questions of its nature to competently deal with other philosophical topics. This is to say that the involvement of critical thinking in philosophical problems or issues is not a widespread practice. Further work on these issues or questions has enormous promise for the enhancement of the philosophy at large for example in areas of religion, education and politics.

We have demonstrated the intractable link between critical thinking and rationality. Essentially, we showed that critical thinking foundations are on the notion of rationality, that is, the link between critical thinking and rationality is *simpliciter*. The notion of rationality has its roots in philosophy. Philosophy deals the rationality as its prime object.

Given this status quo, philosophy is *conditio sine qua non* for critical thinking. Hence, there is the need to amplify the fact that critical thinking must operate within the broad spectrum or realm of philosophy. Hence there is, we urge, fundamental relationship between philosophy and critical thinking.

For example, the philosophical problems and worldviews provide the content of critical thinking. In turn, critical thinking evaluates, reflects on these problems and worldviews. We have also discussed the relationship between logic, epistemology and critical thinking all pointing and confirming our position that that the two are intertwined.

Therefore, the suggestion here is that the link between critical thinking and philosophy is *simpliciter*. Siegel captures this when he writes that:

> My point, however, is that the theory of rationality of critical thinking is ultimately dependent upon the philosophical theory of rationality and other philosophical matters, and that theorists of critical thinking do well to recognize that dependence and take up the pursuit of relevant philosophical matters as their own–or at least recognize the commonalities of purpose between themselves and philosophers independently pursuing such matters.[50]

Following Siegel remarks, the next chapter exposes the link between philosophy and rationality.

2.10 Conclusion

This chapter has focused on analyzing some of the issues, controversies or problems arising within the debate regarding the nature of critical thinking.

As a summary, these legitimate doubts and rational discontents include; one, the issue of definition. Clearly, the philosophical theorists have different definitions of critical thinking. While these various theorists of critical thinking certainly differ with regard to its definition, they also reveal some common emphases. The common emphasis is the affinity to the reasons conception account of critical thinking, that is, reason assessment and critical attitude or critical spirit components. They hold the view that critical thinking requires both skills/abilities and dispositions. What is again common to all is that critical thinking is a normative concept, that is, an activity of thinking viewed commonly as good.

Two, the issue of generalization-domain specificity of critical thinking has dogged critical thinking debate. This is one kind of critique, adequate and worthwhile on its own terms and is referred to as generalizability debate. Centrally, the concerns are whether or not critical thinking skills/abilities and dispositions are generalizable. We concluded that critical thinking involves both general and domain or subject specific skills/abilities and dispositions and that neither is superior to the other.

Three, the question of the role of rationality, logic, epistemology and context in critical thinking was addressed. The chapter affirmed that rationality, logic and epistemology in their proper sense are indispensable to critical thinking. Closely related to this was the issue of rationalistic of foundation of critical thinking which it was argued that it is a universal nature of criteria and principles.

Four, the relationship between critical thinking, creative thinking, higher-order thinking, inquiry, problem solving and decision making was addressed. My take is that these stated dimensions are instances of critical thinking. They are domains of applying critical thinking.

Finally, we looked at the issue of philosophy and critical thinking, arguing the need for more research on how to make the former benefit from the latter.

In accordance to this analysis, it is clear that theoreticians of critical thinking in their endeavours are notorious for their inability to explain their subject matter without legitimate doubts and rational discontents. The discussion has led thus for to the conclusion that such an exposure is vital for it facilitates critical thinking about critical thinking that is, thinking critically about critical thinking. It should pay attention to the criteria of reason assessment as well as the critical attitude or critical spirit, focusing on issues of logic, reasons, rationality, epistemology, context, multiculturalism and philosophy just but to mention a few. Again, there is still a lacuna, which calls for reflection on these matters.

All this pointed to one core issue: how do we teach critical thinking? What is the best approach to teach critical thinking? The consideration of this issue is not possible here hence we have addressed it in chapter six.

In the next chapter, we discuss some models of critical thinking. This will be vital in demonstrating how critical thinking and philosophy interrelate.

2.11 End Notes

1. Harvey Siegel, *Education's Epistemology: Rationality, Diversity and Critical Thinking.* (New York: Oxford University Press, 2017), 7.
2. Sharon Bailin and Harvey Siegel, *Critical Thinking in Blackwell Guide to the Philosophy of Education,* (Eds) Nigel Blake et al., (Blackwell Publishing, 2003), 183.

3. Connie Missimer, *"Perhaps by Skill Alone" Informal Logic*, vol. 12 no. 3 pp. 145- 153.
4. Ibid., 145.
5. See. Robert Ennis, *'Critical Thinking and Subject Specificity: Clarification and Needed Research,"* Educational Researcher,' vol. 18, no. 3 pp. 4-10.
6. Harvey Siegel, *Rationality Redeemed? Further Dialogues on an Educational Ideal*, (New York: Routledge, 1997), 29.
7. Harvey Siegel, *Educating Reason: Rationality, Critical Thinking and Education*, (Routledge, 1988), 38.
8. Harvey Siegel, *Education's Epistemology: Rationality, Diversity and Critical Thinking*, op.cit., 49-50.
9. Ibid., 50.
10. Harvey Siegel, *Rationality Redeemed? Further Dialogues on an Educational Ideal*, op.cit., 13-14.
11. Ibid., 17.
12. Ibid.
13. Ibid.
14. Ibid., 18.
15. Ibid., 19.
16. Ibid.
17. Ibid., 20.
18. Ibid.
19. Ibid., 23.
20. Harvey Siegel, *Education's Epistemology: Rationality, Diversity and Critical Thinking*, op. cit., 143.
21. Harvey Siegel, *Rationality Redeemed? Further Dialogues on an Educational Ideal*, op.cit., 22.
22. Ibid.
23. Ibid., 23.
24. Ibid., 16.
25. Ibid., 24.
26. Ibid., 13.
27. Ibid., 102.
28. Ibid., 104.

29. J. E. McPeck., *Critical Thinking and Education,* (Oxford: Martin Robertson, 1981), 12.
30. Harvey Siegel, *Educating Reason: Rationality, Critical Thinking and Education,* op. cit., 30.
31. Ibid., 135.
32. Ibid., 129.
33. 131.
34. Cf. Harvey Siegel, *Rationality Redeemed? Further Dialogues on an Educational Ideal,* op. cit., 80ff.
35. Ibid., 81.
36. See. Ibid.,
37. Ibid., 73.
38. Harvey Siegel, *Educating Reason: Rationality, Critical Thinking and Education,* op. cit., 132.
39. Ibid., 133.
40. Ibid., 128.
41. Nicholas Rescher, *Rationality: A Philosophical Inquiry into the Nature and Rationale of Reason,* (Oxford: Clarendon Press of University Press, 1988), 43.
42. Harvey Siegel, *Rationality Redeemed? Further Dialogues on an Educational Ideal,* op cit., 102.
43. Ibid., 105.
44. Nicholas Burbules, *Rationality and Reasonableness: A Discussion of Harvey's Relativism Refuted and Educating Reason,* "Educational Theory, vol. 42. No. 2. 250.
45. See. Ibid., 252.
46. Sharon Bailin and Harvey Siegel, *Critical Thinking in Blackwell Guide to the Philosophy of Education,* op.cit., 190
47. Mark Weinstein, "Rationalist Hopes and Utopia Visions," In Audrey Thompson, ed., Philosophy of Education1993: Proceedings of the Forty-Ninth Annual Meeting of the Philosophy of Education Society, Vol, No. 3. 25-36.
48. Harvey Siegel, *Rationality Redeemed? Further Dialogues on an Educational Ideal,* op cit., 185.
49. Cf. Harvey Siegel, *Educating Reason: Rationality, Critical Thinking and Education,* op. cit., 136.
50. Ibid.

CHAPTER THREE
SOME MODELS OF CRITICAL THINKING

As it happens, the notion of rationality is a central focus of investigations throughout philosophy.[1]

It seems fair to say that the notion of rationality constitutes a thread which runs through the entire domain of philosophy; and controversies surrounding that notion lay at the heart of contemporary as well as the traditional philosophical problems.[2]

3 Introduction

The chapter presents a brief historical overview of some models of critical thinking, from ancient philosophers, to the 16th and 17th centuries, the age of enlightenment and the 21st century thinkers. We will expose the ideas of some philosophers such Socrates, René Descartes, John Stuart Mill, Bertrand Russell and Kwasi Wiredu among others who exemplify models of 'critical thinking'. We will discuss these models from a time chronological perspective. Indeed, such an exposure, we hope, will be of help to fostering critical thinking skills/abilities and dispositions to readers of this work.

3.1 A Rationale

A historical approach fosters critical thinking skills/abilities and dispositions. Paul and Elder observe that:

> One of the most powerful ways to open our minds to alternative experiences, and thus to counteract the influence of social conditioning and the mass media, is to read "backward." That is, to read books printed in the past: 10 years ago, 20 years ago, 50 years ago, 100 years ago, 200 years ago, 300 years ago, 400 years ago, 500 years ago, 700 years ago, 800 years ago, even 2000 years ago, and more. This provides us with a unique perspective and the ability to step outside of the presuppositions and ideologies of the present day. When we read only in the present, no matter how widely, we are apt to absorb widely shared misconceptions taught and believed today as the truth.

While Siegel advocates for philosophy of science as the most vital way to foster critical thinking, Paul and Elder champion for reading backwards in order to re-think the present. Further, Paul and Elder justify the role of reading backwards by observing that:

> ...reading widely in the past creates multiple perspectives in the mind that

enable one to better understand the complexities of the present. Critical reading creates a lens through which we come to better understand the role in history in our lives, even the role in history of critical thinking itself.

Accordingly, 'reading backward' facilitates thinking historically and discovering that the idea of critical thinking is old and not a new phenomenon.

Connie Missimer in her challenging paper, *Perhaps by Skill Alone*, asserts that great thinkers or intellectual giants with venal character are not critical thinkers. By providing historical evidence, she questions the link between critical thinking skills/abilities and dispositions:

> Most people assume that the greatest contributors to intellectual progress would be critical thinkers. Yet a number of intellectual giants, including Marx, Rousseau, Bacon, Freud, Russell, Newton, and Feynmann lacked many of the traits which the Character View holds to be necessary for critical thinking. This discrepancy calls into question the connection between having certain dispositions or virtues and the ability to think critically.[3]

For her, critical thinking should be conceptualized as skills view and that it is a misnomer to talk of critical thinking dispositions. She writes that "biographies of several great thinkers suggest that aside from the habit of critical thinking, they have no dispositions or attitudes in common."[4] She then gives examples of various intellectual giants who fit into this category such as Sir Isaac Newton's insensitivity to criticism; Bertrand Russell as a liar; Feynman's rudeness and hedonism; Rousseau superiority complex, playfulness and talking advantage of everybody; Marx was anti-Semitic, Galois rashness; William Harvey temperamental and eccentric tempers; Sir Francis Bacon was a cold fish; and Sigmund Freud lied about his research findings.[5] She then asserts that:

> Given this astonishing range among acknowledged great thinkers, the most reasonable conclusion is that one can be a great thinker without to any significant degree having the traits advocated by the Character View. But is a great thinker necessarily a critical thinker? To answer 'no' lands one in some difficulties.[6]

While it is true that there is overwhelming historical evidence of intellectual giants with venal character, it does not make uncritical thinkers lack critical thinking dispositions. Siegel challenges her perspective by asserting that the account of critical thinking as skills/abilities and dispositions does not call for a thinker to be completely moral or perfect or a saint. In addition, not all character traits are essential for critical thinking. He writes that:

> But in general, the character traits deemed by the character view to be important to our conception of critical thinking are not panoply of such traits, but rather only *those which are involved in our efforts to think critically*. Thus traits such as a willingness to follow an argument where it leads, a disposition to demand evidence for candidates beliefs, a propensity to weigh relevant evidence fairly, a tendency to believe in accordance with such evidence, a frank acknowledgment of fallibility, a willingness to take seriously the arguments of others which challenge one's own basic beliefs and commitments, and the like, are the traits emphasized by the character view as relevant to one's status as a critical thinker.[7]

Hence, the intellectual giants discussed in this chapter are critical thinkers per se. In spite of her protests, Missimer acknowledges the value of historical approach to critical thinking when she writes that:

> According to this version of the Skill View, if students get a glimpse of the wealth of theories which exist in every discipline and activity, they will be more likely to start on a lifetime intellectual journey. If they acquire the habit of critical thinking, we hope that they will go on to contribute their own strands to the weave of intellectual history. By this view the ultimate justification of critical thinking as an educational ideal is that looking at the past acts of critical thinking which form the backbone of each discipline will produce more critical thinking, 'theoretike,' on the part of students in their endeavors in every subject.[8]

She points out that argumentation, rationality and reasoned judgments run through the history of intellectual history have contributed to moral and intellectual benefits. Students will consider and build on 'reading backwards' on these wealth of information while practising critical thinking. Siegel agrees to this extent when he writes that:

> I quite agree with Missimer about pedagogical virtues of this historical study-indeed, I recommend much the same role for the history of science in my discussion of science education.[9]

We have discussed in details of the Missimer perspective in chapter two and it suffices to assert that the above are vital insights that provide the rationale for this chapter.

3.2 The Ancient Period: The Cradle of Critical Thinking

What is philosophy? Why Philosophy? Philosophy is defined as the love of wisdom. Philosophy has largely been an array of thoughts, it is a broad area of study, very general, comprehensive and fundamental. It is a type of inquiry that attempts to say what is true and what is true must be justified by reasons and evidence. Philosophers are known for fearless pursuit of rational argument a very important feature of the ancient Greek philosophers. They follow arguments even if they lead to unwelcomed areas. Against this brief view of the nature of philosophy, we begin the explication with the ancient philosophers.

The ancient pre-socratic philosophers such as the Milesians (Thales, Anaximander, Anaximenes), the Pythagoreans, the Eleatic school (Parmenides, Heraclitus and Zeno) and, the atomists (Democritus and Leucippus) were critical thinkers in their own right. It can be argued that they are the cradle of critical thinking and philosophy in general. Their pure desire to know the nature and principle of things manifested critical thinking.

Stumpf captures this precisely when he writes that:

> Philosophy began when humans' curiosity and wonder caused them to ask the questions "What are things really like?" and "How can we explain the process of change in things?" What prompted these questions was the gradual recognition that things are not exactly what they seem to be, that "appearance" often differs from "reality." The facts of birth, death, growth, and decay-coming into being and passing away-raised not only the questions about personal destiny but also the larger questions of how things and persons come into existence, can be different at different times, and pass out of existence only to be followed by other things and persons. Many of the answers given to these questions by the earliest philosophers are not as important as the fact that they focused upon just these questions and that they approached them with a fresh and new frame of mind that was in contrast to that of the great poets.[10]

Independence of thought, reason/rationality, questioning, replaced the poetic, mythological, religious and cultural explanations of reality with a more philosophic-scientific orientation. There was a progressive explanation of reality from concrete to abstract thought. In addition, the ability to distinguish between appearance and reality was a major breakthrough since the senses were unreliable for most these early philosophers. Stumpf notes and rightly so that "from the very beginning...Greek philosophy was an intellectual activity, for it was not a matter only of seeing or believing but of thinking, and philosophy meant thinking about basic questions in a mood of genuine and free inquiry."[11] These are key tenets of critical thinking as discussed in chapter one. These ancient philosophers and in particular, Pythagoras contributed to the mathematical, scientific, and metaphysical discourses. These early philosophers argued for the use of reason to make meaning of life and also relied on the observation of nature to facilitate understanding of the same.

Fallibilism and skepticism characterized the pre-socratic philosophers. As result of fallibilism or skepticism, there was a shift to the nature of knowledge and ethics from cosmological philosophy. As Stumpf puts it:

> But this very mood, this skepticism, provided the impulse for a new direction for philosophy, for skepticism itself became the subject of serious concern. Instead of debating about alternative theories of nature, philosophers now addressed themselves to the problem of human knowledge, asking whether it was possible for the human mind to discover any universal truth. This question had been further aggravated by the disclosure of cultural differences between various races and peoples so that the question about truth became deeply implicated with the problem of goodness. Could there be a universal concept of goodness if people were incapable of knowing any universal truth? The principal parties to this new debate were the Sophists and Socrates.[12]

This was by itself a manifestation of critical thinking. Scepticism or doubt, fallibilism, truth versus relativism, multiculturalism and ethics which are core dimensions of critical thinking clearly characterized the new philosophical interests.

Human knowledge and ethics took centre stage as reflected by the contrast between Socrates and the sophist's philosophies.

The sophists who included Protagoras, Gorgias and Thrasymachus were mobile teachers who focused on rhetoric and law. Hence, they were less concerned with philosophy. They sought for convenient truth based on relativism and skepticism as Plato tells us. In this respect, their style is referred to as sophistry which implies lack of critical thinking skills/abilities and dispositions. Using the term sophistry derived from the practice of the sophists, Paul and Elder distinguish strong sense critical thinkers who are fair-minded from the weak sense critical thinkers:

> Another traditional name for the weak-sense thinker is found in the word sophist. Sophistry is the art of winning arguments regardless of whether there are obvious problems in the thinking being used. There is a set of lower-level skills of rhetoric, or argumentation, by which one can make bad thinking look good and good thinking look bad. We see this often in unethical lawyers and politicians who are merely concerned with winning. They use emotionalism and trickery in an intellectually skilled

way. Sophistic thinkers succeed only if they do not come up against what we call strong-sense critical thinkers.[13]

Therefore, the sophists were specialists in persuasive speech and not models of critical thinking.

Socrates the Father of "Suicidal Criticality"

The idea of critical thinking as we understand it today can be traced to Socrates and his quest to demonstrate, by a method of questioning, that people could not rationally justify their confident claims to knowledge. His aim was to seek clarification on how one attains reliable knowledge hence he advocated for the practice of disciplined conversation, acting as an 'intellectual midwife.' This is a method called the dialectic or midwifery or meiotic or art or method of questioning that served to facilitate his critical interrogation. The end product of his method was reliable knowledge, knowledge beyond doubt. His critical interrogation developed an in-depth, clarity, rational rigour and logical consistency as fundamental characteristics of critical thinking.

A good example of Socrates' method is found in Plato's *Dialogues* such as the *Euthyphro, Apology, Crito* and *Meno*. In these *Dialogues*, Socrates feigns ignorance, the "Socratic ignorance," about a subject and tries to draw out from the other person, his fullest possible knowledge about it.

For example, in the *Euthyphro*, the subject matter of debate is the definition of piety. Socrates feigns ignorance that he does not know the meaning of piety and then asks Euthyphro to provide one. Euthyphro, who seeks to persecute his own father of impiety, an act Socrates ridicules asserting that, *"not everyone could rightly do what you are doing; only a man who is well advanced in wisdom."* In the process, Socrates realizes that Euthyphro does not understand the meaning of piety.

When Euthyphro is challenged and unable to define piety, he runs away saying *"another time . . . Socrates. I am in a hurry now, and it is time for me to be off."*

In, *Meno*, we see again how Socrates uses his method of questioning in an attempt to achieve reliable knowledge. Socrates enters into a dialogue with Meno on the topic of virtue. Socrates critical questions and rigid arguments aim at *extracting*, as he likes to put it, the proper definition of virtue from Meno. In questioning and cross-examining, he seeks to critically examine what Meno knows about virtue. Socrates is able to demonstrate that Meno pretends to know about virtue and yet he does not know and hence he [Meno] seeks to know. He captures this in form of a question: *"do you think that before he (the slave boy) would have tried to find out that which he thought he knew though he did not, before he fell into perplexity he realized he did not know and longed to know?"*

In the *Apology*, due to his critical nature, Socrates is disliked and hence "falsely" charged. The accusations levelled against him include that "...... *'Socrates is an evil-doer, and a curious person, ... a wise man, who speculated about the heaven above, and searched into the earth beneath, and made the worse appear the better cause; and he teaches the aforesaid doctrines to others.'*

In an attempt to respond to the first charge that he is wise, he observes that his evil name 'wise' was attributable to the oracle of Delphi. He says:

> I will refer you to a witness who is worthy of credit; that witness shall be the God of Delphi—he will tell you about my wisdom, if I have any, and of what sort it is. You must have known Chaerephon; he was early a friend of mine, and also a friend of yours, for he shared in the recent exile of the people, and returned with you. Well, Chaerephon, as you know, was very impetuous in all his doings, and he went to Delphi and boldly asked the oracle to tell him whether— as I was saying, I must beg you not to interrupt—he asked the oracle to tell him whether anyone was wiser than I was, and the Pythian prophetess answered, that there was no man wiser.

The oracle described Socrates as the wisest person but Socrates sort to refute the claim by parading a person who is wiser than him before God. Socrates wants to proof the oracle, in essence God, wrong by presenting a wiser person and remark to God, *'Here is a man who is wiser than I am; but you said that I was the wisest.'* Hence, Socrates would have the proof that God pretends to know and yet he does not know! That though the nature of god is that he cannot lie, on this occasion, he violates his nature. In his critical quest, Socrates observes:

> 'Accordingly I went to one who had the reputation of wisdom, and observed him—his name I need not mention; he was a politician whom I selected for examination—and the result was as follows: When I began to talk with him, I could not help thinking that he was not really wise, although he was thought wise by many, and still wiser by himself; and thereupon I tried to explain to him that he thought himself wise, but was not really wise; and the consequence was that he hated me, and his enmity was shared by several who were present and heard me. So I left

him, saying to myself, as I went away: Well, although I do not suppose that either of us knows anything really beautiful and good, I am better off than he is, — for he knows nothing, and thinks that he knows; I neither know nor think that I know. In this latter particular, then, I seem to have slightly the advantage of him. Then I went to another who had still higher pretensions to wisdom, and my conclusion was exactly the same.'

Socrates concluded that many people pretend to know and yet they do not know. He remarks that *"I found that the men most in repute were all but the most foolish; and that others less esteemed were really wiser and better."* His main agenda was to demonstrate that people may have power and high positions and yet be deeply confused, irrational and are capable of accommodating contradictions. For example, when he asks Meletus to clarify what he means by believing in gods, corrupting the youth among other issues. The outcome is that his accusers cannot clearly articulate these concepts.

Socrates asserts that his mission and vocation is *"above all, I shall then be able to continue my search into true and false knowledge; as in this world, so also in the next; and I shall find out who is wise, and who pretends to be wise, and is not."* In this respect, Socrates as a critical thinker regards and assigns himself the role of a gadfly. As a gadfly his mission and vocation is to buzz around, to discover those who know, those who do not know and more so those who pretend to know. Importantly, as a gadfly to keep people awake and alert or awake them from their dogmatic slumbers:

> ...because he is their heaven-sent friend (and they will never have such another), or, as he may be ludicrously described, he is the gadfly who stirs the generous steed into motion.

> And now, Athenians, I am not going to argue for my own sake, as you may think, but for yours, that you may not sin against the God by condemning me, who am his gift to you. For if you kill me you will not easily find a successor to me, who, if I may use such a ludicrous figure of speech, am a sort of gadfly, given to the state by God; and the state is a great and noble steed who is tardy in his motions owing to his very size, and requires to be stirred into life. I am that gadfly which God has attached to the state, and all day long and in all places am always fastening upon you, arousing and persuading and reproaching you. You will not easily find another like me, and therefore I would advise you to spare me. I dare say that you may feel out of temper (like a person who is suddenly awakened from sleep), and you think that you might easily strike me dead as Anytus advises, and then you would sleep on for the remainder of your lives, unless God in his care of you sent you another gadfly.

The above selected passages from various Plato's *Dialogues*, tell us that Socrates engaged his contemporaries in dialogue and challenged them to examine their ideas and beliefs critically, annoying and antagonizing many in the process. This was the case due to the fact that Socrates had relentless analysis of any and every subject. He had a rational rigour and that he did not claim to know nor pretend to know. His dictum: *"Know thyself"* entail criticality. One should endeavour to understand oneself. This is only possible via self-examination *"for the unexamined life is not worth living."*

Finally, and interestingly, Socrates defined the soul as *"that within us in virtue of which we are pronounced wise or foolish, good or bad."* The implication of this was that Socrates established the fact that one cannot depend upon those in "authority" to have sound knowledge, clarity, and insight.

His sentence handed down to him would guarantee that he would be known as a critical thinker whose "crime" of criticality earned a death penalty. Siegel observes that "Socrates is perhaps the clearest example of a philosopher who argued that education should encourage in all students and persons, to the greatest extent possible, the pursuit of reason."[14] Socrates quest for answers, his reflections on virtues as the means to good life, are key aspects of critical thinking. His method of dialogue has continued to be used by philosophers to date. It is without doubt that Socrates demonstrates how to be an exemplary critical thinker.

Plato

Plato was a key champion of critical thinking, reason and rationality in his various works such as the *Apology, Crito, Phaedo, Republic, laws* among others. There are various aspects of critical thinking articulated such as overcoming illusions (allegory of the cave), the divided line of knowledge, and the precise use of language or terms (*Meno*). In particular, the allegory of the cave is good masterpiece on critical thinking. Below is a diagram of Plato's allegory of the cave.[15]

Some Models of Critical Thinking

This diagram of Plato's Allegory of the Cave represents chained prisoners whose only reality is the shadow world projected on the wall in front of them. They are unaware that behind them is the higher degree of reality of the fire and the statues that are casting the shadows. Still further up is the steep and rugged passage out of the cave to the upper world. A prisoner who follows this path will encounter the world of real objects and the sun.[16]

A lone and liberated prisoner walks up the path to reality (to encounter the world of real objects and the sun) while his colleagues remain prisoners of ignorance. Plato's allegory of the cave reflects the levels of knowledge, some people are on level of imagination, pure sense knowledge and opinions, and others focus on technical knowledge while the few ones actualise to the level of reasoning. Knowledge of "shadows" here connotes low order thinking, ignorance and lack of reasoning skills/abilities. The allegory of the cave laid bare the fact that people have face value, or superficial understanding of themselves and reality. The quest for wisdom and good life entails proper understanding of knowledge and reality in order to avoid assumptions. Plato's artful story reflect logic and critical thinking and assist us to think critically. This artful story assists us in questioning basic acquired beliefs and assumptions:

> It also cautions us to be wary of commonplace knowledge and reminds us that the majority can often be wrong. The great figures in history (philosophers such as Socrates, or scientists, artists, and social reformers) often found themselves in conflict with the basic assumptions of their culture. Likewise, we can be like the prisoners, naively accepting everything we hear. Or we can try to like the lone prisoner who learned to question the assumptions of his contemporaries.[17]

As critical thinkers, we should question commonly held beliefs, assumptions, the opinions of the majority and, more so, what we hear or read.

Plato brings to fore the role of epistemology and fallibilism. Plato reminds us that our sense knowledge is fallible and therefore we should seek to acquire true knowledge or knowledge with certainty. Our discussion on epistemology in chapter one and two, attest to this noble quest.

In addition to skills/abilities of critical thinking, Plato's artful story stresses on dispositions of critical thinking. The act of the liberated prisoner who goes back to the cave to rescue his friends from the yoke of ignorance manifests the inclination, disposition or habit of mind which is a reflection of critical attitude or critical spirit.

As already alluded, Plato featured the Sophists in several of his dialogues, and had a very negative view regarding them. According to him, Sophists made use of argumentation in the service of persuasion, while he championed for the use of argumentation in the service of truth, wisdom and virtue. Accordingly, the Sophists were unscrupulous and practiced fallacious reasoning, for persuasive effect. Plato, therefore, draws the line between critical thinking and argumentation in the service of persuasion.

Aristotle

He was a student of Plato and joined the Plato's academy. Later, he started his own school of philosophy named, the Lyceum. The school was also called *Peripatetic*. Regarding philosophy, Aristotle wrote in the book "Metaphysics" that:

> For it is owing to their wonder that men both now begin and at first began to philosophize; they wondered originally at the obvious difficulties, then advanced little by little and stated difficulties about the greater matters, e.g. about the phenomena of the moon and those of the sun and of the stars, and about the genesis of the universe. And a man who is puzzled and wonders thinks himself ignorant (whence even the lover of myth is in a sense a lover of Wisdom, for the myth is composed of wonders); therefore, since they philosophized order to escape from ignorance, evidently they were pursuing science in order to know, and not for any utilitarian end. And this is confirmed by the facts; for it was when almost all the necessities of life and the things that make for comfort and recreation had been secured, that such knowledge began to be sought.

Aristotle argued that Philosophy begins in wonder. The human person grew up with the pure desire to know, to acquire wisdom and knowledge. This was due the nature of the person's inquiry mind and its eagerness to know how nature works. This search for knowledge and meaning implies the application of critical thinking skills/abilities and dispositions. The paradoxes, contradictions of life and reality, for Aristotle, were the beginning and continuation of knowledge. We still ask the same questions today. In addition, Aristotle is also credited as the father of formal logic. His systematic development of logic clearly laid the foundation for the skills/abilities and dispositions of critical thinking. Siegel asserts that "Aristotle, too, championed rationality, both in theory and practice, and he uttered remarkably modern-sounding ideas concerning education's duty to develop the character traits now associated with the rational person."[18] His elaborate discussions of virtues contribute essentially to the dispositions or character traits of a critical thinker. For him the nature of man is to think about his own thinking. The notion of moderation as an ethical principle is again a good ingredient for a critical thinker. One should not be an extremist, but ought to practice moderation. In addition, Aristotle's discussion of the notions friendship and golden mean reflect critical thinking. His drive that we should be able to distinguish who is a genuine friend is important for critical thinkers. He argued that there are three types of friends namely friends of utility, causal friends and true friends. The latter are rare and few.

Contrary to Aristotle's perspective, people stop wondering, stop questioning and stop attempting to look at things in new ways or non-traditional ways. As critical thinkers we ought to embrace the dictum that *"Philosophy begins in wonder"* and then begin to wonder about what otherwise is taken for granted or assumed to be true, reality good or bad.

Post Aristotelian Thought

The study of the Epicureans, the Stoics, the Sceptics and the Neo-Platonists, covering the main topics is full of philosophical excitement and innovation but that would be beyond the scope of this book. These new schools of thought after Aristotle gave philosophy a new orientation and emphasis. Of significance from critical thinking perspective are the aspects of individuality, wisdom, reason and law, skepticism and the art of living. In particular, these post-Aristotelian schools of thought led people to think independently and to know themselves and more so how as individuals would live a life worth living as individuals.

Critical thinking of the antiquity scholars such Socrates, Plato, Aristotle and the Greek skeptics, all of whom emphasized the role of rationality remains vital to date.

3.3 The Medieval Period

During the medieval age, the tradition of systematic 'critical thinking' was embodied in the writings and teaching of such thinkers as St. Augustine, St. Anselm, St. Thomas Aquinas among others. They brought to our awareness not only of the potential power of reasoning but also of the need for it to be systematically cultivated and "cross examined." For example, St. Augustine followed the thoughts of Plato in seeking to understand and explain religious doctrines such as the trinity, the problem of evil among others. Another example is St. Thomas Aquinas, who following Aristotle developed a systematic approach to truth that could be arrived via logic. Stumpf captures the intellectual atmosphere of the mediaeval period when he writes that:

> For most philosophers in the Middle Ages, the sky hung low, suggesting a close bond between heaven and earth, and, accordingly, between philosophy and theology. Indeed, philosophy in the Middle Ages was virtually the handmaiden of theology, supplying religious thought with a reasoned account of its various doctrines.[19]

The philosophy of the day served the interests and purposes of the church. It promoted the mission of spreading the word of God. In this respect, the philosophical thought of the classical thinkers was modelled to attain this goal. It is important to note that philosophy was viewed as the handmaiden of theology. However, some thinkers like Tertullian and St. Paul questioned the compatibility of the philosophy and theology. There were also concerns with the Moslem Arabian interpretations of the classical or antiquity philosophy. Generally, the medieval scholars in their own rights, championed for fostering of rationality.

3.4 The Renaissance and modern period (15th, 16th and 17th centuries)

We briefly examine this period and its key radical transformations due to critical thinking. It is evident that it is scarcely possible here even to mention the more important philosophical, political, cultural, religious and scientific achievements. Hence we will only spell what we deem to be vital in relation to critical thinking.

This period was also referred to as the age of reason. It was a reaction to the theocentric view, which dominated all domains of knowledge. During this period, there were several scholars who were well known for espousing critical thinking skills/abilities and dispositions. Renaissance and modern periods featured a humanistic over against a theocentric perspective, which helped scientific revolution and the rise of modern philosophy. This meant that the authority of Aristotle and the Catholic Church during the medieval period was subjected to questioning and reflective skepticism. The medieval framework based on catholic orthodoxy and faith was critically evaluated. This led to systematic replacement of faith with reason. In what follows, we expose some of the key spheres of knowledge that evolved in this new direction.

Literature, Arts, Social and Political Theories

Unlike the classical period, which operated "largely on free critical spirit," the attitude of medieval philosophy was different in that its starting point was the doctrines of Christian theology. The dominant culture of the today was that of the church from language, to ethical, social and political theories, to institutions of society such as the family and work, the arts and literature. Those who failed to conform were persecuted. Of course, the classical period also persecuted critical thinkers like Socrates, the martyr of criticality, sanctioned Plato and Aristotle had to flee to exile for fear that the Athens *"sinned against philosophy a second time."* However, the atmosphere was terrible during the medieval period for all teachings and thought needed approval of the "mother church." There was no free inquiry in matters to do with literature, religion, art, society, human nature, social-political theories, law, science and freedom of thought or expression. Virtually all the intellectual, cultural, political and religious atmosphere was dogmatically militarised.

Leading scholars in Europe who sought to think critically regarding intellectual, scientific, educational, cultural, political and religious matters challenged the status quo during the renaissance period. For example, the new theories of politics and ethics developed and advanced shifted their base from the ethico-religious ground prepared by St. Thomas Aquinas' theory of natural law which was influenced by Aristotle's' ethico-political theory. The new theories of politics leaned towards a secular theory of the state advocated by Thomas Hobbes, Nicollo Machiavelli and Jean Jacques Rousseau. The mood was for the separation of the authority of the state from that of the church.

The period was characterized by discoveries in art and literature, which sought to liberate or secularise the human person from religious yoke. The critical works of Dante, Michelangelo, and Mirandola attest to this fact. During this period, there was the "call" to return to original sources over against reading commentaries on classical texts, translations and printing made literary activity readily accessible.

Religion was also to benefit from the wind of change as manifested by the thought and works of John Don Scotus; William of Occam theory of "double truth;" Montaigne; Pascal's new guide to truth; Erasmus and Luther's criticism of the churchmen and religion. These criticisms agitated for new modes of thinking about religion.

Astronomy, Science, Technology, Medicine and Mathematics

Further, the Renaissance mood was embodied in the scientific writings, teachings and inventions. Stumpf captures this when he writes that:

> To enhance the exactness of their observations, they invented various scientific instruments. Tippershey, a Dutchman, invented the telescope in 1608, although Galileo was the first to make dramatic use of it. In 1590 the first compound microscope was created. The principle of the barometer was discovered by Galileo's pupil Torricelli. The air pump, which was so important in creating a vacuum for the experiment that proved that all bodies regardless of their weight or size fall at the same rate when there is no air resistance, was invented by Otto von Guericke (1602-1686). With the use of instruments and imaginative hypotheses, fresh knowledge began to unfold. Galileo discovered the moons around Jupiter, and Anton Leeuwenhoek (1632-1723) discovered spermatozoa, protozoa, and bacteria. Whereas Nicolaus Copernicus (1473-1543) formed a new hypothesis of the revolution of the earth around the sun, Harvey (1578-1657) discovered the circulation of the blood. William Gilbert (1540-1603) wrote a major work on the magnet, and Robert Boyle (1627-1691), the father of chemistry, formulated his famous law concerning the relation of temperature, volume, and pressure of gases. Added to these inventions and discoveries was the decisive advance made in mathematics, especially by Sir Isaac Newton and Leibniz, who independently invented differential and integral calculus. The method of observation and mathematical calculation now became the hallmarks of modem science.[20]

The medieval science based on faith, reason and Aristotle's authority was replaced by a new scientific method of prediction and control. This period lost faith in matters of God, soul, eschatology, and ethics among other aspects. The new desire was to investigate all reality from a non-religious and non-dogmatic perspective. They adopted and opted for the new method of observation advocated by Francis Bacon and mathematical calculation or predication rather than religious speculations.

Critical thinking was manifested and characterized by paradigm shifts in the way people pictured the world from astrology, cosmology, medicine, mathematics, physics and technology.

Studies in Astrology manifested a spectacular success in the use of critical thinking to bring to fore that knowledge was fallible. The ancient Greeks and notably Aristotle sought to explain the motion of the universe based on the geocentric theory.

Ptolemy sustained this theory by developing laws, which later came to be referred to as the Ptolemaic system. Contrary to this, critical perspectives of Nicolaus Copernicus and Galileo Galilei discovered and defended the heliocentric theory. This was a paradigm shift, which saw the geocentric theory replaced with the heliocentric theory. Such a move was driven by the quest for reasons, convincing evidence and truth, which supported the heliocentric theory:

> Galileo claimed that there was very good reason to believe in the existence of moons orbiting the planet Jupiter, namely, observations of the moons made with the use of the recently invented telescope. Galileo held that telescopic observation provided compelling evidence of the moon's existence. His opponents, on the other hand, regarded telescopic observation as problematic, absent a theoretical understanding of telescopic operation which gave us some reason to regard telescopic images as veridical; moreover, they claimed to have very good reasons for thinking that the moons didn't exist, reasons furnished by scripture and by the writings of Aristotle. So: Galileo claimed that telescopic observation provided good reason for believing that the Jovian moons existed, while his opponents demurred; his opponents thought that scripture and Aristotle provided reason for thinking that moons did not exist, while Galileo demurred.[21]

The dispute not only focused on the existence of moons but on the good reasons and compelling evidence for the supporting the same. Galileo Galilei, using the newly invented telescope, validated the Copernican view that it was not the Sun, which moved but the Earth. This led to rejection of the Aristotelian cosmology, Ptolemaic system or theory and the church orthodoxy. Galileo was very unhappy with how scholars were fixated with old views. He wrote to Kepler lamenting that:

> 'My dear Kepler, what would you say of the learned here, who, replete with the pertinacity of the asp, have steadfastly refused to cast a glance through the telescope? What shall we make of all this? Shall we laugh or shall we cry?'

Clearly, he was deeply disturbed with the ignorance manifested by people during his time. His views brought confrontation between him and the Catholic Church. The mother church asserted that:

> 'The view that the sun stands motionless at the centre of the universe is foolish, philosophically false, and utterly heretical, because contrary to Holy Scripture.'

Galileo responded by asserting that:

> 'the intention of the Holy Ghost is to teach us how one goes to heaven, not how heaven goes.'

He further stressed that the scriptures do not teach about the universe since this would be *'irrelevant to the highest goal, that is our salvation.'* Galileo claimed that there were very good reasons based on researched evidence and scientific observations for his position. His opponent, the church, rejected his views as problematic, foolish and at best false, based on the wrong authority of Aristotle and the scripture.

The distinction between appearance and reality was a key contribution by Galileo in respect to critical thinking. He called for a clear distinction between reality and appearance asserting that the latter is inauthentic and at best misleading. He cited the mistake of the church when it asserted that it is the Sun, which moves, and not the Earth as knowledge based on appearance and not on reality. Stumpf writes that "the rigour of Galileo's thinking lay in his method of focusing strictly upon exact mathematical demonstrations and avoiding second hand information based simply upon tradition and opposing conjectures contained in books."[22] This kind of dispute reflects critical thinking by Galileo and uncritical thinking approach by the churchmen. It also shows the role of epistemology and in particular the idea of truth and the fallibility of knowledge. Hence, this is a classical demonstration that knowledge and truth is subject to fallibilism. Bailin and Battersby confirm this when they write that:

> It can happen at the level of academic disciplines, for example, when astronomers rejected the geocentric theory model of the universe (the theory that the earth is at the centre) in favour of the heliocentric model (the theory that the sun is at the centre).[23]

This seeds of doubt sown by Galileo pointed to the fact that knowledge is continuously evolving and changing. This is to say that views in academic disciplines and society are constantly compared, tested, rejected, adjusted and revised. Hence, there is the need to recognize and accept the fact of fallibilism. Hence "this recognition should instil in us the degree of humility and an openness to seriously considering views which differ from our own."[24] This again is a manifestation of critical thinking skills/abilities and dispositions. This dispute contributed to the fact that the human perception of the universe would never be the same.

Other scientists such as Johannes Kepler following Tycho Brahe advocated for the three mathematical laws of elliptical planetary motion of the sun supporting the Copernican system. Nicolaus Copernicus, Galileo Galilei and Giordano Bruno, as well as many of his followers, were critical thinkers in that they derived their reasons for regarding astronomy directly from observed scientific and mathematical evidence and cared about finding the truth regardless of its social implications. They eventually revolutionized the study of Astronomy, radically reoriented philosophical, social, religious, economic, and personal thought.

What emerged as the underlining contentious issue was on the credibility of sources or who was credible on the topic. The church was a credible source but did not guarantee the truth on the topic geocentricism and heliocentricism, for a very credible source can be mistaken or wrong. The scientists provided evidence for their claims and hence they become credible sources on the topic. The vital insight learned here is that a critical thinker or rational person must seek to establish or verify the credibility of sources. Ennis identifies eight basic criteria for credibility:

> These criteria are background experience and knowledge, lack of apparent conflict of interest, agreement with others equally qualified, reputation, established procedures, known risk to reputation, ability to give reasons, and careful habits in similar areas.[25]

These eight criteria ought to be applied with good judgment in determining the credibility of sources. In actual acts of critical thinking, one must evaluate if each criterion is satisfied, be open-minded to revise when it is necessary, be ready to change one's mind about their credibility. Essentially, good judgment is facilitated by critical thinking skills/abilities and dispositions. Appeal to authority is a fallacy label used in the area of credibility of sources. This fallacy occurs when one appeals to wrong authority. For example, the church was appealing to the bible and Aristotle's theories as its source, when it pronounced that the sun moves. As it turned out, the church's sources were wrong. We have discussed in details, this fallacy and others in chapter five. Ideally, the skills/abilities and dispositions of critical thinking must be used in determining credibility of sources.

Sir Isaac Newton, Charles Darwin, and Albert Einstein had excellence in the art of questioning. When we consider the work of these three thinkers, Newton (laws of motion), Darwin (theory of evolution), and Einstein (theories of relativity), we find individuals who were critical thinkers in their endeavours.

Below, we make some detailed examination of the views of Francis Bacon, the renaissance scholar in length for clearly his interest in the method of science and education places him as an outstanding critical thinker.

Francis Bacon

Francis bacon was a chief advocate for critical thinking in the renaissance era who sought to reform philosophy and science in his works, *Advancement of Learning* and *Novum Organum*:

> Francis Bacon (1561-1626), the central thinker of the English Renaissance, is often regarded as the father of modern empiricism. He is a thinker with whose revolutionary works begin the self-conscious study of scientific methodology and the careful investigation of the powers and limitations of the human being as cognizer.[26]

He challenged the methodology employed in scientific research, which identified learning as reading ancient texts replacing it with the empirical method, the method of induction, the "New Organon." He emphasized limitations of the human mind in its quest and ability to acquire knowledge. The earlier approaches placed man as the most important in God's creation, but he argued that man must dominate and control nature that is *"imperium hominis"*. For him, the method of science was the sure way of developing knowledge.

He viewed education as non-performing and stagnant because its chief advocates who included the clergymen were unqualified and they were stabling block to his dictum that *'knowledge is power.'* Stumpf writes that:

> Francis Bacon assigned himself the task of reforming the philosophy and science of his day. His central criticism was that learning had become

stagnant. Science was identified with learning, and learning meant reading ancient texts. The study of medicine, for example, was chiefly literary and was practiced by poets, rhetoricians, and clergymen, whose qualification to practice was their ability to quote Hippocrates and Galen. Philosophy was still dominated by Plato and Aristotle, whose teachings Bacon denounced as "shadows" and "phantoms."[27]

For him, therefore, learning was dogmatic, unreflective, stagnant and useless due to clinging to traditional thought and learning, slavish attachment to the past, so to speak. Particularly science was mixed up with superstitions, religion, theology and its advocates were clergymen who largely preached over against being rational or critical. He described their views as ventures of schoolmen with degenerated and meritless versions of Aristotelianism and at best *"cobwebs of learning, admirable for the fineness of thread and work, but of no substance or profit."* Accordingly, this called for reformations in philosophy and science and a need for a new method. Succinctly put:

> Bacon advocated wiping the slate of human knowledge clean and starting over again, using a new method for assembling and explaining facts. He was convinced that he had discovered such a method, which would unlock all the secrets of nature. He was aware of other attempts to correct the inadequacies of traditional learning, particularly attempts by Gilbert, Copernicus, and Galileo to amend Aristotle's physics. But what impressed him most was Galileo's construction and use of telescopes, an event he considered one of the most important in the history of astronomy because it made possible an advancement of learning. Whereas the ancients did not know the composition of the Milky Way, the telescope made it evident that the Milky Way is a collection of distant stars. Bacon considered the mind as being like a glass or mirror, which had been made rough and uneven both by natural tendencies of passions as well as by the errors of traditional learning. In such a condition, the mind cannot reflect truth accurately. Bacon's method, and his hope, was to make the mind's surface clean and smooth and to supply it with new and adequate instruments so that it could observe and understand the universe accurately. To achieve this, he would have to free science from entrenched and traditional learning, separate scientific truth from revealed truths of theology, and fashion a new philosophy based upon a new method of observation and a new interpretation of nature.[28]

Clearly, he was pessimistic and his vital criticism was that education has stalled due to natural tendencies of passions as well as by the errors of traditional learning which he viewed as based on memorisation and reproducing, leading to inability to acquire the truth accurately. At the same time, he was optimistic that status quo could be changed. Using the analogy of a glass or mirror, which is uneven, rough and in need to be smoothened, he compared this with the human mind. The human mind was "rough and uneven" due to poor scholarship and in need to be "smoothened" with new approaches to knowledge.

This quest required the liberation of science from traditional learning, from religion and theology and more so philosophy must realign itself with the new methods of science. This quest to challenge the status quo is a manifestation of critical thinking by Francis bacon.

He further identified the *distempers of learning* and *idols of the mind* as the major impediments to critical thinking and philosophy in general. Bacon criticized the past ways of thinking in his treatment of the "distempers of learning" and the idols that proceed from the mind, which *"are not sincere, but of an ill and corrupt nature."*

In the *"distempers of learning,"* he identified the fantastical, contentious and delicate learning as the three distempers of learning considering them as vices or diseases of learning. Fantastical learning seeks the use of words, phrases, words, styles, emphasising texts, languages rather than knowledge. Contentious learning has to do with fixed approach to knowledge quoting other thinkers as the starting point of an argument. Delicate learning is based on authoritarian approach to knowledge or pretending to know yet one does not know. These "distempers of learning" are obstacles, diseases, or vices to critical thinking and contribute to the distortion of knowledge.

In Book 1 of the *Novum Organum,* Bacon describes the doctrines of the idols of the mind or "false phantoms." In his analysis of the idols of the mind, he developed a crucial perspective that they are typical ways in which the human mind is fallacious and hence they are obstacles to critical thinking and are distortions of the mind. He argues that the human mind is corrupted and distorted by the four idols namely; Idols of the tribe, cave, market place and theatre. His compares the idols of the mind to beams of light reflected by an uneven mirror asserting that *"for from the nature of a clear and equal glass, wherein the beams of things should reflect according to their true incidence, it is rather like an enchanted glass, full of superstition and imposture."* This leads to inauthenticity, false opinions, superstitions, and deceptions. For Bacon, the idol of the tribe has to do with the preoccupation with opinions. The idol of the cave borrows from the platonic allegory of the cave where from the analogy we see the limitedness of knowledge when one operates in one's ethnic, cultural, religious and certain authorities as the guide to thought. The idol of the market place connotes the daily usage of language. Finally, the idols of the theatre imply paying homage to dogmatic conceptualization of knowledge observing that *"by tradition, credulity and negligence have come to be received."* The doctrine of the idols fosters the idea that we have very good reason to be very suspicious of what we find ourselves believing. Bacon's view is that our minds have become corrupted, awry, led astray and that we must take great pains to avoid pitfalls of fallacious reasoning or persuasions through observation and experimentation, through the inductive or scientific method.

Bacon's point is that the *"distempers of learning"* and *"the Idols of the mind"* demean the power of reason for they make use of uncritical categories of our common-sense understanding of the world. These are obstacles to critical thinking.

Unhappy with the status quo, Bacon advocated for a new method for acquiring knowledge, the method of induction based on observation and experimentations. Such a method would overcome prejudices and see reality as it is.

At one point, he lamented that his public duties slowed his quest as a critical thinker when he wrote: *"I reckoned that I was by no means discharging my duty, when I was neglecting that by which I could of myself benefit man."* This indicates that Bacon was aware that his public political life had interfered with his primary objectives as a thinker. In concluding this section, Bacon's objective was what he termed as the "great instauration" which entailed "the total reconstruction of the sciences, arts and all human knowledge."

Philosophy and Critical Thinking

This new attitude and approach to science contributed to the development of modern philosophy championed by rationalists who argued that all knowledge is via reason and the empiricists who viewed experience as the source of knowledge. The rationalists were René Descartes, Baruch Spinoza and Gottfried Leibniz while the empiricists were John Locke, George Berkeley and David Hume.

The classical philosophy prior to medieval period could venture into subjects of humanity, nature, ethics, God, and political views via the authority of human reason only. However as earlier noted, during the medieval period, philosophy became *'the handmaiden of theology.'* Philosophy was serving theology and religion by providing metaphysical and intellectual resources. This led to domestication of philosophy by the churchmen and freedom of thought was lost and replaced by dogmatisms. Philosophers were churchmen whose mandate was not to promote critical thinking and philosophy but preaching using philosophical language. Hence freedom of thought and more so criticality was in mortal jeopardy.

As a reaction, the renaissance and modern philosophy had to be free to move wherever the pursuit of truth led it. In particular, there was the separation of theology from philosophy. Philosophy was influenced by the new scientific mode of thought and method in two ways namely; the replacement of the earth–centred approach to man–centred approach. Reality was to be understood from a humanistic perspective. Secondly, everything was to be understood from the perspective of motion, in a mechanical model.

Although the extraordinary richness of the modern period can hardly be captured in this brief space, we wish to comment on René Descartes's impact to philosophy and critical thinking.

René Descartes

René Descartes is referred to as the father of modern philosophy and inevitably, he contributed to critical thinking. He aimed at challenging any forms of prejudices by calling to doubt everything that could be doubted.

At a personal level, he was skeptical of the knowledge he had acquired. He says he was educated, *"at one of the most celebrated schools in Europe. . ."* And yet, *"I found myself embarrassed with. . . many doubts and errors."* For example, according to him, theology operated "above our intelligence," poetry was purely imaginative and literature was simply good fables while philosophy was only Aristotelian-Thomistic scholasticism. Knowledge and education was under the Catholic Church, based on authority of Aristotle and any contrary views were met with inquisitions, censuring, sanctions and executions. In particular, he was unhappy with the acceptance of Aristotle's philosophy and views as the only true thought rather than what was based on the evidence of reason. Clearly, he doubted knowledge acquired in his schooling and in general the knowledge of the day.

Well familiar with censuring of Galileo Galilei and Giordano Bruno among others, he opted for allegiance approach and avoided controversy with the "mother church." He asserts:

> That it is unwise to lose one's life when it can be saved without dishonour, and that if a match is very unequal it is better to beat an honourable retreat or ask quarter than stupidly to expose oneself to a certain death.[29]

He then adopted the motto that "to live well you must live unseen." This reflects critical thinking and not acts of cowardice for it is at least reasonable than to have faced the same fate as Galileo Galilei, Giordano Bruno, Nicolaus Copernicus and Giulio Cesare Vanini who were killed for their lack of orthodoxy. His pessimism led him in "…resolving to seek no other science than that which could be found in myself, or at least in the great book of the world, I employed the rest my youth in travel."[30] Descartes travelled a lot to learn from "the great book of the world" in quest to acquire knowledge of certainty.

According to Descartes, philosophy of the day fostered doubts, disputes and not knowledge. Further, philosophy of the day was based on the authority of Aristotle and the Catholic Church. Clearly, he was unhappy with the status quo and wanted a philosophy which was certain and precise like mathematics. One day, he had three dreams, which initiated the paradigm shift for his academic interests and pure desire to discern intellectual certainty based on human reason alone. Descartes:

> …resolved to continue his search for certainty, and on a memorable night, November 10, 1619, he had three dreams, which unmistakably convinced him that he must construct the system of true knowledge upon the powers of human reason alone. Descartes broke with the past and gave philosophy a fresh start. In particular, since his system of truth would have to be derived from his own rational powers, he would no longer rely on previous philosophers for his ideas, nor would he accept any idea as true only because it was expressed by someone with authority. Neither the authority of Aristotle's great reputation nor the authority of the church could suffice to produce the kind of certainty he sought. Descartes was determined to discover the basis of intellectual certainty in his own reason. He therefore gave philosophy a fresh start by using only those truths he could know through his own powers as the foundation for all other knowledge.[31]

Descartes' evolution of thought started with the rejection of the authorities of the day such Aristotelian–Thomistic philosophies and the prevailing customs. He aimed at knowledge based on human reason alone, which was the new way to develop philosophy. He wrote in French and not in Latin, the language of his teachers. He asserted; "I hope that those who avail themselves of their natural reason in its purity may be better judges of my opinion than those who believe in the writings of the ancients."[32] He was absolutely clearly that he would no longer rely on previous philosophers for his ideas or writings. These clearly attest his distaste with the status quo and he aimed at giving philosophy, a new fresh beginning.

This Descartes' quest reflected critical thinking skills/abilities and dispositions as confirmed by Paul and Elder when they assert that:

> ... Descartes wrote what might be called the second text in critical thinking, Rules for the Direction of the Mind. In it, Descartes argued for the need for a special systematic disciplining of the mind to guide it in thinking. He articulated and defended the need in thinking for clarity and precision. He developed a method of critical thought based on the principle of systematic doubt. He emphasized the need to base thinking on well-reasoned foundational assumptions. Every part of thinking, he argued, should be questioned, doubted, and tested.[33]

In this book, *Rules for the Direction of the Mind*, he outlined critical thinking skills/abilities such as systematic thought, clarity, precision, questioning, doubt, verification, and assumptions. He called for the use of reason alone. In addition, just like Francis Bacon, Descartes wanted a method of critical thought based on the principle of systematic doubt that was precise, certain, systematic and orderly which would provide knowledge with certainty. He 'dreamed' that the use of reason and his method of doubt would guarantee that kind of knowledge. Particularly he was impressed by the preciseness and certainty of science and mathematics in acquiring knowledge unlike philosophy, which left many doubts. Descartes writes that he was *"especially pleased with mathematics because of the certainty and self-evidence of its proofs, "*and *". . . was astonished that nothing more noble had been built on so firm and solid a foundation."* In his works, the *Discourse on Method* and *the First Meditation,* he sought to describe the foundations for knowledge. He 'dreamed' of a method that would be precise and accurate like that of mathematics. Equally, he wanted a method for philosophy, which would be clear, precise, and certain to guarantee rational truth.

In his book, *Rules for the Direction of the Mind,* he came up with rational schemes or to be precise 21 rules which guided the human mind in its quests for rational truths by providing clear and orderly procedures. Stumpf notes that:

> Of the 21 rules found in his *Rules for the Direction of the Mind,* the following are among the most important. Rule III: When we propose to investigate a subject, "our inquiries should be directed, not to what others have thought, nor to what we ourselves conjecture, but to what we can clearly and perspicuously behold and with certainty deduce." Rule IV: This is a rule requiring that other rules be adhered to strictly, for "if a man observe them accurately, he shall never assume what is false as true, and will never spend his mental efforts to no purpose." Rule V: We shall comply with the method exactly if we "reduce involved and obscure propositions step by step to those that are simpler, and then starting with the intuitive apprehension of all those that are absolutely simple, attempt to ascend to the knowledge of all others by precisely similar steps." Rule VIII: "If in the matters to be examined we come to a step in the series of which our understanding is not sufficiently well able to have an intuitive cognition, we must stop short there."[34]

These rules may be summarized as follows: do not follow others thoughts on a subject or matter or issue or problem but follow what is intuitively and deductively arrived at with certainty; respect all rules; move step by step intuitively and deductively from the simple to the complex; accept when your reasoning or understanding is incapacitated on a particular matter.

In his work, *Discourse on Method,* he developed four rules similar to the above:

> "The first was never to accept anything for true which I did not clearly know to be such; . . . to comprise nothing more in my judgment than what was presented to my mind so clearly and distinctly as to exclude all ground of doubt. The second, to divide each of the difficulties under examination into as many parts as possible, and as might be necessary for its adequate solution. The third, to conduct my thoughts in such order that by commencing with objects the simplest and easiest to know, I might ascend by little and little, and, as it were, step by step, to the knowledge of the more complex. . . And the last, in every case to make enumerations so complete, and reviews so general that I might be assured that nothing was omitted."

These can be summed as follows: always seek clarity or never accept what is not clear or accept only what is beyond doubt; divide a problem into many parts as possible; always start from the simple to the complex and ensure no omissions. These rules or precepts for him guaranteed knowledge and truth with certainty.

He further argued that the human mind had two mental powers

"intuition" and "deduction" which guaranteed knowledge and truth with certainty when guided by the rules of the mind to avoid illusions. Intuition is simple derivations from the mind via reason while deduction helps us to understand inferences from other facts with clarity and certainty. Deductions here are not to be understood in Aristotelian sense of deriving a conclusion from given premises but rather from facts.

His method was the method of doubt or methodic doubt. This method entails doubting everything. What cannot be subject to doubt is what is founded of the rules or precepts of the mind. Descartes' *Meditations* demonstrates to us how certainty of knowledge may be acquired by following the method of doubt. He pointed out that there is no certainty of beliefs when he wrote in his book, *Meditations* that:

> It is now some years since I detected how many were the false beliefs that I had from my earliest youth admitted as true, and how doubtful was everything I had since constructed on this basis; and from that time I was convinced that I must once for all seriously undertake to rid myself of all the opinions which I had formerly accepted, and commence to build anew from the foundation, if I wanted to establish any firm and permanent structure in the sciences.

Clearly he called to doubt all beliefs and knowledge. Further, he argued that we must doubt all sense knowledge:

> All that up to the present time I have accepted as most true and certain I have learned either from the senses or through the senses; but it is sometimes proved to me that these senses are deceptive, and it is wiser not to trust entirely to anything by which we have once been deceived.

Accordingly, sense knowledge is deceptive and therefore one must doubt what is derived from the senses. For example, you believe that there is a book in front of you; or a student seated in front of you; or you are writing using a pen; or a lecturer, say Dr. Mbithi is in class; or blackboard or desk; or that you are breathing air; that you are supported by the floor; and that I was driving a car and so on. Indeed, all of your beliefs about the world around you are based on sense perceptions which are subject to doubt. Clearly, the senses deceive us. The truth is such beliefs, for Descartes, is dubitable and hence there a need for alternative explanation for the experiences you are having that give rise to these beliefs. Descartes gives the example of a wax. Do we know it via senses or the mind? If the wax is subjected to fire, is it still the same wax?

Some Models of Critical Thinking

Let us examine Descartes dream arguments that lay the ground of doubt for our beliefs about the world and contribute to the problem of intellectual certainty.

The Dream Arguments

Using the dream, the deceiving God and the evil demon arguments, Descartes sort to demonstrate that that all knowledge or beliefs were subject to doubt. This is the basis of the notion of his methodic doubt. For him, we should doubt everything because either we are dreaming or deceived by God or by the Devil.

Regarding the dream argument, he argues that:

> At the same time I must remember that I am a man, and that consequently I am in the habit of sleeping, and in my dreams representing to myself the same things or sometimes even less probable things, than do those who are insane in their waking moments. How often has it happened to me that in the night I dreamt that I found myself in this particular place, that I was dressed and seated near the fire, whilst in reality I was lying undressed in bed! At this moment it does indeed seem to me that it is with eyes awake that I am looking at this paper; that this head which I move is not asleep, that it is deliberately and of set purpose that I extend my hand and perceive it; what happens in sleep does not appear so clear nor so distinct as does all this. But in thinking over this I remind myself that on many occasions I have in sleep been deceived by similar illusions, and in dwelling carefully on this reflection I see so manifestly that there are no certain indications by which we may clearly distinguish wakefulness from sleep that I am lost in astonishment. And my astonishment is such that it is almost capable of persuading me that I now dream.

He demonstrates that one cannot separate, with accuracy, when one is dreaming from when one is awake. We should doubt everything because we are dreaming. For example, are you awake when reading this section of this book? Are surely awake in class or dreaming that you are? How can you prove that you are awake and not dreaming? Therefore, doubt everything because you are not sure if you are dreaming or not. A prior opposed to posterior truths are not derived from experience but are innate. But again should we just accept them? For example, a square or a triangle, are they what we claim they are? Or is just dreaming about them? Hence, one must look for a way that entails knowledge with certainty.

If one is not deceived by dreams, then God is the source of our deception as Descartes points out:

> Nevertheless I have long had fixed in my mind the belief that an all-powerful God existed by whom I have been created such as I am. But how

> do I know that He has not brought it to pass that there is no earth, no heaven, no extended body, no magnitude, no place, and that nevertheless [I possess the perceptions of all these things and that] they seem to me to exist just exactly as I now see them? And, besides, as I sometimes imagine that others deceive themselves in the things which they think they know best, how do I know that I am not deceived every time that I add two and three, or count the sides of a square, or judge of things yet simpler, if anything simpler can be imagined? But possibly God has not desired that I should be thus deceived, for He is said to be supremely good. If, however, it is contrary to His goodness to have made me such that I constantly deceive myself, it would also appear to be contrary to His goodness to permit me to be sometimes deceived, and nevertheless I cannot doubt that He does permit this.

It is without doubt for Descartes, that God deceives us. However, he is aware that people will reject the idea that it is God who deceives us. Informed by his intuition, he introduces the demon as the source of deceptions.

On the argument pertaining to the devil, Descartes writes that:

> I shall then suppose, not that God who is supremely good and the fountain of truth, but some evil genius not less powerful than deceitful, has employed his whole energies in deceiving me...

From the above quotation, it is plausible to infer that the devil is the source of deceptions. He observed that all what we experience "are nothing but illusions and dreams." Descartes is therefore "constrained to confess that there is nothing in what I formerly believed to be true which I cannot somehow doubt."

He concluded by asserting that the only indubitable and certain idea is 'cogito ergo sum' which translates to "I think, therefore I am" and it is the only idea we cannot doubt. This is an idea beyond doubt, absolute and does not require alternative explanation according to Descartes.

Concerning problem solving and decision-making, Descartes writes that *"to live well you must live unseen."* In his Passions of the Soul, he observes "that it is unwise to lose one's life when it can be saved without dishonour, and that if a match is very unequal it is better to beat an honourable retreat or ask quarter than stupidly expose oneself to a certain death."[35] This is manifestation of critical thinking for a critical thinker should be critical about being critical.

Finally, he affirms that his method is the only sure way to certainty of knowledge and rational truth and laments that many scholars of his time failed to realize this and compares them to persons who:

> ...burning with an unintelligent desire to find treasure, continuously roam the streets, seeking to find something that a passerby might have chanced to drop. . . It is very certain that unregulated inquiries and confused reflections of this kind only confound the natural light and blind our mental powers.

Such a venture which is not modelled of the rules or precepts of the mind and the methodic doubt, on clear, distinct ideas, will yield possibilities, doubts and not certainty of knowledge and truth.

In conclusion, for Descartes therefore, the method of doubt developed in his *Rules* and *Discourse* and applied in his *Mediation*, is the guarantee to certainty of knowledge and rational truth with clarity, distinctness, certainty and precision. He was a revolutionary critical thinker who sought only what is clear, precise, certain in the human mind for it ensured infallible knowledge. He rejected the appeal to previous authorities and advocated for epistemological certainty as the way to achieve absolute knowledge and truth. His instance on reason, rationality as the pivotal way to certainty, clarity, preciseness and distinctness reflected critical thinking skills/abilities. His rationalistic program is in essence a critical thinking program.

In concluding this section, it is important to note that the enlightenment philosophy and its thinkers such as Bayle, Montesquieu, Voltaire, and Diderot made significant contribution to critical thinking. The 18th century thinkers of enlightenment such as Immanuel Kant made tremendous contribution to critical thinking skills/abilities and dispositions.

Next, we briefly examine the contemporary period.

3.5 The Contemporary Period

This period comprises of the Germany idealists, the existentialists, the phenomenologists, analytic tradition thinkers, utilitarians and pragmatists. The Philosophers include: F.G.W. Hegel (absolute idealism); Karl Marx (dialectical materialism & social and economic critique); Soren Kierkegaard (on the individual and faith); Friedrich Nietzsche (on the will to power); Schopenhauer (on the blind will); Edmund Husserl (phenomenology & the rigourous method); Max Schelar (the re-examination of values); Martin Heidegger, Jean Paul Sartre, Albert Camus (all focus on the existential hermeneutics); Karl Jaspers, Gabriel Marcel (on retrieving metaphysics); Comte, Spencer, Max Weber, Charles Darwin, Thomas Huxley, Julian

Huxley, Sigmund Freud, Bertrand Russell, John Stuart Mill, Karl Popper (on human social life); Charles Peirce, and William James (on pragmatism).

What is common in general among these thinkers is that they all argued on the importance of the individual personality, human freedom, and the importance of the individual making choices, human social life, reflective and independence of thought which highlights the values of critical thinking. A detailed analysis of their critical perspectives would be going beyond the intended purposes of this book.

I, therefore, expose the ideas of John Stuart Mill and Bertrand Russell in relation to critical thinking.

John Stuart Mill- on Liberty of Thought and Individuality

John Stuart Mill made important contributions to critical thinking especially his advocacy on liberty of thought and individuality.

On liberty, he identifies his topic as "civil or social liberty: the nature and limits of the power which can be legitimately exercised by society over the individual."[36] Mill was concerned with the problem society and sought to examine how the individual and the government should be related. He argued that the "struggle between liberty and authority" in the earlier times focused on the relationship between the political rulers and the subjects. The subjects aimed at protecting themselves from the dictatorships or tyrannical nature of the rulers. Mill was particularly concerned to preserve liberty and set up safeguards by setting limits to the actions of government or society.

Though he argues as if this political culture is no longer in practice, we note that the *status quo* remain to date. In addition to this persisting culture, he points out that the "struggle between liberty and authority" in recent times has to do with tyranny of the majority or numbers. The majority in the society dictate and oppress the minority. Critical thinkers or rational persons should stand up against these forms of oppressions and dictatorships. In particular, the individual must stand up against these forms of absolutisms, which interfere with his liberty.

He asserts that the society can and must only dictate to the individual on two bases namely; self-protection and harm principle. He writes that:

> That principle is, that the sole end for which mankind are warranted,

> individually or collectively in interfering with the liberty of action of any of their number, is self-protection. That the only purpose for which power can be rightfully exercised over any member of a civilized community, against his will, is to prevent harm to others.[37]

This is to say that the only reason why society can and must interfere with the individual's liberty is for self-protection of the individual and for sake of protecting others. These two reasons for him justify why the society may in a reasonable manner impose checks against individual liberties. Otherwise, the individual must remain autonomous if the above principles do not apply.

The individual cannot be sanctioned by the society if, Mill observes that:

> His own good, either physical or moral, is not a sufficient warrant. He cannot rightfully be compelled to do or forbear because it will be better for him to do so, because it will make him happier, because, in the opinions of others, to do so would be wise, or even right.[38]

The individual cannot be compelled to act against his or her interests so long as they do not harm or affect others. The individual therefore has full liberty "in the part which merely concerns himself, his independence is, of right, absolute. Over himself, over his own body and mind, the individual is sovereign."[39]

He identifies three domains of human action which his conception of liberty must protect.

> This, then, is the appropriate region of human liberty. It comprises, *first*, the inward domain of consciousness; demanding liberty of conscience, in the most comprehensive sense; liberty of thought and feeling; absolute freedom of opinion and sentiment on all subjects, practical or speculative, scientific, moral, or theological. The liberty of expressing and publishing opinions may seem to fall under a different principle, since it belongs to that part of the conduct of an individual which concerns other people; but, being almost of as much importance as the liberty of thought itself, and resting in great part on the same reasons, is practically inseparable from it. *Secondly*, the principle requires liberty of tastes and pursuits; of framing the plan of our life to suit our own character; of doing as we like, subject to such consequences as may follow; without impediment from our fellow-creatures, so long as what we do does not harm them even though they should think our conduct foolish, perverse, or wrong. *Thirdly*, from this liberty of each individual, follows the liberty, within the same limits, of combination among individuals; freedom to unite, for any purpose not involving harm to others: the persons combining being supposed to be of full age, and not forced or deceived.[40]

This, for Mill, is the only warranty for freedom or liberty in the society for the individual. These three liberties must be ensured, protected and provided. He sums up by asserting that:

> The only freedom which deserves the name, is that of pursuing our own good in our own way, so long as we do not attempt to deprive others of theirs, or impede their efforts to obtain it. Each is the proper guardian of his own health, whether bodily, or mental or spiritual. Mankind are greater gainers by suffering each other to live as seems good to themselves, than by compelling each to live as seems good to the rest.[41]

In this respect, being a critical thinker entails liberty of the individual from the yoke of the society by being oneself and no one should set the pace or measure or standards of what or how to be.

We now turn to his analysis *"of liberty of thought and discussion"* in which he advocates for freedom of expression and press against any form of authoritarianism or tyranny of numbers or majority. He asserts that:

> If all mankind minus one, were of one opinion, and only one person were of the contrary opinion, mankind would be no more justified in silencing that one person, than he, if he had the power, would be justified in silencing mankind.[42]

We examine the grounds for this assertion. For Mill, we are all subject to infallibility and hence not custodians of the truth. Any opinion may be true or false. An individual must be free to express their ideas, thoughts and beliefs. In refuting falsehoods, then truth is attained. He writes that "there is the greatest difference between presuming an opinion to be true, because, with every opportunity for contesting it, it has not been refuted, and assuming its truth for the purpose of not permitting its refutation."[43] Mill essentially calls for critical evaluation of opinions and other points of view in order to attain the truth. Truth may be persecuted and it has been persecuted but it endures persecutions but he cautions us against this terming it the "piece of idle sentimentality."

> But, indeed, the dictum that truth always triumphs over persecution, is one of those pleasant falsehoods which men repeat after one another till they pass into commonplaces, but which all experience refutes. History teems with instances of truth put down by persecution.[44]

He argues that there many instances in history where truth has been persecuted. On the contrary, truth endures for ever and Mill affirms this when he writes that:

> The real advantage which truth has, consists in this, that when an opinion is true, it may be extinguished once, twice, or many times, but in the course of ages there will generally be found persons to rediscover it, until some one of its reappearances falls on a time when from favourable circumstances it escapes persecution until it has made such head as to withstand all subsequent attempts to suppress it.[45]

It is not truths which are subject to persecutions but also its advocates such as Socrates, and Jesus according to Mill.[46] Mill asserts that:

> No one can be a great thinker who does not recognize, that as a thinker it is his first duty to follow his intellect to whatever conclusions it may lead. Truth gains more even by the errors of one who, with due study and preparation, thinks for himself, than by the true opinions of those who only hold them because they do not suffer themselves to think. Not that it is solely, or chiefly, to form great thinkers, that freedom of thinking is required.[47]

A critical thinker must not hesitate to follow his or her thoughts to their logical conclusion, must think for himself or herself and should avoid opinions of the majority. Freedom of thought aims at forming great critical thinkers for Mill. This again reflects his advocacy for critical thinking.

The society needs persons who can articulate criticism towards it, they should be rewarded, appreciated and not persecuted. Mill writes that:

> Let us thank them for it, open our minds to listen to them, and rejoice that there is someone to do for us what we otherwise ought, if we have any regard for either the certainty or the vitality of our convictions, to do with much greater labour for ourselves.

In our societies today, we have good examples of social critics who embraced individuality and championed for liberty. They include clerics, scholars, university students, political leaders, political and human rights activist to mention a few. The list can go on and on but it suffices here to assert that some individual critical thinkers have stood against the oppressions of the society.

On Individuality, as "*One of the Elements of Wellbeing*," Mill provides an elaborate defence of individuality and liberty, the idea that people should be free to adopt their own life styles "without hindrance, either physical or moral, from their fellow-men, so long as it is at their own risk and peril." The individual has absolute liberty to do whatever he wants in so far as it does not affect or infringe on the freedom of others.

However, there is limitation of the liberty of the individual. Mill writes that the individual *"...must not make himself a nuisance to other people. But if he refrains from molesting others in what concerns them, and merely acts according to his own inclination and judgment in things which concern himself,"* then this is liberty.

Mill further observes that *"...there should be different experiments of living; that free scope should be given to varieties of character, short of injury to others; and that the worth of different modes of life should be proved practically, when anyone thinks fit to try them."* This facilitates the freedom to try, taste and judge what deems to be the best for oneself. Hence, *"it is desirable, in short, that in things which do not primarily concern others, individuality should assert itself"* on what pleases and maximises one's happiness.

But unfortunately this is never the case and Mill confirms this when he observes that the *"individual spontaneity is hardly recognized by the common modes of thinking as having any intrinsic worth, or deserving any regard on its own account."* The majority have the say and the individual must conform to their ideals. He writes that:

> The majority, being satisfied with the ways of mankind as they now are (for it is they who make them what they are), cannot comprehend why those ways should not be good enough for everybody; and what is more, spontaneity forms no part of the ideal of the majority of moral and social reformers, but is rather looked on with jealousy, as a troublesome and perhaps rebellious obstruction to the general acceptance of what these reformers, in their own judgment, think would be best for mankind.

Therefore, it is only acceptable practice to follow the majority and to conform to the stipulated standards of expectations than standing out of the crowd so to speak. This according to Mill is killing individuality and his liberty at the altar of the masses or tyranny of numbers or majority. As an individual, he or she is unique and they should not replicate each other as machines. Individuality calls one to appreciate his or her uniqueness devoid of controlled life or copy one another.

Customs are good but they must be subject to critical evaluation. They must not be obstacles to the full expression of individuality. Mill writes that:

> Nobody denies that people should be so taught and trained in youth, as to know and benefit by the ascertained results of human experience. But it is the privilege and proper condition of a human being, arrived at the maturity of his faculties, to use and interpret experience in his own way. It is for him to find out what part of recorded experience is properly

> applicable to his own circumstances and character. The traditions and customs of other people are, to a certain extent, evidence of what their experience has taught them; presumptive evidence, and as such, have a claim to this deference: but, in the first place, their experience may be too narrow; or they may not have interpreted it rightly. Secondly, their interpretation of experience may be correct but unsuitable to him. Customs are made for customary circumstances, and customary characters: and his circumstances or his character may be uncustomary. Thirdly, though the customs be both good as customs, and suitable to him, yet to conform to custom, merely as custom, does not educate or develop in him any of the qualities which are the distinctive endowment of a human being.

It is plausible to infer from this quotation that individuality and criticality, according to Mill, calls us to challenge our customs, traditions, cultures and religions appreciating the good aspects and denouncing the unacceptable or out-dated practices.

In addition, Mill advocates for critical thinking as a practical tool for living in this world when he asserts that:

> He who lets the world, or his own portion of it, choose his plan of life for him, has no need of any other faculty than the ape-like one of imitation. He who chooses his plan for himself, employs all his faculties. He must use observation to see, reasoning and judgment to foresee, activity to gather materials for decision, discrimination to decide, and when he has decided, firmness and self-control to hold to his deliberate decision.

Here he calls for the use of the skills/abilities of thinking as well as the dispositions to do so.

The individual cannot be reduced to a machine for he or she is a human person and not an object. Hence Mill asserts that *"human nature is not a machine to be built after a model, and set to do exactly the work prescribed for it, but a tree, which requires to grow and develop itself on all sides, according to the tendency of the inward forces which make it a living thing. Unlike machines we require a unspontaneous healthy free living."* The individual ought to be given the space to nature himself or herself freely. This will ensure their free and full self-development.

The problem is that, the initial attempts by the society to control the excess of the individual have changed since for Mill and rightly so *"society has now fairly got the better of individuality; and the danger which threatens human nature is not the excess, but the deficiency, of personal impulses and preferences."* This is what we must also interpret as crucial for us critical thinkers. Our societies, yes oppresses us today, but not by checking our excesses but by marginalising our life styles due to poverty, lack of education, poor health care, wars and poor democracy if any.

Our individuality and liberty is also at stake, as Mill and again rightly so observes that, *"in our times, from the highest class of society down to the lowest every one lives as under the eye of a hostile and dreaded censorship."* In today's society, we lack freedom since we are constantly being monitored or under surveillance.

Variety is important and Mill asserts that *"to give any fair play to the nature of each, it is essential that different persons should be allowed to lead different lives."*

Critical thinking is manifested when:

> It will not be denied by anybody, that originality is a valuable element in human affairs. There is always need of persons not only to discover new truths, and point out when what were once truths are true no longer, but also to commence new practices, and set the example of more enlightened conduct, and better taste and sense in human life.

The Genius *ex vi termini*, that is, *more individual than any other people*, and their brilliance in thought and originality are not appreciated in society particularly. Mill rightly confirms this when he writes that:

> *If from timidity they consent to be forced into one of these moulds, and to let all that part of themselves which cannot expand under the pressure remain unexpanded, society will be little the better for their genius. If they are of a strong character, and break their fetters they become a mark for the society which has not succeeded in reducing them to common-place, to point at with solemn warning as "wild," "erratic," and the like; much as if one should complain of the Niagara river for not flowing smoothly between its banks like a Dutch canal.*

> *I insist thus emphatically on the importance of genius, and the necessity of allowing it to unfold itself freely both in thought and in practice, being well aware that no one will deny the position in theory, but knowing also that almost every one, in reality, is totally indifferent to it. People think genius a fine thing if it enables a man to write an exciting poem, or paint a picture. But in its true sense, that of originality in thought and action, though no one says that it is not a thing to be admired, nearly all, at heart, think they can do very well without it. Unhappily this is too natural to be wondered at. Originality is the one thing which unoriginal minds cannot feel the use of. They cannot see what it is to do for them: how should they? If they could see what it would do for them, it would not be originality. The first service which originality has to render them, is that of opening their eyes: which being once fully done, they would have a chance of being themselves original. Meanwhile, recollecting that nothing was ever yet done which some one was not the first to do, and that all*

> good things which exist are the fruits of originality, let them be modest enough to believe that there is something still left for it to accomplish, and assure themselves that they are more in need of originality, the less they are conscious of the want.

The genius should be given the atmosphere of freedom to flourish. On the contrary, collective mediocrity flourishes more in society than the few individual geniuses, a truth long confirmed by Socrates. He writes that *"in sober truth, whatever homage may be professed, or even paid, to real or supposed mental superiority, the general tendency of things throughout the world is to render mediocrity the ascendant power among mankind."* This is the case or reality today. Both Mill and Soren Kierkegaard shared this perspective, that the individual is lost in the group. This is manifested in politics, religion, educational institutions where the individual of genius material, of originality and criticality is persecuted by the "collective mediocrity" and the unoriginal minds.

Mill calls us to encourage the few individuals and exceptional genius to be different and stand out for the betterment of the society as Socrates attempted to do as the "gadfly" of Athens. He captures this when he asserts that

> It does seem, however, that when the opinions of masses of merely average men are everywhere become or becoming the dominant power, the counterpoise and corrective to that tendency would be, the more and more pronounced individuality of those who stand on the higher eminences of thought.

The individual must promote nonconformity and champion individualised thought. The exceptional individuals should be motivated in acting and thinking differently from the collective mediocrity or masses and they are not to be suppressed or deterred. Mill avers that we cannot afford to be satisfied or contented because in so doing we forget the need for an opposition to keep us on our intellectual vigilance, and to remind us of the values of critical thinking. Such satisfaction or contentedness leads to the stifling of genius critical individuals who are agents of progressive change. Mill then asserts that:

> In this age the mere example of non-conformity, the mere refusal to bend the knee to custom, is itself a service. Precisely because the tyranny of opinion is such as to make eccentricity a reproach, it is desirable, in order to break through that tyranny, that people should be eccentric. Eccentricity has always abounded when and where strength of character has abounded; and the amount of eccentricity in a society has generally

been proportional to the amount of genius, mental vigor, and moral courage which it contained. That so few now dare to be eccentric, marks the chief danger of the time.

Mill clears values eccentricity, that is, the courage to challenge conventionality but frowns that only few stand up for it and again, Socrates services as a good example of person who was eccentric. Here we see dispositions like courage viewed as fundamental and criticality characterized by mental rigour as advocated by Mill.

Finally, Mill concludes his considerations on individuality, by asserting that:

The despotism of custom is everywhere the standing hindrance to human advancement, being in unceasing antagonism to that disposition to aim at something better than customary, which is called, according to circumstances, the spirit of liberty, or that of progress or improvement.

Custom and its related concepts such as religion, morals just but to mention a few are the major obstacles to the full development of the individual. We are constantly under the yoke and censorship of customs. Some customs stand out as obstacles to the progress of the individual and they must be critically challenged. Following Wilhelm von Humboldt, he notes that freedom and variety of situations are important for the individual development but laments that variety is under persecution.

Mill on *"of the limits to the authority of society over the individual"* examines the relationship between society's legitimate authority over the individual beyond the spheres of freedom of thought, discussion and lifestyle. Mill asks:

What, then, is the rightful limit to the sovereignty of the individual over himself? Where does the authority of society begin? How much of human life should be assigned to individuality, and how much to society?[48]

He asserts that "to individuality should belong the part of life in which it is chiefly the individual that is interested; to society, the part which chiefly interests society."[49] The individual has rights which are outside the society or state but also needs the society to realize his rights.

In spite of such noble views, it astonishes that Mill a champion of freedom, liberty, autonomy and by extension civilisation advocated for colonisation and domination of those he referred to as "barbarians or primitive societies." These societies are lacking in maturity of thought or faculties and need to be taken care of like children.

He asserts that:

> For the same reason, we may leave out of consideration those backward states of society in which the race itself may be considered as in its nonage.... Despotism is a legitimate mode of government in dealing with barbarians, provided the end be their improvement, and the means justified by actually effecting that end.[50]

His examinations were exclusive over against been inclusive and this is a short fall in his ideals and endeavours as a critical thinker and a champion of critical thinking. His ideal on liberty and individuality must embrace universality over against particularity in its conceptualization otherwise, they are tainted with racialism, prejudices or biases at best.

Mill was generally concerned with the problems of society in relation to the individual. His perspective *on liberty* was an argument for individualism. These considerations comprise and rightly so, the ideal of critical thinking as understood by John Stuart Mill. In the next section, we examine Bertrand Russell's perspective.

Bertrand Russell - On Appearance and Reality

Although Russell does not use the term "critical thinking," this ideal is central to his philosophy. His writings have a rich conception of critical thinking, which includes not only skills/abilities but also dispositions or attitudes habits of mind or traits of mind. William Hare wrote a paper entitled "Bertrand Russell on critical thinking,"[51] in which he extracted from Russell's social, political and educational writings a rich conception of critical thinking as skills/abilities and dispositions or attitudes comparable to the major advocates of critical thinking such Siegel, Ennis and Richard Paul and Linda Elder. However, the link between Russell and critical thinking is contentious and cannot be addressed in this work.

For our interests and purposes, we restrict ourselves to Russell's book *Problems of Philosophy* and particularly to chapter one on, *Appearance and Reality* which manifest his conception of critical thinking.

In this work, Russell begins by asking: *"is there any knowledge in the world which is so certain that no reasonable man could doubt it?"* His intention is to demonstrate that all forms of knowledge must be subjected to radical doubt and this will lead to re-evaluation of all our daily assumptions. He avers that:

> This question, which at first sight might not seem difficult, is really one of the most difficult that can be asked. When we have realized the obstacles in the way of a straightforward and confident answer, we shall be well launched on the study of philosophy, for philosophy is merely the attempt to answer such ultimate questions, not carelessly and dogmatically, as we do in ordinary life and even in the sciences, but critically, after exploring all that makes such questions puzzling, and after realizing all the vagueness and confusion that underlie our ordinary ideas.

Therefore, for him, we must not take anything for granted but critically question and doubt everything to avoid contradictions, vagueness, and confusion. This is the only guarantee to the attainment of certainty of knowledge.

Like René Descartes, he raises issues with sense knowledge as deceptive. We cannot trust knowledge which comes via our senses and it must be 'reasonably doubted.' What he means is that one should not doubt for the sake of doubting but rather one ought to embrace reflective doubt. He then uses the example of a table to illustrate his theses. All facts of the table from colour, shape, size, texture, sense of touch among others can be called to question. In other words, we do not know the real table per se. This is because sense knowledge is deceptive. He gives the distinction between sense data as the things known to us through sensation such as colour, shape among others, while sensations is the experience of immediate awareness of these things. As sources of knowledge, they cannot be trusted.

Critical thinking therefore should separate appearance from reality, a distinction between what things seem to be and what they actually are. Critical thinking and:

> Philosophy, if it cannot answer so many questions as we could wish, has at least the power of asking questions which increase the interest of the world, and show the strangeness and wonder lying just below the surface even in the commonest things of daily life.

Russell follows early philosophies of pre-socratics, Plato, St. Augustine, Berkeley, and Descartes who sought the distinction between what is from what appears to be. He demonstrated how deceptive appearances can be and hence stressed the distinction between appearance and reality emphasising that we cannot trust appearances as a reliable path to truth.

3.6 Recent times

In the 20th Century recent pronouncements of critical thinking can be attributed to Claude summer, John Dewey, C. Wright Mill, and Ludwig Wittgenstein. These scholars raised questions regarding education as indoctrination (Sumner), the analysis of language (Wittgenstein), the nature of democracy (Mill) and the role of pragmatism of human thought (Dewey). More so a systematic approach to critical thinking has been developed as reflected in the discussions found in chapter one and two in this book.

3.7 *African philosophy and Critical Thinking*

The central issue within the debate on African philosophy has centred on the notion of rationality. The discussions advanced are either in support that Africans are capable or incapable of exercising rationality or reason.[52] This has led to two schools of thought namely; Eurocentricism and Afrocentricism.

Eurocentricism in essence is a form of prejudice or biasness regarding one group, the Africans. The form of biasness or prejudice inevitably singles Africans as outside the domain of critical thinking since in denying rationality is in essence, denying the former. These assertions, which are unethical and epistemological depictions regarding Africans are largely based on racial prejudices or biasness. The key advocates of this school of thought include Hegel, Carothers, Levy Bruhl, Karl Marx, and David Hume among others.[53] Afrocentricism seeks to set the records straight by refuting the theses of Eurocentricism. The general line of argument is that Africans are not free or lacking in rationality, in critical thinking. Their position and argument is that the so-called philosophy has its origin in Africa, that Africans practised a collective rationality and more so there is a professional philosophy in Africa. In addition, within the traditional African set up, there are individuals who are capable of philosophising outside the masses.

The key scholars of this school of thought include; Martin Bernal, Henry Olela, Claude Sumner, George James, Kwasi Wiredu, John S. Mbiti, Odera Oruka to mention a few.

This further can be seen in the light of Universalist versus particularistic perspective. The universality champion that rationality and philosophy in general is universal and applicable to all while the particularistic regard them as cultural or domain specific. Eurocentricism adopts a particularistic perspective. It regards philosophy and rationality as the preserve of the western culture. The Afrocentricism seeks to assert a universality perspective as demonstrated by the professional philosophy when its advocates (Hountoundji, Wiredu, and Appiah) assert that rationality and philosophy are universal and not particular.

The key point is that rationality and philosophy are universal aspects and are not a prerogative of any particular culture. In any culture we find individuals who are capable or incapable of philosophising or who lack or have critical thinking skills/abilities and dispositions.

Besides the above debate, African philosophy seeks to address some pertinent issues revolving philosophising within the context of Africa. To discuss all the African philosophers who have contributed from this perspective would beat the logic or rationale of this book. Hence, we will briefly examine the critical thoughts of Kwasi Wiredu.

Kwasi Wiredu - Philosophy and an African Culture

One outstanding scholar of African philosophy is Kwasi Wiredu, a Ghanaian who in his book, *Philosophy and an African Culture*, identifies three major problems or vices which philosophy and in particular critical thinking must address in Africa.

These vices are anachronism, authoritarianism and supernaturalism. Ochieng'-Odhiambo asserts that "the first two, in particular have greatly and adversely afflicted African society by enhancing the communal folk thought at the expense of modern African philosophy and modernisation in general."[54]

Anachronism is the inability to appreciate and acknowledge that something or ideas have out lived their utility. This is a big problem in Africa, which stifles criticality. Africa continues to produce raw materials and import finished products from Europe, America and Asia as second hand goods whose time and utility is no longer viable. The failure to acknowledge this has made Africa to be a dumping site of all manner of things from out dated technologies to second hand clothes. Philosophy and critical thinking in particular must address this vice in order to promote creativity and innovation in Africa. This will ensure originality of both ideas and products and more so autonomy.

By *Authoritarianism* Wiredu implies the unquestioning appeal to things or person(s) in power. This is a vice, which has stifled democracy in Africa. This has led to a situation where freedoms, political and social rights have no room. Wiredu writes that African society "...was deeply authoritarian. Our social arrangements were shot through the principle of unquestioning obedience to superiors, which often meant elders.... but it is rare to come across any which extol the virtues of originality and independence of thought."[55] The despotism of culture or customs must be challenged for it suppresses criticality. It crushes expressions of individuality and hence a great obstacle to human development. Wiredu thinks that African cultures tend to stifle development because they are static. Without freedom and variety in society as the Prussian philosopher Wilhelm Humboldt asserted, African will never progress or develop, and even if it does, it would be following anachronistic ideals and at a stagnating pace. The practice of democracy in Africa is by paper and therefore it does not exist in reality. In essence the status quo is fostered by the authoritarianism of the African cultures. The politics of succession in Africa have followed this authoritarian criterion. Philosophy and in particular, critical thinking can and must address this pressing issue. Siegel notes that one fundamental value of critical thinking is to promote democracy. Siegel avers that "it is not simply an intelligent citizenry, but a critical one, which democracy wants."[56] This is vital for challenging the authoritarian nature of the African societies. Critical scrutiny cannot be wished away but it must be embraced if democracy is to flourish in Africa. Corruption has taken toll in Africa because it very difficult if not impossible to question those in authority. Again we see the need for courage to scrutinise this matter. Moreover, although this agitation for critical scrutiny and eccentricity may irritate some, we prefer it rather than miserable conformity and with good reasons as outlined above.

By *Supernaturalism,* Wiredu implies that certain beliefs are harmful to people. The African society for Wiredu and other scholars such as John S. Mbiti, Fr. Placide Temples among others associate Africans with excessive obsession with religion, at best that "Africans are notoriously religious..."[57] This has negative impact to human development for religion is known to stifle development and the advanced countries in science and technology have divorced religion. This is what Wiredu is thinking when he lists supernaturalism as a vice in African society. He gives the example of family planning methods and how religion has rejected it. The same must be said of the use of contraceptives and the spread of HIV/Aids in Africa.

Leadership issues again are tainted with false beliefs that leaders are anointed by God. Hence philosophy and in particular critical thinking is the 'messiah' so to speak to address this vice according to Wiredu.

The fundamentality of reasoned procedures and critical talents and attitudes is indispensable in addressing these vices. In essence fostering of critical thinking skills/abilities and dispositions is essential for a better Africa. Such an approach will ensure critical and questioning citizenry.

3.8 *Conclusion*

This chapter has focused on exposing from a historical perspective of critical thinking as manifested by various key philosophers. In accepting the inseparability of critical thinking from rationality, the chapter showed how this fact has guided philosophers in their quests. We explored how the ideal of critical thinking, as reason and rationality, has been central in the history of philosophy from the pre-Socratics, to the medieval thinkers, to modern and contemporary philosophers. This historical approach has no doubt examined how critical thinking ideal is of value and this is good since it would guide readers in fostering critical thinking skills/abilities and dispositions.

The sampling of the models of critical thinking enabled us to acquire invaluable insights that deepened and widened thinking about critical thinking. It also guided us in recognizing some of the prejudices, stereotypes and misconceptions from a historical perspective. For critical thinkers, such efforts are indispensable in understanding society today. It important to note that proponents of some of these models had questionable traits but that does not mean they were not critical thinkers as Connie Missimer sought to argue.

In essence, this chapter demonstrated that the history of critical thought heightens our awareness of the necessity of critical thinking. It suffices to say that philosophy is critical. Moreover, critical philosophy permeates all domains of knowledge from science to law. In this regard critical thinking has a role to play in any field of study.

In the next two chapters, we will demonstrate the relevance of logic both –formal and–informal to critical thinking.

3.9 End Notes

1. Harvey Siegel, *Educating Reason: Rationality, Critical Thinking and Education,* (Routledge, 1988), 127.
2. Ibid., 128.
3. Connie Missimer, *Perhaps by Skill Alone* Informal Logic, XII.3, Fall 1990, 145.
4. Ibid., 146.
5. Cf. Ibid.
6. Ibid., 147-148.
7. Harvey Siegel, *Rationality Redeemed? Further Dialogues on an Educational Ideal* (New York: Routledge, 1997), 59.
8. Connie Missimer, *Perhaps by Skill Alone* Informal Logic, op. cit., 150-151.
9. Harvey Siegel, *Rationality Redeemed? Further Dialogues on an Educational Ideal,* op cit., 65.
10. Samuel E. Stumpf, *Socrates to Sartre: A History of Philosophy,* (Boston: McGraw-Hill college, 1999), 5.
11. Ibid., 6.
12. Ibid., 29-30.
13. Paul, R. & Elder, L. *Critical Thinking: Tools for Taking Charge of Your Learning and Your Life.* (Pearson/Prentice Hall, 2008), 17- 18.
14. Harvey Siegel, *Education's Epistemology: Rationality, Diversity and Critical Thinking.* (New York: Oxford University Press, 2017), 3.
15. William F. Lawhead, *The Philosophical Journey: An Interactive Approach* (5th Ed), New York: McGraw-Hill, 2011), 31.
16. Ibid.,
17. Ibid., 36.
18. Harvey Siegel, Education's *Epistemology: Rationality, Diversity and Critical Thinking,* op. cit., 3.
19. Samuel E. Stumpf, *Socrates to Sartre: A History of Philosophy,* op.cit., 189.
20. Ibid., 203-204.
21. Harvey Siegel, *Rationality Redeemed? Further Dialogues on an Educational Ideal,* op cit., 19.

22. Samuel E. Stumpf, *Socrates to Sartre: A History of Philosophy,* op cit., 204-205.
23. Sharon Bailin & Mark Battersby, *Reason in the Balance: An Inquiry Approach to Critical Thinking,* (Cambridge: Hackett publishing Company, Inc.2016), 16.
24. Ibid.
25. Robert H. Ennis, *Critical Thinking* (Prentice–hall, Inc, 1996), 69.
26. Dion Scott-Kakures and Susan Castagnetto et al, *History of Philosophy,* (New York: Harper Perennial publishers Inc 1993), 98.
27. Samuel E. Stumpf, *Socrates to Sartre: A History of Philosophy,* op cit., 207.
28. Ibid.
29. René Descartes, *The Philosophical Writings of Descartes,* Vol. I, trans. John Cottingham, Robert Stoothoff, Dugald Murdoch, and Antony Kenny (Cambridge: Cambridge University Press, 1985), 404.
30. René Descartes, *The Philosophical Writings of Descartes,* Vol. III, trans. John Cottingham, Robert Stoothoff, Dugald Murdoch, and Antony Kenny, op. cit., 250-251.
31. Samuel E. Stumpf, *Socrates to Sartre: A History of Philosophy,* op. cit., 223.
32. René Descartes, *The Philosophical Writings of Descartes,* Vol. III. op.cit., 151-152.
33. Paul, R. & Elder, L. *Critical Thinking: Tools for Taking Charge of Your Learning and Your Life,* op. cit., 169.
34. Samuel E. Stumpf, *Socrates to Sartre: A History of Philosophy,* op cit., 225-226.
35. René Descartes, **T**he *Philosophical Writings of Descartes,* Vol. I. op. cit., 404.
36. John Somerville and Ronald E. Santoni, *Social and Political Philosophy: Readings from Plato to Gandhi,* (New York: Double Day, 1963), 302.
37. Ibid., 310.
38. Ibid.
39. Ibid.
40. Ibid., 312-313
41. Ibid., 313.
42. Ibid., 316.

43. Ibid., 318-319.
44. Ibid., 327.
45. Ibid., 327.
46. Cf. ibid., 323-332.
47. Ibid., 331.
48. Ibid., 337.
49. Ibid.
50. Ibid., 310.
51. William Hare, *"Bertrand Russell on Critical Thinking," Proceedings of the Twentieth World Congress of Philosophy,* http://www.bu.edu/wcp/Papers/Educ/EducHare.htm [visited 16 December 2002]. Also published in the Journal of Thought, 36(2001): 7-16.
52. Cf. Julius Wambua Mbithi, *A Critical Exposition of the Concept of and the Reality on the Debate on African Philosophy.* A paper published in *African Tomorrow Journal,* A Salvatorian Institute of Philosophy and Theology Journal, Morogoro, 2006.
53. Ibid.,
54. F. Ochieng'-Odhiambo, *African Philosophy: An Introduction,* (Nairobi: Consolata Institute of Philosophy Press, 2002), 85.
55. Kwasi Wiredu, *Philosophy and African Culture.* (Cambridge: Cambridge University Press, 1980), 4.
56. Harvey Siegel, *Educating Reason: Rationality, Critical Thinking and Education,* 61.
57. John S. Mbiti, *African Philosophy and Religions,* (London: Heinemann Publishes, 1969), 1.

CHAPTER FOUR
CRITICAL THINKING AND ARGUMENT ANALYSIS

... that *formal* logic as well informal logic is relevant to critical thinking course.[1]

This conception of critical thinking links naturally with argumentation. For good argumentation involves good reasoning, and so the skilled assessment of probative forces of reasons; it also involves the normative impact of reasons, insofar as the arguer is one who is not only skilled at argumentation, but who also regularly engage in high quality argumentation and is appropriately directed-moved-by it.[2]

4 Introduction

So far we have demonstrated that critical thinking is a process of acquiring a set of thinking skills/abilities and dispositions. These skills/abilities enable one to construct or take apart arguments, examine the credibility of the source(s), read, write carefully and be assertive on one's own ideas with clarity, accuracy and precision. In addition, one must be inclined to do so. One major issue that arose in chapter two is the link between logic and critical thinking. Hence this chapter seeks to investigate the relevance of logic to critical thinking.

4.1 The Relevance of Logic to Critical Thinking

Some of the critical thinking theorists have argued that logic is relevant to critical thinking.

For example, Siegel writes that there are two reasons as to why logic is relevant to critical thinking: "first, formal logic can be seen as providing a paradigm of good argumentation."[3] Since critical thinking entails good reasoning, the connection between premises and conclusion, then logic provides the means to this good argumentation. When we assert that good argumentation involves good reasoning or good argument, it entails the grounds for accepting or affirming the given conclusion. Good or bad reasoning or arguments connote the degree to which the given premises support the conclusion. Good argumentation offers justification for accepting the claim or conclusion because the premises are reasonable. On the contrary, bad reasoning or argumentation entails that the justifications offered do not support the conclusion or the premises are not reasonable. Therefore, formal argumentation is central to critical thinking.

The second reason for considering logic as relevant to critical thinking, according to Siegel, is that, logic is the source of clear reasons:

> A second reason for thinking formal logic to be relevant to critical thinking is that the latter is fundamentally concerned with the proper assessment of reasons, and formal logic provides an excellent source of clear reasons.
>
> ...formal logic is relevant to reason assessment, and so to critical thinking (and exposure to formal logic is desirable for the critical thinking student, for it illustrates well the fundamental relation of "is a reason for.")"[4]

Logic provides excellent source of clear reasons or "reasons for," which are vital for critical thinking in proper assessment of reasons

These two reasons, for Siegel, provide the rationale of logic to critical thinking for "logic is relevant to the determination of the goodness of reasons. Such determination is central to critical thinking."[5] Critical thinking entails the determination of good reasons and hence logic becomes handy in this respect. Therefore, formal and informal logic is relevant to critical thinking.

4.2 Basic Concepts of Logic

In this section, we will focus on the basic concepts of logic.

4.2.1 Logic

"Logic is the study of the methods and principles used to distinguish correct from incorrect reasoning."[6] Thus, it seeks to understand if reasons are good or bad in an argument. In essence, it deals with the analysis of arguments evaluating the relations between premises of an argument and its conclusion. It analyzes whether the given premises support (provide probative or putative forces) or do not support the given conclusion.

4.2.2 Argument

An argument is defined as a set of premises or statements with one and only one conclusion. Here is an example of an argument:

1. All humans are mortal- 1st premise
2. Socrates is a human- 2st premise
3. Therefore, Socrates is mortal – 3rd premise known as the conclusion.

Arguments either serve to persuade others or as a tool to discover the truth. Political or ethical debates largely make use of arguments as a tool to persuade others to accept or reject a certain perspective.

In matters of crime, a detective may use argument to discover the truth.

Conclusion

Conclusion is derived, affirmed, or inferred from the given premises; it necessarily or follows from the given premises. The premises must provide *good reasons* for believing that the conclusion is true. The premises must support or provide probative and putative forces for accepting or affirming the truth of the conclusion. However, it is not always the case that the given premises support the conclusion and when that occurs, then we infer that the argument is, invalid. And if premises support the conclusion as demonstrated by the above example, then it is declared valid. In worthy to note that in some instances there are unstated conclusions hence a critical thinker must be able to recognize such instances.

Conclusion indicators include: this shows that..., so..., therefore..., consequently..., hence..., it follows that..., subsequently..., thus..., in conclusion..., accordingly..., this suggests that..., this proves that..., this implies that...

Premises

From the above example, 1, 2 & 3 are referred to as premises. The third premise is known as the conclusion. Premise (s) is a statement or statements in an argument. The premises provide probative and putative forces of reason for accepting or supporting the conclusion. Premises provide *good reasons* for supporting or affirming the conclusion as true. Hence it is critical to ask, are the given premise(s) relevant to the conclusion? Do they support the conclusion? Are the premises reasonable? Are the sources credible? Are the premises clear, precise, or are they vague or ambiguous? Are they evidentially strong or weak? This requires critical thinking skills/abilities as well as the dispositions to do so.

Premise have common indicators which include; because..., since..., in the light..., whereas..., given that..., for the reason that..., for..., in view of..., this is implied by...

I. Unstated premises

Arguments can also have unstated premises. For instance:

You can't withdraw money from ATM machine without a card. So, Kioko won't be able to make a withdrawal.

The unstated premise must be: Kioko has no ATM card.

Therefore, a critical thinker ought to identify unstated premises.

I. Independent and dependent premises

By independent premises, the implication is that the falsity one of the premises would not cancel the support of the other premises in support of the conclusion. For example:

1. Providing free condoms will increase immorality.
2. In addition, doing so will increase marriage breakdowns.
3. So, we should not provide free condoms.

The premises in this argument are independent of each other. In essence it is a case of one conclusion derived from two arguments.

On the other hand, by dependent premises, the implication is that the falsity of one premise would warrant lack of support for the conclusion. For example:

1. Raising wages will waste resources.
2. We don't have resources to waste.
3. Therefore, we should not raise wages.

The premises in this argument are dependent on each other in derivation of the conclusion such in absence of one, the conclusion would not be supported.

Statement/Proposition

A statement or proposition is a sentence, which is either true of false. The following are examples of statements:

1. All catholic priests are male. (T)
2. All catholic nuns are female. (T)
3. Some dogs are Germany shepherds. (T)
4. All unicorns are flying animals. (F)

Statements 1, 2, 3 are true while 4 is false. Ideally, there are two truth-values of statements namely: truth and falsehood. It is important to note that questions, expressions or commands are not propositions.

4.2.3 *Valid and Invalid, Strong and Weak Arguments*

An argument is valid or invalid, strong or weak.

Validity and Invalidity

An argument is either valid or invalid.

I. Valid Argument

A valid argument has this basic structure: the conclusion is completely or absolutely and necessarily derived from the given premises; given that the premises are true, the conclusion cannot be false; from true premises, the conclusion is also true. In other words, the conclusion cannot be false given true premises.

Example 1:
1. All eucalyptus are trees.
2. All trees are plants.
3. Therefore, All eucalyptus are plants.

Example 2:
1. All Germany shepherds are dogs.
2. Some animals are not dogs.
3. Therefore, some animals are not Germany shepherds.

These examples are valid since the premises are true and the conclusion is true. The focus is on the linkage between the premises and the conclusion. It is important to note that an argument can have false premise but still be valid because the determination of validity is independent of its actual truth value of the premises. As noted here, validity focuses on logical connectivity of the given premises and the conclusion.

II. Invalid Argument

An invalid argument has the following general characteristics: first if its conclusion is false though its premises are true. Second, if the premises do not support the conclusion and third, if the premises are true with a false conclusion.

Example 1:
1. All physicists are materialists.
2. Karl Marx was a materialist.
3. So, Karl Marx was a physicist.

Example 2:
1. All birds are animals.
2. All dogs are animals.
3. Therefore, all dogs are birds.

Example 3:
1. All priests are celibate.

2. All nuns are celibate.
3. Therefore, all nuns are priests.

Example 4:
1. If Grace is a woman, then she is a catholic nun.
2. But Grace is not a catholic nun.
3. Therefore, Grace is not a woman.

The above examples of arguments have true premises but the conclusions are false hence invalid.

4.2.4 Deductive and Inductive Arguments

Arguments are either deductive or inductive.

Deductive Arguments

Deductive logic is concerned with determining the validity and invalidity of arguments. Deductive arguments can be valid or invalid, sound or unsound. In this section, we examine the concepts of sound or unsound deductive arguments.

Deductive Sound and Unsound Arguments

Deductive arguments are either valid or invalid as discussed above. In addition, they are either sound or unsound.

Deductively Sound Argument

Deductively sound argument has the following features; it's valid and with true premises.

Example 1:
1. All mammals have lungs.
2. All Bats are mammals.
3. Therefore, All Bats have lungs.

Deductively Unsound Argument

Deductively unsound arguments have the following features:
a) Valid but at least has a false premise
b) Invalid with true premises.
c) Invalid with one false premise.

An example of deductively valid but unsound argument;
1. All birds are animals.
2. Some Germany shepherds are not animals.
3. Therefore, some Germany shepherds are not birds.

This is deductively valid but unsound because of the 2nd premise is false.

Example of deductively invalid and unsound argument:
1. All nuns are single.
2. All priests are single.
3. Therefore, All priests are nuns.

This is invalid and unsound because it has true premises but false conclusion.

Here is an example of deductively invalid argument with one false premise:
1. All trees are animals.
2. All Germany shepherds are animals.
3. Therefore, All Germany shepherds are trees.

Validity and Truth

As explained above validity relates to the premises and the conclusion in an argument. Truth and falsehood apply to single propositions/statements. Validity of an argument is independent of the truth value of the propositions. An argument can be valid but with false propositions or invalid with true conclusion. A valid argument may contain all true premises, one false premise, two false premise, and false conclusion. Recall our discussion (above) regarding validity and soundness of an argument.

The validity or invalidity of an argument is not determined by the truth or falsity of an argument's conclusion neither is validity of an argument a guarantee of the truth of its conclusion.

Inductive Arguments

Inductive arguments necessitate a degree of probability, that the conclusion is determined by the strength of the given premises. The support from the given premises is not sufficient to guarantee with certainty the conclusion. In essence there is a gap between the given premises and the conclusion, an inductive leap.

Inductive arguments are either strong or weak, or cogent or uncogent.

A Strong Inductive Argument

A strong inductive argument is probable such that it is unlikely (though possible) that its conclusion is false while its premises are true. We then talk of slightly, moderately or very strong inductive argument depending of the degree of strength of the given premises. Therefore, validity or invalidity does not arise when it comes to inductive arguments.

Here is an example:

Gold is an expensive rare mineral.

Silver is an expensive rare mineral.

Bronze is an expensive rare mineral.

Tanzanite is an expensive rare mineral.

Quartz is an expensive rare mineral.

Therefore, rare minerals are expensive.

A Weak Inductive Argument

Essentially, a weak inductive argument is not likely that if its premises are true then its conclusion is true. Here is an example;

Copper is a good conductor of heat

Iron is a good conductor of heat

Therefore, Metals are good conductors of heat.

Inductively Cogent and Uncogent Arguments

An inductive argument is either cogent or uncogent. Similar to the concept of soundness for deductive arguments, a strong inductive argument with true premises is termed cogent. A weak inductive argument is termed as uncogent. It is cogent if the premises are strong and true hence sound; uncogent if the premises are weak and some are false, hence unsound. Below is an example of inductively cogent sound argument:

1. All presidents in republic of Kenya have been men.
2. Therefore, the next president would be a man.

Here is an example of inductively uncogent unsound argument:

a) It always rains by the 15th of October every year. Therefore, probably it will rain on the 15th of October this year.

This argument is weak in the sense that it is unlikely to establish the truth of the conclusion.

As a summary, in this section, we have introduced the basic concepts of logic. We explained what logic is and why it is necessary or relevant to critical thinking. We have discussed various concepts of logic such as propositions, premises and the types of arguments.

We have explained the fundamental difference between deductive arguments and inductive arguments. Finally, we discussed validity and invalidity as contrasted with truth and falsity exploring the key relations between validity and truth.

The following section of the chapter is devoted to the analysis of language and its crucial role in critical thinking.

4.3 *Language and Critical Thinking*

Language can and has been used to manipulate or persuade our thoughts or reasoning. It is a source of errors and misunderstanding due to carelessness, lack of clarity, impreciseness and ambiguity. Hence below is an examination of the uses or functions of language.

Cognitive and Emotive Functions

Language can be used in cognitive and emotive sense. It is used cognitively when information is conveyed. Here is an example;

a) The initial composition of East Africa was three countries namely; Kenya, Tanzania and Uganda. By the year 2018, the composition had increased to comprise Burundi, Rwanda, and South Sudan.

This is cognitive use of language. Hence, from this example, one is able to know the number of countries that compose the East African block with accuracy.

Language is used in the emotive sense to the extent that a sentence evokes emotions. For example, abortion is killing an innocent and mercilessly, unborn child. The words killing, innocent, mercilessly and unborn are used in the emotive sense.

Logic is "chiefly concerned with language used informatively–affirming or denying propositions, formulating or evaluating arguments, and so on. In reasoning it is this informative function of language that is the principal concern."[7] This is crucial for critical thinkers since it useful to understand the link between the informational content of propositions, between cognitive and emotive usages of language. Critical thinkers must be aware of emotionally loaded language because it is an obstacle to critical thinking.

Ambiguity and Vagueness

Critical thinkers must be able to identify ambiguity and vagueness in the usage of language. These two terms connote two different things: "An ambiguous claim has two or more possible meanings, and the context does not make clear which meaning is intended. A **vague claim**, by, contrast, has a meaning that is indistinct or imprecise."[8] A classic example of an ambiguous claim is: You have heard it from the horse's mouth! Some indicators of vagueness are; relatively, significantly, old, rich, young among others. For example, the research has significantly showed that... is a vague claim.

Ambiguity entails more than one meaning and lack of a proper context. For example, the words; argument, record, one, father, sister, person, baby, coach, chair, bar, good, minutes, look, press just but to mention a few, are in many cases are used ambiguously. The ambiguities of these words arise due to the fact they have more than one meaning and can mean different things in different contexts.

Ambiguity can arise due to semantics, that is, with the meaning of words or what they symbolise or signify. For example:
- a) She is hot.
- b) He is cool.
- c) Grow up!

These are ambiguous statements due to the use of the words hot, cool or grow. These are examples of semantically ambiguous claim due to a particular term or phrase.

Syntactically ambiguous claims occur due their structure such as punctuation, grammar sentence structure or word order. Consider the following example:
- a) Critical thinkers must be able to identify and avoid ambiguity and vagueness.
- b) The DOS saw the student leaders with Dr. O.
- c) The soldiers saw the immigrants with binoculars.
- d) He cleaned the house with his wife.
- e) I have been driving for many years when I fell asleep and caused an accident.
- f) Keep distance.
- g) Dr. K. to Students of African traditional religion: we meet tomorrow for witchcraft and sorcery.
- h) The ultimate goal of the project is to provide a guide for use by people who will work with university students who are at –risk of radicalisation or who have been radicalised.
- i) I have discussed in details, this fallacy and others in five.

These examples are syntactically ambiguous claims.

There is also grouping ambiguity, which occurs when we do not clearly define or make it clear regarding our reference, that is, are we taking of the group or the individuals of the group? For example:

    a) High school teachers earn more than university lecturers.

This is ambiguous statement since it is not clear if we are comparing individuals in the groups or the group as a whole.

Signs are often ambiguous. Some examples of ambiguous signs are:

    a) "Automatic washing machines: please remove all your clothes when the light goes out!
    b) We exchange anything - bicycles, washing machines, etc. why not bring your wife along and get a wonderful bargain?"[9]
    c) Hotel parking.
    d) This is a corruption free zone.
    e) This is drug free zone.

Ambiguity as we will demonstrate in the next chapter leads to fallacies reasoning. A fallacy is an error or mistake in reasoning. The major fallacies of ambiguity are:

> Equivocation (where there's a shift of meaning in a word or phrase leading to an incorrect conclusion), accent (where the emphasis of a word or phrase leads us to an incorrect conclusion) and amphiboly (where the sentence structure or use of grammar creates ambiguity, leading to an incorrect conclusion).[10]

We have discussed and given relevant examples of the fallacies of ambiguity in the next chapter. Therefore, critical thinkers must be able to identify and avoid the use of ambiguity and vagueness.

Rhetoric

Some rhetoric devices such as **loaded, hedged, descriptive, sexist, racial, images, metaphorical, asymmetrical, cultural, exclusive and inclusive uses of language** manipulate thinking hence critical thinking comes in handy to expose and eliminate them. Critical thinkers must identify words when they are used as slanters, or slanting devices such as euphemisms, dysphemism, persuasive comparisons, explanations, stereotypes, innuendos, loaded questions, weaselers, downplayers, horselaugh or ridicule or sarcasm, hyperboles, and proof surrogates. Critical thinkers should not allow themselves to be fooled, persuaded or influenced by these linguistic tactics. We explore some of these language devices or tactics below.

Concerning **euphemisms and dysphemism**, the former entails excessive positive remarks while the latter is the converse entailing negativity. For example, the terms "rebels" or "guerrillas" are neutral. But when the term "freedom fighters" is used, it connotes euphemism. The term "terrorist" would connote dysphemism when used instead of "rebels" or "guerrillas." Union officials would connote euphemism while troublemakers or activists would connote dysphemism. Euphemisms and dysphemism are used to influence our thoughts.

A persuasive comparison entails unfair comparisons. For example, comparing a person's beauty with an ostrich!

Persuasive explanations are used in a flattering sense where the goal is to persuade rather than give good reasons. For example, the reason I gave up on my Ph.D. research is because I married. There could be other better reasons such as fees or incompetence to pursue the programme.

Stereotype is a false image created with no evidence. For example, Dr. K. describes Dr. M. as eccentric. Stereotype is common when it comes to ethnic groups whereby one ethnic grouping regards the other in stereotype manner. For the example:

a) "According to the Bororo (a tribe of Northern Brazil), the Trumai (a neighbouring tribe) spend the night at the bottom of the river."[11]

Innuendos communicate in a condemnatory manner about something without actually saying it. A classic example of an innuendo goes like this; *"I didn't say the meat was tough. I said I don't see the horse that is usually outside,"* or your presentation is good though have you used vernacular language. Another example would go like this:

1. Eng. M: Dr. M., is Dr. O and Dr. K saying the truth?
2. Dr. M: Yes, this time and on this occasion.

Some other examples would be to remark that: the priests are competent in many regards! Or that Dr. K. is competent, I suppose or he is useful so far or surprisingly he has a Ph.D. in shrines!

Loaded questions or complex questions entail a question with a yes or no answer. It is also known as the fallacy of complex question. For example, have you stopped been corrupt? Or have stopped beating or cheating on your wife? Do you sill drive while drunk? Are you still cheating or stealing? Are you still cheating in exams? Are you still abusing drugs? A critical thinker must demand the question(s) is simplified or broken down.

Weaselers are words used in a claim to water down or weaken criticisms and provide an escape route. Such words include; reportedly, it is arguable that, some would say that, perhaps, it may well be that, in what may be the most obvious, possibly, maybe, assuming, presuming, and may be. Here is an example:

a) In what may be the most obvious indicator of a government's priorities, when the electoral board **reportedly** rigged the elections, they are not in jail.

Reportedly is not the necessary and sufficient condition for the board members to be jailed. Critical thinkers must be alert to detect these weaselers.

Downplaying is to demean a position in order to make it appear insignificant or less important or trivial. For example, a posts in the university group WhatsApp platform reads; do not mind Dr. M, he is eccentric, liberal and at best, a trouble maker. This example demonstrates how words such as; the so-called, just another, mere or merely among others are used as downplayers. Most of the above serve as downplayers. Quotation marks also are used as downplayers. For example, he "picked" or "fished" his "Ph.D." from a university near the Indian Ocean or he "researched" or "collected" his Ph.D. in the neighbouring war torn country.

Horselaugh, ridicule, or sarcasm entails the use of ridicule of all manner or kinds. Laughing is a powerful tool of denigrating a person rather than her ideas. One may simply laugh at a claim ("appoint him DOS or Registrar? Har, har, har). This is common in debates where one person may keep laughing and making funny remarks as his or her tool to win rather than addressing the subject matter or argument at hand. Others examples are: after a seminar or workshop a participant remarks: I really would want and love to appreciate your facilitation and value of our time..., or our able facilitator..., for me who was listening..., my expectations are met only that i struggled to remain attentive..., or this hotel is comfortable relatively..., when the facilitator is requested to give handouts, he remarks; that is very good and tempting but it would disable your musing..., or I would love to be available for you again... all these are examples of sarcasms which entails communicating the opposite of one's intentions. Critical thinkers must able to detect when such devices are been used.

Hyperbole entails exaggerating or overstatement. To describe that responding to his remarks is equivalent to hitting a mosquito with a hammer is hyperbole.

A proof surrogate is simply lack of evidence or authority in spite of suggesting the availability of the same. Examples of indicates of proof surrogate are; there is every reason to believe, our informed sources say, it is obvious that, studies show that, among others. This tactic is common among lawyers and in advertisements.

In concluding this section, it is important for critical thinkers to know these linguistics tactics which can obscure good reasoning. In addition, language can be of positive value for critical thinkers. It can be used as liberation tool or voice, as tool to break oppressive language.

Definitions

Critical thinkers must be familiar with the various types of definitions and how they can be used to manipulate one's thought. Definitions if not properly used contribute to ambiguity, impreciseness, and vagueness as reflected in the Plato's dialogues and highlighted in chapter three. In this section, we will examine various types of definitions and their importance to critical thinking.

The Structure of Definitions: Extension and Intension

It is important to distinguish between extension and intension of term or symbol. The extension of a term comprises of the set of things to which the term connotes. Thus the extension of the term fish consists of mud fish, jelly fish, cat fish, tilapia and so on. The intension of the term consists of properties a thing must have in order to be included in the term's extension, in the case of "fish," the extension includes fins, scales and so on. Further the extensional definitions are divided into two namely: ostensive (non-verbal) and enumerative (verbal). Ostensive definitions specify the meaning of a term by pointing to objects in its extension. For example, pointing a tree or rock or frogs and so on.

An enumerative (verbal) definition entails specifying the meaning of a term by naming the individual members of the extension individually or in groups. For example, East Africa initially meant Kenya, Uganda and Tanzania.

Types of Definitions

Definition by genus and difference

Definiendum and definiens are two commonly used technical terms in discussing definitions:

> The definiendum is the symbol being defined. The definiens is the symbol (or group of symbols) used to explain the meaning of the definiendum. Put otherwise, the definiendum is the term to be defined and the definiens is the definition of it. However, it would be a mistake to say that the definiens is the meaning of the definiendum—rather, it is another symbol (or group of symbols) that has the same meaning as the definiendum.[12]

Definiendum is the word or symbol being defined while definiens are the words or symbols that do the defining.

Genus is the main class while species is simply a proper subclass. For example, fish is genus while the subclass includes cat fish, mud fish, and tilapia just to mention a few. The difference is the aspect that distinguishes the members of a given species from others in the same genus.

In line with this, there are five types of definitions namely; (1) stipulative, (2) lexical, (3) precising, (4) theoretical, and (5) persuasive. We will consider each in turn.

A. Stipulative Definition

Stipulative definition entails a meaning that is deliberately assigned to some symbol independent of its established use. For example, "Muthama" is used as name of person in Kenya but in "Sheng" a slant/street language in Kenya, it means mother or a woman.

B. Lexical Definition

A lexical definition reports the meaning which is established by the symbol or term. Good examples of lexical definitions are from dictionaries. For example, "immanent" means existing.

C. Precising Definitions

Precising definitions reduces the vagueness ambiguity or of a term by imposing limits on the use or conventional meaning making it more exact. For the example the terms "dead" or "velocity" or "abortion" or "person" or "matter" or "force" need precise definitions.

D. Theoretical Definitions

A theoretical definition attempts to provide adequate understanding of the thing(s) to which the symbol or term applies. For example, in the Euthyphro, "right" means approved by gods," or the definition of piety as discussed by Socrates and Euthyphro, or when Socrates struggles to find the correct definition of "justice" in Plato's Republic, or in Meno when he seeks to extract the meaning of virtue. Within the debate on abortion, there are attempts to theoretically define terms such as the human person, child, rights among other aspects.

E. Persuasive Definition

Persuasive definition seeks to influence attitudes or stirring emotions in definitional attempts. For example, abortion is killing of unborn child; capitalism is man eat man economic system; government by the people, of the people, with the people, make A great again.

Using Definitions to Evaluate Arguments

Definitions are vital in evaluating arguments to determine their validity or invalidity, soundness or unsoundness. Due to lack of good definitions, equivocation and verbal disputes occur.

Equivocation occurs when a term is used with more than one meaning. Here is an example;

1. The sign read "fine to play loud music," and since it was fine, I played loud music.
2. Judge to accused: I want you to set the record straight. The accused responds: thank you.

The words record and fine are understood differently in these contexts.

The word "fine" is used with two different meanings. Fine to mean penalty and also in the second sense to imply it is okay.

Verbal disputes occur when two or more disputants appear to disagree because of an ambiguous word. William James a psychologist provides a classical example of a verbal dispute:

> Some years ago, being with a camping party in the mountains, I returned from a solitary ramble to find every one engaged in a ferocious ...dispute. The corpus of the dispute was a squirrel- a live squirrel supposed to be clinging to one side of tree trunk; while over against the tree's opposite side a human being was imagined to stand. This human witness tries to get sight of the squirrel by moving rapidly round the tree, but no matter how fast he goes, the squirrel moves as fast in the opposite direction, and always keeps the tree between himself and the man, so that never a

glimpse of him is caught. The resultant...problem now is this: Does the man go round the squirrel or not? He goes round the tree sure enough, and the squirrel is on the tree; but does he go round the squirrel? In the unlimited leisure of the wilderness, discussion had been worn threadbare. Everyone had taken sides, and was obstinate....

The dispute is, does the man go round the squirrel or not? One party is for while the other is against. William James resolves the dispute by clarifying the meaning of going round:

> Mindful of the scholastic adage that whenever you meet a contradiction you must make a distinction, I immediately sought and found one, as follows: "which party is right," I said "depends what you practically mean by 'going round' the squirrel. If you mean passing from the north of him to the east, then to the south, then to the west, and to the north of him again, obviously the man does go round him, for he occupies these successive positions. But if on the contrary you mean being first in front of him, then on the right of him, then behind him, then on his left, and finally in front again, it is quite as obvious that the man fails to go round him, for by the compensating movements the squirrel makes, he keeps his belly turned toward the man all the time, and his back turned away from him.

The whole dispute from this example is as result of the meaning of "going round." Plato in his various books/*Dialogues* depicts Socrates who engaged in dispute over the meaning words such piety, justice, good and virtue just but mention a few.

As a summary, we have in general looked at the use of language, definitions and their significance for critical thinkers. As Gottlob Frege noted that it is vital to *"indicate the pitfalls laid by language in the way of the thinker."* In this respect, critical thinkers must be alert of language when it contributes to fallacious or incorrect reasoning or argumentation.

In the next section, we look at the common basic argument forms.

4.4 *Common Basic Argument Forms*

It is important to know the various argument forms which determine if either an argument is valid or invalid because of their structure. This knowledge is helpful in establishing whether an argument is valid or invalid.

Prior to a detailed examination of the arguments forms, there is the need to understand conditional statements. Below is an example of argument with conditional statements:

    1. If it is a lemon, then it is green
    2. It is a lemon.

3. So, it is green

From this example, the following characteristics of conditional statements are deduced:

A. It comprises of two components namely antecedent and consequent.

If ... (**Antecedent**)... then... (**Consequent**) also referred to as clauses.

   i. Antecedent (Lemon)
   ii. Consequent (Green)

B. Conditional statements are hypothetical in nature.

Conditional statements by the fact that they are hypothetical imply that the truth of the antecedent and the consequent is not stated.

C. Necessary and Sufficient Conditions

Necessary and sufficient conditions have important logical relationships, which are key in understanding claims and evaluation of arguments. Sufficient conditions are the conditions which are minimally required for something, that is, A provided that B, which is symbolised as (A → B). Sufficient condition warranties whatever it is a sufficient condition for something to happen and they are expressed as the antecedent of the conditional claims. For example, to claim that being born in Kenya is a sufficient condition for Kenyan citizenship implies that all one needs to be a Kenyan citizenship is to be born in Kenya. In an argument structure this will be as follows:

1. If Anne is born in Kenya (P), then she is a Kenyan citizen. (Q)
2. Anne was born in Kenya. (P)
3. Therefore, Anne is a Kenyan citizen. (Q)

The antecedent (P) is the sufficient condition for deriving the truth of the consequent (Q). It is vital to note "If" clause introduces sufficient condition. The claim "If Anne is born in Kenya (P), then she is a Kenyan citizen (Q)" states that being born in Kenya is a sufficient condition to infer that one is a Kenyan citizen. Hence the "If" clause, expresses sufficient condition.

Necessary condition entail the essential conditions for something, that is, something B can only be because of A, that is, "only B because of A." In other words, A is necessary condition for B, i.e. B

only if A. If there is no A then no B. this is symbolised as (¬A→ ¬B) or B→A. Note that: **Only if** introduces necessary condition.

1. If Michael is a Roman Catholic priest, then he is a male.
2. Michael is a Roman Catholic priest.
3. Therefore, Michael is a male.

Being a male is a necessary condition for Roman Catholic priesthood; he is celibate **only if** he is a Roman Catholic priest. Clearly being a male is not sufficient for priesthood since there are so many males who are not priests.

Another example to illustrate necessary condition is "If you fuel your car, then the car will start" states that fuel is a necessary condition for the car to start. The car requires fuel necessarily for it to start. Clearly, the consequent clause states a necessary condition for the antecedent. If the consequent conditions are not met, then the antecedent is false and the argument is invalid.

NB: One thing can be a necessary and a sufficient condition for something else. For example: If Michael is a Roman Catholic priest, then he is celibate. It's a sufficient condition for one to be a Roman Catholic priest, one has to be celibate. But it is also a necessary condition for one to be celibate to be a priest. The moment one ceases to be celibate, one ceases, to be a catholic priest. In symbols: P→C and C→P respectively. Here are some examples:

1. Being a Roman Catholic male (M) is a necessary condition for priesthood (P), expressed symbolically: P→M.
2. "A valid argument is one in which the premises support the conclusion *completely*. More formally, a valid argument is one such that *it is impossible for its conclusion to be false while its premises are true.*"[13]

To say that A is a sufficient condition for B is to say that if B is present, then A must (or will) also be present. To say that A is a necessary condition for B is to say that it is impossible to have B without A. Bailin and Battersby observe that:

> In summary, in the sentence form "If P then Q," P specifies a sufficient condition for Q while Q specifies a necessary condition for P. We know that whatever something happens, whether it is fire or a running car, all necessary conditions (including gas or oxygen) must be present. After all, if they are really necessary conditions you can't have an event without them. And once all the necessary conditions are present, they will be sufficient for the event to occur.[14]

All sufficient conditions and also necessary conditions must be met or fulfilled for an event to happen. For example, for one to be employed in Kenyan public university, one must meet all academic requirements and also be of integrity. The sufficient conditions for employment are simply meeting all the necessary conditions.

As a summary, the definitions of "sufficient condition" and "necessary condition" can, equivalently, be put as follows:

(1) "A is a sufficient condition for B" means the same as "A logically entails B."

(2) "A is a necessary condition for B" means the same as "B logically entails A."

A necessary condition is whose absence an event would not occur while a sufficient condition is one whose presence is a must for an event to occur.

Siegel classical example of the relationship between reason assessment and critical attitude or critical spirit components illustrates further the point on sufficient and necessary conditions. He writes that:

> There is first, the ability to assess reasons properly. Call this the *reason assessment* component. There is second, the willingness, desire, and the disposition to base one's actions and beliefs on reason; that is, to *do* reason assessment and be guided by the results of such assessment. This I call *critical attitude* or *critical spirit component* of critical thinking. Both components are, I claim, essential to the proper conceptualisation of critical thinking, the possession of which is necessary for the achievement of critical thinking person. They are jointly sufficient as well.[15]

His argument is that both reason assessment and critical attitude or critical spirit is sufficient as well as necessary conditions for critical thinkers. For neither one is sufficient by itself "for being able to assess reasons is not sufficient for being a critical thinker, though necessary."[16] Accordingly, one requires both aspects to be a critical thinker.

Finally, understanding the concepts of sufficient conditions and necessary conditions is significant for determining whether an argument is valid or invalid.

Basic Argument Forms

The basic argument forms are either valid or invalid. Some of these basic arguments have names while other don't. Let us consider the forms without names first.

Forms and counterexamples

Form 1: has this form:
1. All A are B.
2. All B are C.
3. Therefore, All A are C.

We do substitution instance:
1. All Germany shepherds are dogs.
2. All dogs are animals.
3. Therefore, all Germany shepherds are animals.

This form 1 is representation of the pattern of reasoning which is valid based on the form regardless of its content.

Form 2: has this structure:
1. All A are B.
2. Some C are not B.
3. Therefore, some C are not A.

We do substitution instance:
1. All gold are gems.
2. Some stones are not gems.
3. Therefore, some stones are not gold.

Here are some examples:

Example 1:
1. All flowers are roses.
2. Some plants are not roses.
3. Therefore, some plants are not flowers.

Example 2:
1. All Germany shepherds are dogs
2. Some animals are not dogs.
3. Therefore, animals are not Germany shepherds.

Example 3:
1. All lemons are green.
2. Some fruits are not green.
3. Therefore, some fruits are not lemons.

All arguments with this form are valid.

Form 3: has this structure:
1. All A is B.

2. All C is B.
3. All A is C.

We do substitution instance:
1. All catholic priests are celibate.
2. All catholic nuns are celibate.
3. Therefore, all catholic priests are catholic nuns.

Below is another example:
1. All flowers are plants.
2. All roses are plants.
3. All flowers are roses.

The form of this argument is invalid for it has true premises and a false conclusion.

Form 4: has this structure:
1. All A are B.
2. Some B are not C.
3. Therefore, some C are not A.

We do substitution instance:
1. All Germany shepherds are ferocious animals.
2. Some ferocious animals are not fish.
3. Some fish are not Germany shepherd.

In this instance, the premises are true but the conclusion is false hence the argument form demonstrates that the argument is invalid.

Form 5; it has this structure:
1. No A are B
2. All B are C.
3. Therefore, No A is C.

We do substitution instance:
1. No democrats are republicans.
2. All republicans are mammals.
3. Therefore, no democrats are mammals.

This form is invalid for the premises are true while the conclusion is false.

Hence, there is a fundamental relationship between argument form, validity and invalidity. It therefore important to identify the form of the argument for in so doing one is able to determine if an argument is valid or invalid. However, this is not without challenges, difficulties and complications. For example, this method cannot demonstrate that a valid form is valid. We can have substation instance of true premises and true conclusion but it does imply validity of the argument. For example, based on form 5; (No A are B; All B are C; So, No A are C) whose structure is invalid but we can make substitution instance which is valid.

    1. No dogs are human beings. (True)
    2. All human beings are two legged beings (True)
    3. No dogs are two legged beings. (True)

Nevertheless, the form 5 is invalid since there are instances as we have seen which we have true premises but false conclusion.

Two, this method cannot be used to show if an argument is strong or weak.

Valid Argument Forms with Names

In logic there are five arguments forms with names, which are valid. The first one is:

I. Modus Ponens

This argument has this form:
1. If P, then Q.
2. P.
3. Therefore, Q.

Modus pones connotes mode of positing. It sets down as a fact i.e. the second premise posits the first premise. It is also termed as affirming the antecedent. Example 1;

1. If there is combustion, then phlogiston substance will be produced.
2. There is combustion.
3. Therefore, phlogiston substance will be produced.

Example 2;

1. If the physical universe has existed for an infinite period, then all energy in the universe is spread evenly.
2. The physical universe has existed for an infinite period.
3. Therefore, all energy in the universe is spread evenly.

These are valid arguments because the antecedent (sufficient condition) is present and therefore the consequent is realized.

II. Modus Tollens

It connotes the way or mode of removing. It is also referred to as denying the consequent. It has the following form:
1. If P, then Q.
2. ¬ Q.
3. Therefore ¬ P.

Example 1:
1. If Isaac newton was correct on laws of motion, then Albeit Einstein is wrong on relativity theory.
2. Albeit Einstein was not wrong on relativity theory.
3. Therefore, Isaac newton was not correct on laws of motion.

III. Disjunctive Syllogism

This is an either/or argument, i.e. Either P or Q. The statements which comprise this argument are referred to as disjuncts. Either can imply inclusive (both disjuncts) or exclusive sense (not both but one).

Example 1: exclusive sense disjunctive syllogism
1. Either Gilbert is sitting near the fence or he is in the classroom.
2. Gilbert is not in the classroom.
3. Therefore, Gilbert is sitting near the fence.

This is an example of the exclusive sense disjunctive syllogism.

Example 2: Inclusive sense disjunctive syllogism.
1. Either to get a job in a Kenyan public university you must have Ph.D. in relevant area or M.A., teaching and research experience.

Clearly one with both is not excluded from applying. Both variations of the arguments are valid.

IV. Pure Hypothetical syllogism

This argument form comprises of hypothetical or conditional statements i.e.
1. If P, then Q.
2. If Q, then R

3. Therefore, if P, then R.

Example 1:
1. If it is raining, then the ground will be muddy.
2. If the ground will be muddy, then the car will get stuck.
3. Therefore, If it is raining, then the car will get stuck.

Example 2:
1. If God is the creator, then he created the devil.
2. If God created the devil, then God is morally irresponsible.
3. Therefore, if God is the creator, then God is morally irresponsible.

V. **Constructive and Destructive dilemma**

It is important to get some background information on dilemmas:

> In ancient Greece, people used to talk about being stuck on the horns of dilemma. This means being faced with two choices, each of which has serious consequence; yet you have to pick one or the other. So you choose one- and then have to deal with the set of consequences that follows.[17]

A critical thinker must be able to solve dilemmas without being trapped since:

> The premises of the syllogisms so combined are formulated disjunctively, and devised in a way designed to trap the opponent by forcing him to accept one or the other of the disjuncts. Thus the opponent is forced to accept the truth of the conclusion of one or the other of the syllogisms combined. When this is done successfully, the dilemma can prove to be a powerful instrument of persuasion.[18]

To be "in" a dilemma or on the horns of a dilemma implies to choose between two alternatives, both of which are bad or unpleasant or an unacceptable conclusion. There are two types of dilemmas namely complex and simple.

> A complex dilemma entails "an argument consisting of (a) a disjunction, (b) two conditional premises linked by a conjunction, and (c) a conclusion that is not a single categorical proposition (as in a simple dilemma) but a disjunction, a pair of (usually undesirable) alternatives ...
>
> A simple dilemma consists of an argument designed to push the adversary to choose between two alternatives, the (usually undesirable) conclusion in either case being a single categorical proposition."[19]

Critical Thinking & Argument Analysis

Three Ways of Refuting Dilemmas

The techniques of refuting dilemmas have been developed "known as "going (or escaping) between the horns," "taking (or grasping) it by the horns," and "rebutting it by means of a counter dilemma."[20] The aim is not to determine validity of invalidity but to escape the traps of or to counteract the dilemma.

"Going (or escaping) between the horns," entails rejecting the disjunctive premises since it easy to establish it's false.

"Taking (or grasping) it by the horns," entails rejecting the premises which is a conjunction by denying some of its parts showing that it is false.

"Rebutting it by means of a counter dilemma," entails constructing another dilemma to rebut the current one by coming up with conclusion different from the original. In essence it diverts attention from the original argument. Copi and Cohen notes that:

> A classic example of this elegant kind of rebuttal concerns the legendary argument of an Athenian mother attempting to persuade her son not to enter politics:
>
> If you say what is just, men will hate you; and if you say what is unjust, the gods will hate you; but you must either say the one or the other; therefore, you will be hated.

Her son rebutted that dilemma with the following one:

> If I say what is just, the gods will love me; and if I say what is unjust, men will love me. I must say either the one or the other. Therefore, I shall be loved![21]

Below is another example by the same authors that focuses on an argument between an optimist and pessimist:

> If I work, I earn money, and if I am idle, I enjoy myself. Either I work or I am idle. Therefore, either I earn money or I enjoy myself...

A "pessimist" might offer the following counter dilemma:

> If I work, I don't enjoy myself, and if I am idle, I don't earn money. Either I work or I am idle. Therefore, either I don't earn money or I don't enjoy myself.[22]

Copi and Cohen provide classical lawsuit between Protagoras and Euathlus:

Protagoras, a teacher who lived in Greece during the fifth century BCE, specialized in teaching the art of pleading before juries. Euathlus wanted to become a lawyer, but not being able to pay the required tuition, he made an arrangement according to which Protagoras would teach him but not receive payment until Euathlus won his first case. When Euathlus finished his course of study, he delayed going into practice. Tired of waiting for his money, Protagoras brought suit against his former pupil for the tuition money that was owed. Unmindful of the adage that the lawyer who tries his own case has a fool for a client, Euathlus decided to plead his own case in court. When the trial began, Protagoras presented his side of the case in a crushing dilemma:

If Euathlus loses this case, then he must pay me (by the judgment of the court); if he wins this case, then he must pay me (by the terms of the contract). He must either lose or win this case. Therefore, Euathlus must pay me.

The situation looked bad for Euathlus, but he had learned well the art of rhetoric. He offered the court the following counterdilemma in rebuttal:

If I win this case, I shall not have to pay Protagoras (by the judgment of the court); if I lose this case, I shall not have to pay Protagoras (by the terms of the contract, for then I shall not yet have won my first case). I must either win or lose this case. Therefore, I do not have to pay Protagoras![23]

Another classical example is the *Euthyphro Dilemma* named after a particular exchange between Socrates and Euthyphro in Plato's dialogue, *Euthyphro*. In a famous passage, Socrates asks, *"Is the pious loved by the gods because it is pious, or is it pious because it is loved by the gods?"*

Below is another example of a classical dilemma derived from the Plato's dialogue:

The Meno begins just like any other early dialogue. Meno professes to know what virtue is and Socrates sets about testing that knowledge. After a series of failed attempts to say what virtue is, Meno admits to being at a loss (aporia). He contends that Socrates' sting has numbed both his mind and his tongue. There upon Socrates, in his customary way, disavows his own knowledge and exhorts Meno to join him in the search for the knowledge they both lack. But for the first time in the dialogues, Meno questions how such a search is to be carried out. The problem he suggests can be put as follows:

1. Either we know what we are searching for or we do not.
2. If we know what we are searching for, the search is pointless.
3. If we do not know what we are searching for, the search is impossible.
4. So, the search is either pointless or impossible.

> The question, of course, is why we should accept 3. Meno argues that if we fail to know at all what something is, we will not know what to set up as the object of our search nor be able to recognize it should we come upon it. We will not know what to look for nor when we have found it.[24]

Another classical dilemma is by King Croesus. He sought advice on whether to attack Persian alone or seek alliance. The oracle responded with ambiguity that *if King Croesus you go to war, a might empire will be destroyed*. King Croesus interpreted that he was to win the war but on the contrary, he lost terribly. When he came back and questioned the oracle, the response was that he was told that *a mighty kingdom will be destroyed*!

We conclude this section with another classical example of a dilemma that Socrates faced when he had the option to escape from prison found in the book, *Crito*:

> And what a life should I lead, at my age, wandering from city to city, ever changing my place of exile, and always being driven out! For I am quite sure that wherever I go, there, as here, the young men will flock to me; and if I drive them away, their elders will drive me out at their request; and if I let them come, their fathers and friends will drive me out for their sakes.

In essence, a critical thinker must be familiar with these tactics of resolving dilemmas.

We now examine two more aspects of dilemmas namely; constructive and destructive dilemmas.

A. Constructive dilemma

Most of the examples above are constructive dilemmas. This argument combines both disjunctive and hypothetical statements and has the form below:

1. Either P or Q.
2. If P, then R.

3. If Q, then S.
   4. Therefore, either R or S.

For example, "the age-old problem of evil can be put in the form of a constructive dilemma:

   1. If God cannot prevent suffering, then god is not omnipotent.
   2. If God does not want to prevent suffering, then God is not perfectly good.
   3. But either God cannot prevent suffering or God does not want to prevent suffering.
   4. So, either God is not omnipotent or God is not perfectly good."²⁵

Another example is Pascal's wager below:

   1. If God exists, I have everything to gain by believing in Him.
   2. And if God does not exist, I have nothing to lose by believing in Him.
   3. Either God exists or God does not exist.
   4. Therefore, I have everything to gain or nothing to lose by believing in Him.

B. Destructive Dilemma

The destructive dilemma is similar in form to the constructive dilemma, but instead of affirming the truth of the one of the antecedents, it denies one of the consequents. The conclusion, which follows validly from two modus tollens steps, results in the denial of at least one of the antecedents.

   1. If P, then Q.
   2. If R, then S.
   3. Either ¬ Q or ¬ S.
   4. Therefore, either ¬ P or ¬ R.

For Example:

   1. If this soup contains spices, then Caro will like it,
   2. If this soup contains pepper, then Agnes will like it.
   3. Either Caro will not like it or Agnes will not like it.
   4. Therefore, either this soup does not contain spices or this soup does not contain pepper.

It is important to note that there is no specific order for the premises in a dilemma.

In following section, we explore the invalid argument forms.

Invalid Argument Forms

The two invalid argument forms are:
  I. Fallacy of Denying the Antecedent.
  II. Fallacy of Affirming the Consequent.

I. Fallacy of Denying the Antecedent

This is usually confused with modus tollens. This argument has this form:
  1. If P, then Q
  2. ¬ P
  3. Therefore, ¬ Q

Here is an example:
  1. If there is fire, then there is oxygen
  2. There is no fire.
  3. Therefore, there is no oxygen.

But, this sort of conclusion is mistaken. For instance, just because there is no fire does not guarantee that there is no oxygen.

II. Fallacy of Affirming the Consequent

It is often confused with modus ponens. This argument has this form:
  1. If P, then Q.
  2. Q.
  3. Therefore, P

Here is an example:
  1. If there is fire, then there is oxygen
  2. There is oxygen.
  3. Therefore, there is fire.

But, this sort of inference is mistaken. For instance, just because there is oxygen does not guarantee there is fire. There is oxygen everywhere and yet we are not burning.

Understanding these common argument forms helps in recognizing whether or not certain arguments are valid or invalid, that is, if they are grounded on good reasoning.

4.5 *Categorical logic:*

Categorical logic associated with Aristotle deals with deductive arguments. It is a mode of studying logical inferences based on the relations of inclusion and exclusion of classes or categories or sets. Categorical logic is significant since it contributes to clarifying, and analyzing arguments, fostering skills/abilities such as precision, carefulness, and accuracy. Further, the reasons for accepting claims are set forth by the relationship between classes, sets or categories. Hence, they are important for determining good reasoning. Categorical logic helps in understanding the logical structure of everyday use of language, in identifying the meaning of claims, analyzing contracts or leases and unravelling logical implications of claims.

I. Categorical Statements or Claims

There are four categorical statements that relate two classes, sets or categories. Here are four examples of the categorical statements/claims:

1. All Germany shepherds are animals.
2. No priests are nuns.
3. Some Catholics are priests.
4. Some politicians are not honest.

The logical implications of these categorical statements respectively are that:

1. Every member of the class of Germany shepherd is an animal.
2. The classes of priests and nuns exclude each.
3. (Some) meaning at least one member of the class of Catholic's is a member of the class of priests.
4. At least one member of the class of politicians is not a member of the class of honest.

Note that: by a class it means a collection of all objects that have the same specified characteristics in common.

II. Components of Standard Form Categorical Syllogism

There are four standard form categorical syllogisms namely:

	Quantity	Quality	Type	Quantifier	Subject term	copula	Predicate term
1.	Universal	Affirmative	A	All	S	Is/Are	P
2.	Universal	Negative	E	No	S	Is/are	P
3.	Particular	Affirmative	I	Some	S	Is/are	P
4	Particular	Negative	O	Some	S	Is/are	P

NOTE:
1. Quantity means either the categorical statement is universal or particular, that is, it applies to all members of the class or only to some.
2. Quality of categorical statement is either affirmative or negative. By affirmative, it implies wholly or partially including some members of the class and negative states that wholly or some members are not included.
3. Type: the four categorical statements are represented by capital letter (**A, E, I** and **O**) respectively.
4. Quantifiers are represented by the words **all, some** and **no,** determine the quantity (how much) of the subject class is or is not in the predicate class.
5. Subject terms and predicate terms are the first term and the *second* or *last* terms respectively. These terms must be classes, not merely adjectives, adverbs, etc.
6. Copulas are represented by verb *is/are*. They are the linking verbs between the subject term and the predicate term.
7. Finally, "each type of categorical statement has both a standard and multiple *stylistic variants.*"[26]

Universal Affirmative:
All S are P.
Each S is a P.
S are P.
Any S is a P.
 If anything is an S, then it is a P.
Things are S only if they are P.

Universal Negative
No S are P
Nothing that is an S is a P.
All S are non-P.
If anything is an S, then it is not a P.
Nothing is an S unless it is not a P
Only P are S

Particular affirmative	**Particular affirmative**
Some S are P	**Some S are not P**
There are S that are P	At least one S is not a P
At least one S is a P.	Not all S are P
There exists an S that is a P.	Not every s is a P.
Something is both an S and a P.	Something is an S but not a P.
There is an S	that is not a P.

In summary, the four standard form categorical syllogisms are:

1. (A): All S is P
2. (E): No S is p
3. (I): Some S is P
4. (O): Some S is not P.

Note that: Only P are S is interpreted as, all S are P and not that all P are S. One must translate with exact equivalence the above ordinary claims to standard form categorical syllogism for the A-claim. The term **"only"** when used by itself, introduces the predicate term while phrase **"the only"** introduces the subject term for the A-claim.

For example;

1. **Only** men are catholic priest, translates as: All catholic priests are men.
2. Germany shepherds are **the only** good dogs, translates as: all Germany shepherds are good dogs.

The phrase "whenever" hints the A or the E claims. Also it is important to note that claims about individuals are treated as **A or E claims**. For example;

1. Socrates is a mortal translates as all people identical with Socrates are mortal.
2. Plato is not right handed translates as all people identical with Plato are not right handed.

To avoid awkwardness, it is recommended that it is translated just as either A or E claim.

Venn Diagrams and the Categorical Statements

Venn diagrams are named after British logician John Venn. Venn diagram as shown below use circles to represent classes or categories or set named by the term.

Critical Thinking & Argument Analysis

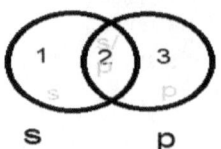

Nb: the letters S & P connote classes or set or categories while the numbers 1, 2 & 3 in the cirlces show where a member(s) of classes are located.

In either representing or diagramming classes in the Venn diagrams, one shades for the universal statements or an x is used to represent the particular classes. In this case, if an area has shade, it represents an empty class while if contains an X, it denotes the existence of at least one member of the class i.e. that it is not an empty class.

A blank area means that we cannot say if it is either empty or has some members. The diagrams for the four categorical statements are:

1. The universal affirmative (A): All S are P.

The A- claim i.e. All S are P, means that there are members of S who are not members of P. This in a venn diagram is represented as above. S (area 1) is an empty class and All S that is P, is represented by not shading the area where S is P is, (the area where s & p overlap).

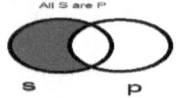

2. The universal negative (E): No S are P.

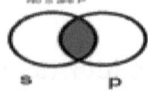

The E-claim, i.e. No S are P, means that no members of S are members of P. S class and P class exclude each other. In this case, we shade area 3 where we find both S and P.

3. Particular affirmative: (I): Some S are P:

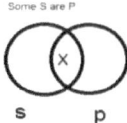

Some means at least one. The I- categorical statement, i.e. Some S are P, in the Venn diagram, an x is used to connote or represent at least one member. As shown above an X is placed at area 3 where both s and p are found.

4. Particular negative: (O): Some S are not P.

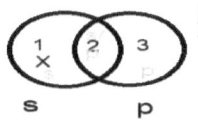

Some S is not P means at least one S is not P. In the venn diagram an x is used to connote or represent at least one s is not a member of p. As shown an X is placed at area 1 where an S which is not p where is found.

Categorical Statements II:
The Traditional Square of Opposition and its Immediate Logical Inferences

The diagram below illustrates how a traditional square of opposition looks like. It also provides the logical relationships.

Traditional Square

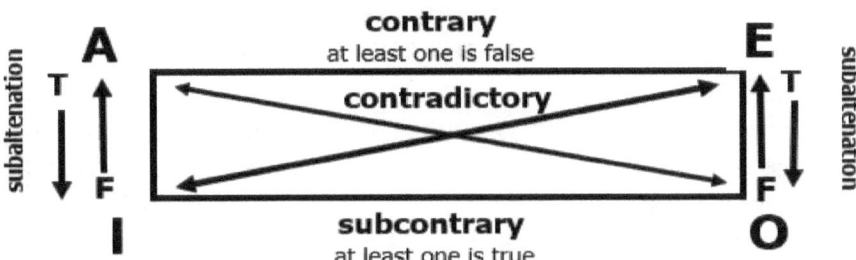

Contraries cannot both be true.
Subcontraries cannot both be false.

The categorical statements in Aristotelian logic are referred by the letters, that is:

1. (A): All S is P.
2. (E): No S is P.
3. (I): Some S is P.

4. (O): Some S is not P.

The square of opposition provides immediate logical relationships between standard form categorical statements with the same subject and predicate terms.

Consider the following:
1. All Germany shepherds are dogs.
2. No Germany shepherds are dogs.
3. Some Germany shepherds are dogs.
4. Some Germany shepherds are not dogs.

The Logical Relationships are:
1. Contradictories: A/O & E/I- they can't both be either true or false i.e. if one is false, the other is true.
2. Contraries: A/E-both can be false but not true at the same time.
3. Sub contraries: I/O- both cannot be false but both can be true.
4. A/I & E/O – implies the true value downwards and not upwards and both imply false value upwards.

Immediate logical Inferences from the Traditional Square of Opposition

Given the truth value of one categorical claim it is possible to infer the truth value of the corresponding three types. However, it is not possible to determine the truth values of the other three. It is important to note that:

> So here are the limits on what can be inferred from the square of opposition: beginning with a true claim at the top of the square (either A or E), we can infer the truth values of all of the remaining claims. The same is true if we begin with a false claim at the bottom of the square (either we or O): we can still deduce the truth values of the other three. But if we begin with a false claim at the top of the square or a true claim at the bottom, all we can determine is the truth value of the contradictory of the claim in hand.[27]

With this information the following immediate inferences are made from the traditional square of opposition.
1. A = T, E = F, O = F & I = T.

2. E = T, A = F, I = F & O = T
3. O = F, E = F, A = T & I = T
4. I = F, A = F, E = T & O = T
5. A = F, E =?, O = T & I =?
6. E = F, A =?, I = T & O = ?
7. O = T, E = ?, A = F & I =?
8. I = T, A = ?, E = F & O = ?

These are the logical relationships of the traditional square of opposition.

It is worthwhile to note that Venn diagrams introduced earlier reflect these logical relationships. This notwithstanding, some of the inference from the traditional square of opposition have been rejected and hence the modern square of opposition derived.

The Modern Square of Opposition

In this section, we will discuss the modern square of opposition. George Boole, a British logician rejected some of the implications of the traditional square of opposition. This is referred to as the Boolean interpretation of categorical propositions. Essentially the traditional square of opposition entails nonempty classes, a notion not accepted by Boole and other logicians of modern times.

From the traditional square of opposition, I & O definitely are not empty classes laying the foundation for the issue or source of controversy. To understand the problem, issue or the controversy it must be seen that some propositions have existential import, and some do not and which was the outcome of Boolean interpretation of categorical propositions. Consider the following example:

1. Some Germany shepherds are dogs.
2. Some Germany shepherds are not dogs.

Both of these categorical statements imply that at least one dog is Germany shepherd and at least one Germany shepherd is not a dog. Hence they do not connote empty categories or classes. They have existential import when they assert the existence of objects of some kind.

It was noted that A/I & E/O – implies the truth value downwards and not upwards and both imply false value upwards. Given this status, such inference creates problems because there is existence of classes where such existence does not exist. Since categorical statements refer to non-empty classes (I & O). This results to a problem termed as the existential import i.e. giving existence to non-existing classes.

To illustrate this, consider the following:
1. All Germany shepherds are dogs and some Germany shepherds are dogs.
2. No Germany shepherds are dogs and some Germany shepherds are not dogs.

Here there is a contradiction, all Germany shepherds are dogs and some dogs are Germany shepherds & no dogs and at least one dog is Germany shepherd contradict each other. (I & O) categorical statements have existential import. They imply that at least one member of the class exists. Given that (A & E) which have empty classes imply their truth of (I & O) which do not have empty classes, then existence is given to non-existing classes. This is a problem with the traditional square of opposition. (A & E) categorical statements must have existential import, because a statement with existential import cannot be derived from one lacking existential import. The logical relationship between (A & O) & (E & I) collapses since truth by implication is no longer tenable.

Venn diagrams become handy in illustrating this:

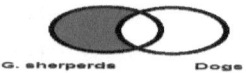

For the I-claim we need an X which is not represented in the Venn diagram. This clearly says that A claim does not imply that I –claim. Let us consider the E and O claims.

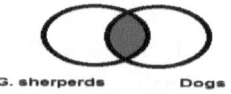

An X must appear at the class of Germeny shepherds for the O claim, but this is not the case.

The implication is that E – claim does imply the O- claims. Therefore, I & O claims are not subcontraries and A & E claims are not contraries.

This necessarily leads to the modern logicians rejecting the traditional square of opposition and adopting a new one. This is also termed as the Boolean logic. Below is the diagram for the modern square of opposition.

Boolean logic endorses and retains the diagonal logical relationships termed as the contradictories namely (A&O) and the (E & I) as shown above.

Categorical Statements III: Immediate Inferences
Conversion, Obversion and Contraposition

A. Conversion

Converse entails switching the subject term with the predicate term.

Type	Statement	Converse	
A	All lemons are green	All green are lemons	Invalid
E	No priests are nuns	No nuns are priests	Valid
I	Some stones are minerals	Some minerals are stones	Valid
O	Some trees are not blue gums	Some blue gums are not trees	Invalid

E & I, are valid while the A & O, are invalid converse. It is also important to note that E & I and their converse retain the same truth value. This is termed as logical equivalence.

B. Obversion

The obverse is attained by changing its quality and replacing its predicate term with its complement. Each category contains a complement. Complement of a class entails all members who do not belong to that class. The term compliment refers to word or phrase that denotes the class compliment.

Type	Statement	Obverse	
A	All lemons are green	No lemons are nongreen.	Valid
E	No priests are nuns	All priest are nonnuns	Valid
I	Some stones are minerals	Some stones are not nonminerals.	Valid
O	Some trees are not blue gums	Some trees are nonbluegums.	Valid

Any categorical statement is equivalent to its obverse and therefore valid.

C. Contraposition

It results from switching the order of the terms and replacing each term with its compliment.

Type	Statement	Converse	
A	All lemons are green	All nongreen are nonlemons	valid
E	No priests are nuns	No nonnuns are nonpriests	invalid
I	Some stones are minerals	Some nonminerals are nonstones	invalid
O	Some trees are not blue gums	Some nonblue gums are not nontrees	valid

The categorical statements A & O, valid while the E & I, are invalid contrapositives. A and O contrapositives have the same meaning. The implication is that A and it contrapositive are logically equivalent and also, O and its contrapositive are logically equivalent.

5. Aristotelian Logic: Categorical Syllogisms

In this section, the objective is to understand categorical syllogism and their rules. Such knowledge is important for a critical thinker. It is essential to know that:

> A syllogism is a two-premise deductive argument. A categorical syllogism (in standard form) is a syllogism whose every claim is a standard – from categorical claim and in which three terms occur exactly twice in exactly two of the claims.[28]

For example:
1. All physicists are scientists……………………………..premise 1
2. Some philosophers are not scientists…………………premise 2
3. Therefore, some philosophers are not physicists… conclusion.

When a categorical syllogism is in the standard form:
  a) Its first premise contains the major term (the predicate of the conclusion).
  b) The second premise contains the minor term (subject term of the conclusion).
  c) Conclusion is stated the last.

From the given example:
  a) 1 & 2 are the premises while 3, is the conclusion.
  b) The first premise is the major premise, the source of the major term (P), i.e. physicists.
  c) The second premise is the minor premise, the source of the

minor term (S), i.e. philosophers.

d) Middle term (M) is the term which occurs twice in a categorical syllogism, i.e. scientists and it never in the conclusion.

The rationale is that if both premises support conclusion, then the argument is valid. The premises provide reasons for supporting the conclusion. If not, then it is invalid. Essentially, "if the proper connections between S and P are established via the middle term M - then the relationship between S and P stated by the conclusion will follow - that is the argument is valid."[29]

Mood and Figure

Syllogisms are different because of their mood and figure. Mood depends upon the type of propositions (A, E, O or I). It is a list of the types beginning with the major premise and ending with the conclusion while the figure depends on the arrangement of the middle terms in the proposition. There are four possible figures as shown below:

First Figure	Second figure	Third Figure	Fourth Figure
1. M — P	P — M	M — P	P — M
2. S — M	S — M	M — S	M — S
3. So, S — P	So, S — P	So, S — P	So, S — P

The form of the syllogism is defined by its mood and figure, which in Aristotelian logic results to valid and invalid forms. In essence, the Aristotelian logic uses mood and figure to determine validity and invalidity of arguments. With these analytical tools, we can identify every possible categorical syllogism by mood and figure. If we were to list all the possible moods, beginning with AAA, AAE, AAI, AAO, AEA, . . .and so on, we would eventually have enumerated sixty-four possible moods. Each mood can occur in each of the four figures; 4 × 64 = 256. It is certain, therefore, that there are exactly 256 distinct forms that standard-form syllogisms may assume. Of these 256 possible forms, only a few are valid forms while others are invalid. There are fifteen valid forms of the categorical syllogism namely:

First figure: AAA, EAE, AII, EIO.

Second Figure: EAE AEE EIO AOO.

Third Figure: IAI, AII OAO EIO.

Fourth Figure: AEE, IAI EIO.

Logicians gave a unique name to every valid syllogism, each characterized completely by mood and figure, information we shall not deal with at this level. The above information is necessary for identifying syllogism form and their validity or invalidity. This method of determining validity and invalidity is tedious hence there are two other methods for determining whether an argument is valid or invalid namely the Venn diagrams and the rules of syllogism.

The Venn Diagram Method of Testing Validity

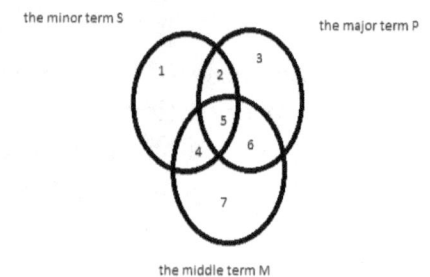

Figure 1

Earlier we introduced the Venn diagrams. Here we will demonstrate how they used to determine if an argument is valid or invalid. To construct Venn diagrams, we draw three circles overlapping each to represent the three terms, i.e. the major term (P), the minor term (S) and the middle term (M) in a standard form categorical syllogism. The S circle is the left hand side overlapping with the P circle at the right side and the M circle overlaps at the bottom as shown below.

Figure 1 above represents a venn diagram.

The next step entails determining whether a syllogism is valid or not using the Venn diagram method. To determine this, follow the steps below:

1. Diagram the premises, i.e. 1 & 2.
2. Determine whether the diagram of the premises tells us that the conclusion is true. This works if you do not need to diagram the conclusion. In other words, the argument is valid if the conclusion is already diagrammed or represented in the process. If you must represent or diagram the conclusion, then the argument is invalid.

3. In constructing Venn diagrams, one indicates that the various areas of the diagram are either containing something or they are empty. Recall that categorical statements are about exclusion or inclusion of classes!
4. An X (I &O) represent at least one object, by shading (A & E) indicates an empty class, and when there is no shade or X, it implies that there is no information about it.
5. If a syllogism contains both universal and particular premises, one must diagram the universal premises first, and then followed by the particular.
6. To diagram the X which represent either the I or O categorical statements there is the need for one to be extremely careful on where to put the X as will be demonstrated later.

It important to revise the Venn diagrams and the standard form categorical statements discussed earlier.

Let us diagram the following categorical syllogisms:
1. All Germany shepherds are dogs
2. No cats are dogs
3. No cats are Germany shepherds

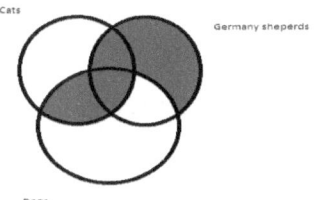

Figure 2

The figure above represents a valid argument since the conclusion is already diagrammed.

As noted the I & O categorical statements can be tricky when it comes to diagraming the X. consider the following categorical syllogism.
1. All philosophers are atheists
2. Some scientists are not atheists
3. Some scientists are not philosophers.

Critical Thinking & Argument Analysis

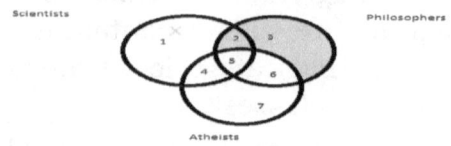

Figure 3

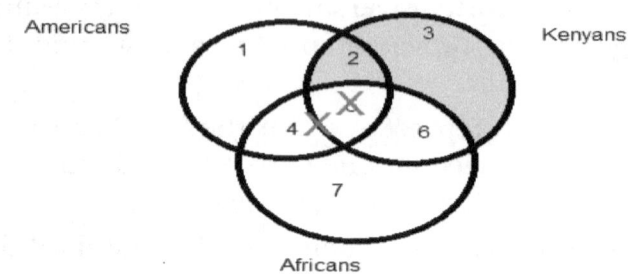

Figure 4 above represents a valid argument since the conclusion is already diagrammed. Note that this is a bit easy.

Consider the following.
1. Some Americans are Africans.
2. All Kenyans are Africans.
3. Therefore, some Americans are Kenyans.

The above figure represents an invalid argument since there is the need to diagram the conclusion. The X for particular statement goes on line between 4 & 5 since it not clear whether to place it in 4 or 5. Further the X for the conclusion tells us that it must go in areas 2 & 5 but 2 tells us that it is empty. In such a case, the X goes to 5. Hence it makes the argument invalid since between it only partially represents the class and not wholly. In essence, for the argument to be valid, the X must be wholly within the appropriate area. In this particular case, the X is partially in the appropriate and therefore fails to establish the conclusion.

The Rules for Testing Validity of Categorical Syllogism

The diagram method is tedious in determining validity or invalidity of arguments. The use of rules based on the notion of distribution, the affirmative and negative claims is quicker method for determining the validity and invalidity of arguments.

Notion of Distribution

In order to understand how the rules of categorical syllogism apply, one must know the meaning of distribution. Distribution is attributed to the subject and predicate terms. A term is distributed if it says something about all members of the class and undistributed if it does not. The four categorical statements have the terms distributed as illustrated below:

Type	Form	Terms Distributed
A	All S are P	S
E	No S are P	S and P
I	Some S are P	None
O	Some S are not P	P

I-claim distributes both terms, A-claim distributes the S term while O distributes the P term. The A & E statements distribute the subject term(S) while the, O & I statements distribute the predicate term (P). This notion of distribution is important in evaluating syllogisms.

The Rules and Fallacies

It is important to note that some logicians argue that there are four or eight rules of syllogism. In most cases, those who argue that they are four simply condense them. in addition, it is vital to note that the rules are based on three aspects namely; those that violate structure, distribution and quality. If any of the rules is violated, then a formal fallacy occurs and accordingly, the syllogism is invalid. With these understanding, then we can state the set of rules of syllogism for determining the validity or invalidity of arguments.

I. In a valid standard–form categorical syllogism must contain exactly three terms, and each must be used with the same meaning throughout the argument. For example:

    1. "Killing innocent human beings is wrong.
    2. The fetus is an innocent human being.
    3. Therefore, killing the fetus is wrong."[30]

The phrase "human being" is being used in two different senses. On the one hand it is being used to refer to genetically human beings, while on the other hand it is being used to refer to a "human member of the moral community." For example:

    1. Everything Kenyan runs well.

2. All cars run well.
   3. Therefore, All cars are Kenyans.

The fallacy thus committed is called, the fallacy of four terms.

II. In a valid standard–form categorical syllogism, the middle term must be distributed in at least one premise. If it is not distributed, then the fallacy of undistributed middle occurs. For example:
   1. All priests are holy.
   2. All sisters are holy.
   3. Therefore, All sisters are priests.

The term holy is undistributed and therefore the argument is invalid.

III. In a valid standard–form categorical syllogism, a term distributed in the conclusion must also be distributed in the premises. This is vital for if it happens then the conclusion is giving more information than the given premises. If it occurs, then it commits the fallacy of either illicit major or illicit minor. An example of illicit major:
   1. All priests are holy.
   2. No sisters are priests.
   3. Therefore, No sisters are holy.

The term holy is distributed in the conclusion and not in the premise hence, it commits the fallacy of illicit major.

The fallacy of illicit minor occurs when the minor term is distributed in the conclusion and not the second premise. Here is an example of illicit minor:
   1. All philosophers are rational persons.
   2. All philosophes are psychologically disturbed persons.
   3. Therefore, All psychologically disturbed persons are rational persons.

IV. In a valid standard–form categorical syllogism, the number of negative premises must be equal the number of negative conclusions. Given this fact a syllogism violating this rule commits one of the following fallacies:
   i. Fallacy of exclusive premises.
   ii. Fallacy of inferring an affirmative conclusion from a negative premise.

iii. Fallacy of inferring a negative conclusion from affirmative premises.

An example of the fallacy of exclusive premises: Any categorical syllogism with two negative premises is invalid.

1. No scientists are believers
2. Some philosophers are not believers
3. Therefore, some philosophers are not scientists

Below is an example of the fallacy of inferring an affirmative conclusion from a negative premise. If one of the premises is negative, the conclusion must be negative otherwise the argument is invalid.

1. Some mathematicians are scientologists
2. No philosophers are mathematicians
3. Therefore, Some scientologists are philosophers

Below is an example of the fallacy of inferring a negative conclusion from affirmative premises. A syllogism is invalid if it has negative conclusion while all the premises are positive.

1. All Germany shepherds are dogs
2. Some animals are Germany shepherds
3. Therefore, Some animals are not dogs.

V. In a valid standard–form categorical syllogism, it is impossible to derive a valid argument from universal premises and a particular conclusion. Here is an example:

1. All philosophers are scientists
2. All philosophers are atheists
3. Therefore, Some atheists are scientists

So far, we have dealt mainly with the structure of arguments, how they are formulated and how to determine their validity or invalidity, strength or weakness. From the above, we conclude by quoting Siegel's remark that:

> Thus logic (both formal and informal) is relevant to reason assessment, and so to critical thinking...logic is relevant to the determination of goodness of reasons. Such determination is central to critical thinking.[31]

Such an understanding of logic, as seeking to determine good reasons or 'reason for,' is relevant to critical thinking which deals reason assessment.

In the next chapter, we continue to demonstrate the relevance of logic to critical thinking by discussing fallacies.

4.6 Conclusion

In this chapter, we have demonstrated that studying argumentations proof to be valuable skills/abilities or tools for critical thinking. In examining both the deductive and inductive arguments, we have shown that there are indispensable to critical thinking in understanding the patterns of reasoning. These patterns of reasoning are in daily use and hence the need to understand them.

Critical thinking calls for understanding of the relationships among claims in arguments. As noted earlier, good argumentation entails good reasoning, that is, a justification for accepting the conclusion based on the assumption that from true premises the conclusion is true. It is important to ask if the given premises are reasonable, i.e. are the premises true, and whether or not the premises support the conclusion. In doing so, one critically determines whether an argument is valid or invalid, sound or unsound, strong or weak, cogent or uncogent. In essence critical thinking is a skilled assessment of evidential and alleged forces of reasons. In understand arguments one must seek to see if the probative and putative forces of reason support or entail accepting the conclusion. A critical thinker ought to evaluate if the given reasons support the conclusion. This is necessary but not sufficient, because the identification of good arguments also involves the normative impact of reasons, that is, the arguer is not only *appropriately* moved by the forces of reasons but is appropriately *moved* too.

A critical thinker should pay attention to arguments since it is not easy to identify them. Some have complicated structure, others are spoken hence not easy to get the premises and conclusion, others are fallacious or weak or poor.

Finally, this task undertaken in this chapter, is essential in clarifying and understanding both academic and everyday encounters with arguments for in so doing is to affirm that argumentation has rationality, reasonableness as its basis.

4.7 End Notes

1. Harvey Siegel, *Educating Reason: Rationality, Critical Thinking and Education,* (Routledge, 1988), 2.
2. Harvey Siegel, *Rationality Redeemed? Further Dialogues on an Educational Ideal,* (New York: Routledge, 1997), 4.

3. Harvey Siegel, *Educating Reason: Rationality, Critical Thinking and Education,* op. cit., 26.
4. Ibid.
5. Ibid.
6. Cohen, C. and Copi, I. *Introduction to Logic* (12th Edition), (New Jersey: Prentice Hall, 2005), 2.
7. Ibid., 69.
8. Brooke Noel Moore and Richard Parker, *Critical Thinking 6th Ed,* (Boston: McGraw-Hill publishes, 2001), 60.
9. Ibid., 53.
10. Wanda Teays, *Second Thoughts: Critical Thinking from a Multicultural Perspective,* (California: Mayfield Publishing Company, 1996), 144-145.
11. F. Ochieng'-Odhiambo, *African Philosophy: An Introduction,* (Nairobi: Consolata Institute of Philosophy, 2002), 7.
12. Cohen, C. and Copi, I. *Introduction to Logic,* op.cit., 98.
13. C. Stephen Layman, *The Power of Logic,* (Boston: McGraw Hill Companies, Inc 2002), 3.
14. Sharon Bailin & Mark Battersby, *Reason in the Balance: An Inquiry Approach to Critical Thinking,* (Cambridge: Hackett publishing Company, Inc.2016), 66.
15. Harvey Siegel, *Educating Reason,* op. cit., 23.
16. Ibid., 38.
17. Wanda Teays, *Second Thoughts: Critical Thinking from a Multicultural Perspective,* op. cit., 380.
18. Cohen, C. and Copi, I. *Introduction to Logic,* op.cit., 289.
19. Ibid.
20. Ibid.
21. Ibid., 291.
22. Ibid.
23. Ibid., 292.
24. Dion Scott-Kakures and Susan Castagnetto et al, *History of Philosophy,* (New York: Harper Perennial publishers Inc 1993), 28.
25. C. Stephen Layman, *The Power of Logic,* op.cit., 38.
26. Ibid., 129-131.
27. Brooke Noel Moore and Richard Parker, *Critical Thinking* op. cit.,

302-303.
28. Ibid., 310.
29. Ibid.
30. Mary Anne Warren, on the *Moral and Legal Status of Abortion, In Intervention and Reflection: Basic Issues in Medical Ethics* (5th Edition), (Belmont: Wadsworth Publishing Company, 1996), 85.
31. Harvey Siegel, **E***ducating Reason: Rationality, Critical Thinking and Education,* op. cit., 26.

5 CHAPTER FIVE
CRITICAL THINKING AND FALLACIES

Logic–both formal and informal–provides a large set of general criteria by which reasons are evaluated.[1]

5.1 Introduction

In this chapter, we will seek to explicate the meaning and types of fallacies. Further, we will elucidate how to distinguish these types giving relevant examples. In addition, we will demonstrate how to avoid fallacious thinking. This is important since fallacious or erroneous reasoning attempt to influence or persuade our thinking coloured as reasonable arguments. Hence, critical thinkers must and ought to be aware of fallacies since they are defective arguments that lack putative or probative forces of reasons. Further, the chapter will be to demonstrate that informal Logic provides a large set of general criteria by which reasons are evaluated and hence relevant to critical thinking. In this respect, we will discuss some of the critical thinking theorists who have contributed to the notion of fallacious reasoning and its impact to critical thinking. Finally, it is important to note that this chapter cannot purport to expose or discuss all fallacies and their attendant issues.

5.2 The Meaning of Fallacy

Fallacy has several meaning such error, mistake, an omission, fault, poor judgement or conclusion. In this book, a fallacy implies "an error in reasoning."[2] Further, "a logical fallacy occurs when the premises do not imply the conclusion."[3] If the given premises do not support the conclusion, then a fallacy occurs. It is a flaw of reasoning.

Some of the critical thinking theorists notably, Harvey Siegel, Robert Ennis, Bailin and Battersby, Paul and Elder have contributed to the notion of fallacious reasoning and its impact to critical thinking.

Harvey Siegel, in his various works asserts that fallacious reasoning entails lack of evidential or probative force or weight:

> That is, the crucial thinker must be able to tell whether a putative reason is a genuine one; whether it strongly or weakly supports some claim or action for which it is offered as a reason; and whether she ought on the

basis of the reason under consideration, to accept the claim or perform the action in question. The beliefs and actions of the critical thinker, at least ideally, are *justified* by reasons for them which she has properly evaluated; when the beliefs and actions, in other words, are based on good reasons. But when are reasons good ones? How do we distinguish good reasons from not-so-good ones?[4]

According to Siegel, Informal logic, which entails "subject-neutral logical reasons,"[5] is one of the standards for evaluating reasons. It helps to identify that the reasons offered do or do not support a given claim, are putative, genuine, strongly or weakly support a claim, action, or belief. Such a task seeks to identify fallacious reasoning, which entails lack of good reasons and hence bad or not-so-good reasons to justify or support a belief or action.

Paul and Elder conceptualize fallacy as:

> An error in reasoning; flaw or defect in argument; an argument that doesn't conform to rules of good reasoning (especially one that appears to be sound); containing or based on a fallacy; deceptive in appearance or meaning; misleading; delusive.

Notably Ennis asserts that:

> There are a large number of terms (such as circular argument) that are used to identify fallacious thinking. Knowing them can be helpful because they can save time in communication with those who know them, and because they are reminders of common errors that people make. They are dangerous, though. They can easily be used specifically, and can intimidate people who do not know them.[6]

A critical thinker or a rational person must be familiar with certain technical terms, often in Latin language, that have been used to refer or to identify fallacies. In addition, knowing fallacies is important since a critical thinker or a rational person easily identifies flawed thinking, and cannot be intimidated or misled.

According to Bailin and Battersby, "a fallacy is a common weak (or even terrible) type of argument that nonetheless has considerable persuasive power."[7] Fallacious reasoning occurs due to persuasive power of an argument. Defined on the basis of persuasion and lack of logical evidential worth, "a fallacy is an argument pattern whose persuasive power greatly exceeds its evidential worth (or, in legal terms, its probative value)."[8] Hence, fallacies have logical weakness as well as persuasive effects or power. They occur when the persuasive effect or power outweighs the logical evidence:

> Sometime the persuasive effect is just to change the topic and get us off course in the argument. In other fallacies, the effect can be to convince us of a claim for which inadequate evidence has been presented. Sometimes the effect is more nebulous, such as creating a negative association with a particular point of view.[9]

A critical thinker should identify these intentional or unintentional persuasive effects or powers, which lack logical evidence and which lead to fallacious reasoning. In addition, such a thinker should avoid, counteract, or guard against them.

In relation to this, they point out that "one of the most obvious barriers to the spirit of inquiry is the use of fallacious arguments. As we know, fallacies are arguments which are logically weak but which have considerable persuasive power..."[10]

They are obstacles to critical inquiry for they "divert the inquiry from its rational course..."[11] hence violating the role of reason in the process of critical inquiry. This occurs when the rational discourse is substituted by illicit persuasions. Bailin and Battersby advices that:

> We must also carefully monitor our arguments in order to avoid the use of fallacious reasoning. Being aware of common fallacies such as ad hominem, appeal to popularity, and hasty generalization and assiduously avoiding their use can help keep inquiry on its rational track and thus respect the commitment to reason which characterizes the spirit of inquiry.[12]

From the above, it is plausible to infer that it is important to be aware and familiar with fallacious reasoning in order to avoid them and ensure good argumentation. In addition, there is the need to consider how to respond to fallacious reasoning:

> This is especially an issue in a dialogue because, in the heat of the moment, it is easy to fall prey to the persuasive effects and not recognize the logical errors.[13]

A critical thinking ought to be aware of the persuasive effects of fallacious reasoning because it entails logical errors. Such a rational person must overcome these fallacious reasoning.

5.3 Reasons why Fallacies Occur

Fallacies occur due to people's ideological commitment, religious, political, economic and cultural principles. People tend not to be open-minded and open to alternative views or perspectives. They occur due to ignorance, careless habits of mind, intentionally or unintentionally, or due to lack of education. Further, fallacies occur when "...people...accept or reject claims when they have no good grounds for doing so."[14] This is to imply that fallacies occur when they are no good grounds to support certain claims or conclusions. In addition, they occur due to grammatical constructs, emotional, or psychological gimmicks, irrelevance, presumptions and unrelated cause among other causes. In particular, they are deliberately employed or used for economic gains such as in advertisements or sales; for political mileage or persuasions; for religious conversions and for legal practices by lawyers. Hence, fallacies are powerful tools for pushing agendas in the domains of academics, economics, legal, political and religions.

5.4 Types or Classification of Fallacies

There are two types of fallacies namely; formal and informal fallacies. Formal fallacies have to do with logical structure of an argument. We have already discussed various formal fallacies in previous chapters. The informal fallacies do not involve the structure of the argument but the content of the argument such as language.

The patterns of language can be deceptive or misleading leading to poor argumentation or its content can be ambiguous, vague, imprecise, and inconsistent resulting to fallacies reasoning. This chapter concerns itself with the informal fallacies and how critical thinking helps in identifying and avoiding them.

5.5 Informal Fallacies

It is essential to note that fallacies are categorised differently by different authors:

> This classification of fallacies is a controversial matter in logic. There is no one correct taxonomy of fallacies. Logicians have proposed lists of fallacies that vary greatly in length; different sets have been specified, and different names have been given to both the sets and the individual fallacies.[15]

The have been attempts to classify informal fallacies which dogged with controversies. Ideally, there is no one correct taxonomy of informal fallacies for they vary in length, grouping or classification, and have been given different names. The presentation that follows divides informal fallacies into three namely;

1. The fallacies of relevance or irrelevance premises.
2. The fallacies of presumption or unwarranted assumptions.
3. The fallacies ambiguity.

We will examine each group, and each individual fallacy, in detail in the following sections.

5.5.1 The Fallacies of Relevance or Irrelevant Premises

Fallacies of relevance or irrelevant premises occur when the premises given do not reasonably support the conclusion. They are irrelevant to the conclusion given, that is, they are beside the point. There is no logical connection or evidence between the given premises and the conclusion drawn, though there might be a persuasive, psychological or emotional connection. Some fallacies of relevance are:

A. Argumentum ad Hominem

The argument against the person, which derives its name from Latin phrase, *Ad hominem*, meaning "against man" occurs when one avoids the issue at hand and maliciously attacks the person who advances the argument. This is contrary to providing a rational critique of the issue or argument itself. Generally, the attempt is to offer a defence or a response by attacking the opponent rather than the opponent's argument. The attack is based on economic, religious, social classes, level of education, gender, sexual orientation, national origin, race, individual characteristics such as weight, age among other factors.

Here is a general example:

a) John: abortion is killing innocent life.

   Mercy: how would you know? You just a lazy man and a tout and at best a village idiot who suffers from poverty of the mind or simply intellectual poverty!

The argument on abortion is side lined and Mercy labels John as masculine, lazy and uneducated based on his job as a tout. This fallacy takes three forms namely; abusive ad hominem, circumstantial ad hominem, Tu quoque (you, too).

I. Abusive ad Hominem

Abusive *ad hominem* occurs when there is a direct attack on the person and not the argument. It occurs when there is a complete shift from the issue at hand to the person who was putting forth his perspective. Below is an example:

1. Student remarks that Logic is a difficulty area of study and the Lecturer retorts: I am not surprised your mind is made for either for touting or farming and harvesting bananas!
2. A politician remarks to his opponent that he will lose the primaries because he is a village cock!
3. Dr. M retorts to Dr. O and Dr. K: Your line of musing reflects that you must have picked your Ph.D. like farmers pick tea leaves or garbage collectors collect trash in Mumbai!
4. Seminar facilitator remarks: Dr. N of Mathematics Department: Your ideas are only good if you do not present them in vernacular and more so if they are not obscured by your computer illiteracy!

II. Circumstantial ad Hominem

This fallacy occurs when the attempt is to discredit by calling attention to the circumstances of the person advancing an issue or argument. The circumstances include; social, sexual orientation, cultural, economic, political, religious, race or colour, to affiliations such as membership of a group, club, organisations or sect. The argument is not pursued to its logical conclusion but unrelated circumstances are introduced to divert attention. Here are some examples:

a) Of course, he opposes university fees increment. His father is member of county assembly.
b) Engineer Peter advocates for the canonisation of the Cardinal because he is bleeding-heart staunch catholic.

The difference between *Ad hominem* from *Ad hominem circum*stantial is that the former discredits the person's character while the latter attacks the circumstances surrounding of the person. The former is also called character assassination.

III. Tu Quoque

Tu quoque, is a Latin phrase, meaning "you, too or you," "you are another." It occurs when the issue or argument is not addressed but attention is directed to opponent as hypocrite or inconsistent. In essence, it operates on the idea that, "practice what you preach!" For example:

a) If a student A finds another, B smoking marijuana in the hostel and question her, B retorts to A, we have seen you smoke too.

The general structure of the argument is not to address the matter at hand but the person. Similar variations of this fallacy include genetic fallacy, poisoning the well and pseudorefutation. Pseudorefutation entails rejecting a person's claim on basis of inconsistent of something else advocated by the same person. Poisoning the well entails tarnishing or mud smearing a person refutation or name in advance. Here is an example of poisoning the well:

a) Dr. K: what! Dr. M? How can you appoint him the Chair of the Department? He is an activist, eccentric and perennial critic of everything. I say this, appoint him at you own peril!

Dr. K. is poisoning the minds of the appointing authority using character assassination as his tactic.

B. Argumentum ad Baculum [Appeal to Force]

Ad Baculum is a Latin phrase meaning "force." This fallacy is identifiable with the presence of a threat or force or coercion that is either explicit or subtly disguised. It occurs when appropriate use of reasons or evidence in support of argument is replaced with coercions or force or threats. Our cultural, educational, political and religious systems rely extensively on an implicit appeal to force. The following are some examples of *Ad Baculum*:

1. Dean K to Dr M: Dr. M, you either pay homage to me and my office like the ancestors worshiped shrines or I will do all it takes to have your position as chair of department revoked!

2. DOS: You have not attended today's meeting and the appointing authority has noted with concern.

3. You are either with us or against us.

4. Agnes, I remind you that the promotions are round the corner and I am chairing the panel. By the way I am having dinner at the night Club Haven at 7 p.m. come dressed sexy. It pays back you know...
5. God exists because believing otherwise takes you to hell.

All these examples are not based on any good reasons for accepting the claims but on scare tactics. Their bases are pure threats such a keeping a position, fear, threats, sexual harassment, blackmail, bribery, extortion, life of eternal condemnation and as such ad Baculum.

C. Argumentum ad Populum [Appeal to People or Masses]

The phrase *Populum* is Latin meaning "people, populace, or nation." This fallacy occurs when rather than giving good reasons or providing evidence to support the conclusion in an argument or issue, there is an attempt to appeal to mass sentiment or patriotism or to create excitement. The appeal to the populace occurs in arguing that everyone does it, it is valued or accepted by all and therefore it must be good and the conclusion is based on assertions about commonly or traditionally held beliefs. Hence, it does not rely on putative or probative evidence and rational argument. The issue is that the nation, group, populace or consensus or the masses are the measure of the truth. Its common occurrence is in political rallies or religious crusades. Below are some examples:

1. Thousands of catholic believe in Heaven, so you too must hold the view there is heaven!
2. Be cool! Take a beer! All university students do!
3. Political or campaign slogan: Make *A* great again!

Historically, Adolf Hitler used this fallacy in his oratories in order to convince his fellow Germanys of his atrocities. This fallacy has various forms namely: 1) Bandwagon, 2) common practise.

I. **Bandwagon**

It is simply joining the majority since one does not wish to be left out of the group form of thinking. It occurs in politics and in advertisements. Its main tool of operation is appeal to the mob mentality using slogans such as; comrades power for students' unions, or solidarity for ever for workers' unions. Political parties will come with slogans or words or music which will push citizens to their side rather than developing policies. Critical citizenship should be alert to detect such fallacious reasoning.

II. Common Practise

It takes the form "everybody does it" since one does not appeal to reasons or good grounds for accepting a claim or position but simply appeals to populace.

D. Argumentum ad Vercundiam [Appeal to Authority]

John Locke, a British philosopher, came up with the Latin name, *Ad Verecundiam*, which translates to inappropriate authority. This fallacy is identifiable in an argument based primarily on the premise that some expert (or some publication) reports that S is true and so it must be the case without verification. This fallacy occurs when the person (or publication) is not relevantly qualified or is biased. Here is an example:

1. The mother church/catholic church once argued through its leadership that Galileo Galilei was wrong and committed a heresy when he challenged the geocentric theory and advocated for the heliocentric theory. The church noted with deep concern that Galileo was ignorant because the bible says that it is the sun which moves and not the earth. The church retorted that *'the view that the sun stands motionless at the centre of the universe is foolish, philosophically false, and utterly heretical, because contrary to Holy Scripture.'*

Clearly, the bible or the church is not the legitimate authority on matters of cosmology for it is the earth which moves and not the sun.

It is good to seek legitimate authority or competent authority and not simply appealing to people who are famous. For example, it would be good to appeal to St. Thomas Aquinas on matters to do with morality/ethics and not Albeit Einstein or Isaac Newton. In advertisement we are constantly pushed, so to speak, to buy clothing such as t-shirts, shirts, shoes, tracksuits, or cars because a famous person such as footballer or a golf player affirms their superiority and uses such items.

A critical thinker must use critical thinking skills/abilities and dispositions to determine the credibility of the sources. Some basic criteria as noted in chapter four include but not limited to: *background experience and knowledge, lack of apparent conflict of interest, agreement with others equally qualified, reputation, established procedures, known risk to reputation, ability to give reasons, and careful habits.*

E. Argumentum ad Misericordiam [Appeal to Pity]

Misericordiam is Latin meaning "mercy or pity." This fallacy occurs when the premises appeal to your sorrowful circumstances or pity or sympathy and not to good reasons or evidence to support the conclusion in an argument. The statements purely evoke mercy or sympathy and have no logical connection with the conclusion. Here are some examples:

a) A student who has failed in her exams appeals to be given an A because the contrary will result to her scholarship withdrawn.

b) A person kills his wife and argues to be set free because if jailed he will remain a bachelor for life.

c) A man kills his parents and in court, begs clemency on the basis that he is an orphan

Clearly, from the above examples, there are no good reasons provided to support the conclusion but only appeal to emotions or pity. A classic example from the book, *Apology*, by Plato, is Socrates trial:

> Well, Athenians, this and the like of this is all the defence which I have to offer. Yet a word more. Perhaps there may be someone who is offended at me, when he calls to mind how he himself on a similar, or even a less serious occasion, prayed and entreated the judges with many tears, and how he produced his children in court, which was a moving spectacle, together with a host of relations and friends; whereas I, who am probably in danger of my life, will do none of these things. The contrast may occur to his mind, and he may be set against me, and vote in anger because he is displeased at me on this account. Now if there be such a person among you, —mind, I do not say that there is, —to him I may fairly reply: My friend, I am a man, and like other men, a creature of flesh and blood, and not 'of wood or stone,' as Homer says; and I have a family, yes, and sons, O Athenians, three in number, one almost a man, and two others who are still young; and yet I will not bring any of them hither in order to petition you for an acquittal. And why not? Not from any self-assertion or want of respect for you. Whether I am or am not afraid of death is another question, of which I will not now speak. But, having regard to public opinion, I feel that such conduct would be discreditable to myself, and to you, and to the whole state. One who has reached my years, and

who has a name for wisdom, ought not to demean himself. Whether this opinion of me be deserved or not, at any rate the world has decided that Socrates is in some way superior to other men. And if those among you who are said to be superior in wisdom and courage, and any other virtue, demean themselves in this way, how shameful is their conduct! I have seen men of reputation, when they have been condemned, behaving in the strangest manner: they seemed to fancy that they were going to suffer something dreadful if they died, and that they could be immortal if you only allowed them to live; and I think that such are a dishonour to the state, and that any stranger coming in would have said of them that the most eminent men of Athens, to whom the Athenians themselves give honour and command, are no better than women. And I say that these things ought not to be done by those of us who have a reputation; and if they are done, you ought not to permit them; you ought rather to show that you are far more disposed to condemn the man who gets up a doleful scene and makes the city ridiculous, than him who holds his peace.

From this long passage, it plausible to infer that Socrates refuses to appeal to pity or mercy.

F. Argumentum ad Ignorantiam [Appeal to Ignorance]

This fallacy occurs when a conclusion is based upon an absence of proof or evidence, that is, either declared true or false because of lack of proof or evidence.

a) Nobody has ever proved that there is God, therefore, there is no God.

b) There is no scientific proof that there is heaven, therefore there is no heaven.

c) There is no scientific proof that heaven is not there, therefore heaven is there.

d) Nobody has ever proved that there is ancestral world in African culture. Therefore, there is no ancestral world.

A classic example is this:

> An argument from ignorance was confronted by Galileo, whose newly invented telescope, early in the seventeenth century, plainly revealed the mountains and valleys of the moon. In his day, the "truth" that the moon was a perfect crystalline sphere was unquestioned; it had to be perfect because that was what Aristotle had taught. Confronted by the evidence the telescope revealed, Galileo's Aristotelian opponents responded with an argument that seemed irrefutable: Any apparent irregularities on the moon's surface are filled in with a crystalline substance that is, of course, invisible! This hypothesis saved the moon's perfection, was in

accord with what Aristotle had taught—and could not be proved false. This fallacy deserved ridicule. Galileo answered with an argumentum ad ignorantiam of his own, absurd enough to expose his critics: The moon is not a perfect sphere, he replied, because there are surely crystal mountains—invisible! —rising high from its surface. Because my theological critics cannot prove the claim false, we cannot conclude that such mountains are not there![16]

G. Missing the Point (Ignoratio Elenchi)

It is also referred to as fallacy of irrelevant conclusion and mistaken refutation. The Latin word *elenchi* is derived from a Greek word that means a "disproof," or a "refutation." An *ignoratio elenchi* is a mistaken refutation or simply ignorance of proof. It occurs when the given premise of an argument point to a specific conclusion yet the arguer draws a different conclusion. The new conclusion resembles the actual one, that is, non sequitur, meaning it does not follow. It should not be confused with argumentum ad ignorantiam above. Here is an example:

a) As an example, suppose that Cs for education emphasizes how important it is to increase the number of teachers for the public schools by lowering the entry requirements. The teacher's union responds by insisting that a there many teachers who are jobless, who require better working conditions and pay rise and more so to continue upgrading the current teacher's education as a pressing priority than lowering entry requirements.

That assertion is entirely reasonable, of course, but it misses the point of what was said earlier. One party presents an argument for P, to increase the number of teachers; his interlocutor counters with an irrelevant Q, about the importance of teacher's welfare such pay rise etc. The union misses the point, it provides a mistaken refutation, and at best it refutes, or tries to refute, a claim other than that which was originally at issue. Here is another example:

b) Suppose that some very controversial amendment to the tax code is proposed. Such an increase is argued would double taxation and burden the already overburden taxes payers. In responding, the government argues that such taxes are fair, because the government needs that money to implement its agenda.

This response is an *ignoratio elenchi*. The amendment to the tax code may certainly be defended, but the need for the resulting funds misses the point of the argument that had been put forward: the claim of unfair double taxation and burden of the already overburden taxes payers.

5.5.2 The fallacies of Presumption or Unwarranted Assumptions

The fallacies of presumption occur when unstated assumptions cause the argument to be accepted. Some fallacies of presumption or unwarranted assumptions include:

A.   Petitio Principii [Begging the Question]

It is also known as arguing in circle or circular reasoning. The Latin expression *petitio principii* means "begging the first principle or begging the question." Note that, it is pronounced as *"peh-TIT-ee-o pri-KIP-ee-ee."* This fallacy occurs when the argument assumes the point to be proved, that is, the argument, reply, or question assumes already the very issue under debate. *Petitio principii* argument may appear to offer legitimate and independent support for the conclusion. However, closer examination reveals that it is not the case. The inadequate premises do not support the conclusion or repeats the premises in the conclusion in different words or by reasoning in circle. Some examples are:

1. Aristotle writes that, "all men mean by justice that kind of state of character which makes people disposed to do what is just and makes the act justly and wish for what is just."[17]

2. When Jehovah's witnesses come to my door, and argue that I should believe in the divinity of the bible because (for the reason that) the bible proclaims itself to be the divine and so authoritative word of God, it does not take any theological or other subject-specific information or criteria to realize that the reason offered does not in fact support the claim it is offered in support of. Rather it begs the question. (Similar remarks apply to the argument that pro–life persons make against abortion, namely that abortion is wrong because it involves a violation of the right to life of the "baby" –so that abortion is just "baby killing." No biological or other subject-specific knowledge is needed to recognize that this argument (more exactly, the reason provided by the premise) begs the

question against the "pro-choice" person who denies that fetus is a person who has a right to life. (Of course the question whether or not the fetus is properly thought of as a person with a right to life can be addressed, but it is not addressed by this "pro-life" argument.))[18]

3. "How do we know, for example, that

   p: abortion is baby killing

   Is a bad reason for

   q: abortion is morally wrong;

   While

   r: a fetus is sentient and has a concept of self,

   if justified, would be a *good* reason for q? In this example our evaluation of the forces of reasons p and r for claim q is straightforward: p is a bad or weak reason for q because p begs the question against those who think that abortion is morally permissible since a fetus is not in relevant respects like a baby and so has no "right to life";"[19] while r offers good reason based on sentient and concept of self which is not based on question begging.

4. God created the world because the bible says so. But how do I know that what the bible says is true? Because it is the word of God.

5. The student is not guilty of cheating in the exam for she is innocent of having committed it.

From the above examples, the conclusions of the arguments are rephrased version of the given premises. It also clear that the premises are identical to their conclusion. The given premises have assumed the truth of the claim of the matter at hand. Therefore, the truth of the conclusion is affirmed by the truth of the premise or simply restating the conclusion as evidence. These type arguments do not lead to the truth but are only persuasive in nature. For the truth-value to be attained, each premise must be different from the conclusion. Siegel asserts that the:

> ...the example of begging the question illustrates this: a reason which begs the question- that is, one which assumes the very point for which it purports to be a good reason- is bad reason,

with no probative weight. This is true no matter what the context happens to be. Begging the question functions as a general criterion of reason assessment, in that any putative reason which begs the question will fail to be a good reason, i.e. will fail to provide warrant or justification for the claim for which it purports to be a reason.[20]

Such arguments, which beg the question, do not constitute good reasons that would establish prima facie support for the conclusion. Begging the question lacks putative or probative weight for it assumes the very point for which it purports to be a good reason.

B. Complex Question

The fallacy of complex question occurs when in asking a question it illegitimately assumes the conclusion alluded to in the question. Below are some examples:

   a) Have you stopped cheating in the exam or sneaking out of school?
   b) Have you stopped handling stolen goods? Or been corrupt?
   c) Are you still smoking cocaine?
   d) Have you stopped battering your wife?

Any answer, either a yes or no, to these questions implies guiltiness. Any question has one or more assumptions or presumptions.

C. False Dichotomy or Bifurcation

It is also known as the fallacy of the excluded middle. This fallacy occurs when a situation or choice is presented as an either –or situation when in fact, there are other choices. Examples of false dichotomy:

   a) Dr K says: The university: love it or leave it.

Dr K. is limiting the choices about the university, one can criticize it, promote its activities, and participate in research or workshops among many other choices.

D. False Analogy

The fallacy of false analogy occurs when a comparison is drawn between incompatible things thus creating false analogy. It is frequently used in advertisements. An example of false analogy:

   a) A good woman is just like smoking this cigar or driving this car!

b) An advertisement reads: when you drink this beer, you become as strong as a lion.

In this analogy, what is similarity between a good woman and a cigar or a car or drinking beer and the strength of a lion? The two have no connections whatsoever.

E. False Dilemma

It occurs when one uses a premise that unwarrantedly reduces the number of alternatives to be considered. For example;

a) Dean: Look, here's the choice: either resign or shut up! For I am tired of some lecturers in the school of humanities and social sciences criticizing their own university. What I say is this: they are paid by the university, shop, pay rent, fees for their children, etc. using university salary. And since these dons do not resign from the university, they should love it instead of criticizing it, period!

Of course, this is not real choice. Democracy must prevail and the solution is to address the matters raised and to not giving option of resigning.

F. Fallacy of False Cause

The fallacy of false cause occurs when one possible cause of phenomenon is assumed to be the cause of others. This fallacy has three forms namely; 1) Post hoc, ergo propter hoc, 2) Non causa pro causa 3) Oversimplified cause.

I. Post hoc, ergo propter hoc

The fallacy gets its name from the Latin phrase, *Post hoc, ego propter hoc* meaning "after this, therefore because of this." This fallacy occurs when an event is assumed to be the cause of another without any valid reasons. There is illegitimate assumption that phenomenon x preceded event y, therefore, x caused y. Some examples are:

a) I saw a priest in the morning and we won the bet.

b) I was crossed by a dog or cat and we failed the job interview.

II. Non causa pro causa

Non causa pro causa is Latin which means "not for the cause". This fallacy occurs when a cause is assumed and presented as the cause. For example:

a) I prayed at the shrine and we passed the national exam.

One can pass national exams because of well preparations and not because of praying.

III. Oversimplified cause

It occurs when one cause is singled out as the cause of the others hence oversimplification. For example:

a) The quality of religious life has been declining of late; surely teachers of religious studies are teaching African traditional religions and not doing their work properly.

Definitely they are many others reasons as to why the quality of religious life is declining such secularisation, new cultures and religions and not because of poor teaching.

G. Slippery Slope

This fallacy occurs when an argument is advanced that if A is allowed, then B which is worse than A, will occur without providing evidence that the alleged consequences will occur. Here are examples of this fallacy:

a) Dr. K: I tell you, Dr. M. and Dr. O., if we support the legalisation of cutting of trees in Kenya, the next thing will be legalisation of cutting all shrines and religious shrubs. So don't support legalisation of cutting of trees.

b) Allowing high school students to have mobile phones in school will lead to may strikes.

The fallacy occurs when there is no sufficient reason, logical or credible evidence to support the deemed consequences or chain reaction and only serves to persuade one to abandon an action or policy.

H. Hasty Generalisation

This fallacy of hasty generalization occurs when a generalization is drawn on the basis of too small sample. The fallacy occurs when a person uses one case to support a generalization. Here are some examples of hasty generalization:

a) Persons who are in pain can get a dose of marijuana. Therefore, everyone should be able to use marijuana whenever they want!

b) I looked for a vacant house in the neighbourhood and I could not find one. Certainly there is housing problem in Kenya.

These are good examples of the fallacy of hasty generalization, which entails taking very limited evidence, small samples, little information, or an unrepresentative group and treating it as if it strongly supports a generalization. A critical thinker should be able to realize that one case cannot support such a generalization. This fallacy has another form namely, the anecdotal evidence.

I.   Anecdotal Evidence

Bailin and Battersby assert that, "by far the most common basis for a hasty generalization is a generalization based on anecdotal evidence or an individual experience."[21] This fallacy happens when anecdotal or individual experience is used to provide evidence or prima facie support for a generalized conclusion. Here is an example:

a) I don't believe in a good God for my father suffered from cancer which led to his death.

I.   Accident

This fallacy of accident is the converse of hasty generalization and it occurs when a general rule or principle is applied to a special case where such a rule or principle does not apply. For example:

a) Dr. K: The bible says, "Thou shall not kill"; therefore, police officers should not kill armed robbers who pose danger to them and the populace.

Clearly, the general rule does not apply and this leads to the fallacy of accident.

J.   Question –begging Epithets

This fallacy occurs when language is used in circular manner to divert attention from the argument. It takes two forms namely: eulogistic and dyslogistic.

Eulogistic entails excessive praise or extreme positive remarks, while dyslogistic is the converse for it is extremely negative in terms of description of people or events or situation. Below are some examples of question-begging epithets:

Dyslogistic:

a) Dr. K: Don't believe what those student leaders say about students' rights; they are just a bunch of mealy–mouthed, peanut brained with no sense of demands of intellectual or democratic life.

b) Dr. M. lecturers have become the leeches on society since they are constantly on strike demanding better pay.

Eulogistic:

a) Dr. K: You should believe whatever those politicians say about increasing their salaries, because they are hardworking citizens, with the interest of the country at heart.

The language is used in circular manner, loaded, prejudicial and hence not objective.

K. Straw Man/Person fallacy

The straw man/person fallacy occurs when an opponent's position is connoted as being more extreme hence regarded as outrageous or unacceptable or indefensible. It occurs when one changes the subject at hand or presupposes a proposition that actually is at issue, or attributes a false assumption to one's position, or misinterprets or misdescribes a person's position and attack the resulting easy target. Here is an example:

a) Dr. K. Don't even think about his position. Supporting the abolishment of African Traditional Religious studies at the university level is tantamount to advocating for atheism.

The argument forwarded connotes an extreme situation than the actual case. A critical thinker must question the change of subject matter, misdescription or misinterpretation.

L. Red herring

This fallacy occurs when a diversion or distraction from the main issue is introduced from the main point been made. It is also referred to as smoke screen. It is common in literature, courts and movies. For example:

a) Dr M to Dr. K: Why are you intimidating the faculty?

   Dr. K: I am excited by the fact that in my research I have concluded that shrubs and stones have religious significance in African culture!

b) An attorney general responded to a question raised by a lawyer in the supreme court regarding election malpractice in Kenya as follows.... since ad nausea, I have been saying we should raise the bar for those who are to be admitted to the supreme court and apparently there is sufficient evidence to that effect!

The issue of intimidation or election malpractice has not been addressed rather a new line of thought or topic is introduced which is irrelevant to the argument. This fallacy uses the tactic of distortion, distraction, changing or shifting focus or introducing irrelevant issue from the matter, issue or question at hand. It is important to appreciate that the term red herring... "has an interesting background: A herring cured in salt (which is reddish in colour) has a powerful odor before it is cooked. If one is dragged across the trial of an animal that dogs are tracking, the dogs will give up the original scent and follow the herring."[22]

M. Biased Statistics

The fallacy of biased statistics occurs when an inference is drawn from a sample that is not diverse enough. This is common in opinion polls meant to discredit a politician or an issue. An example of biased statistics:

a) The opinion polls of KLB found that 57% of Kenyans are unhappy with the election results which were won by the ruling party. The survey was conducted within the opposition zone.

Such statistics is biased since it is one sided since there is a shift from the sample population to the target population.

N. Fallacy of misleading vividness

This fallacy is closely connected with statistics and sample studies. It occurs when striking or vivid counterexample is given at the expense of strong evidence. For example:

a) Dr. K. to Dr. O: The overwhelming evidence is that smoking marijuana reduces pain.
b) Dr. O. to Dr. K: Really, I have been smoking it while sailing in Indian Ocean and I still have stomach pain!

5.5.3 The Fallacies of Ambiguity

Fallacies of ambiguity also known as linguistic fallacies occur as a result of structural issues in language. They happen when the same words have different meanings, or open to different interpretations, unclear sentence structure, and grammar. They include:

A. Equivocation

A term is equivocal when it is predicated of diverse things according to an entirely different concept. For example, coach has the following meanings; a trainer, a vehicle, or seal; hide can mean the skin of an animal, to seek protection or concealment; run can mean to spring or flow; evolution as a theory in the Darwin sense means random, unguided change or the common usage means loosely some change; fine can mean okay or some penalty. The fallacy of equivocation also referred to as semantic fallacy occurs when a word or words or phrases in an argument are used to present different meanings or senses in the same context. This fallacy is common in advertisements and among politicians. The following are some examples of the fallacy of equivocation:

Example 1:
1. The sign reads, "Fine to play loud music," and since it was fine, I played loud music.

Example 2:
1. Only illegal are Criminal actions.
2. Every murder trials are criminal actions.
3. Therefore, all murder trials are illegal.

Example 3:
1. Every river has a bank
2. Equity is a bank
3. Therefore, Equity is a river.

Example 4:
1. "A feather is light.
2. What is light cannot be dark.
3. Therefore, a feather cannot be dark.

The meaning of light is obviously different in the two senses and therefore, despite the apparent formal validity of the argument, the argument is not valid."[23] A critical thinker must identify the word/phrase that is equivocal, point out the different meanings and make the necessary distinctions.

B. **Accent**

This fallacy occurs when, a word or phrase is visually or verbally emphasized or repeated leading to inferring a false conclusion. It is commonly used in advertisement, in newspaper headlines, in magazines, promotional schemes, in political rallies or religious crusades or misquoting someone out of context. For example:

a) FREE SHIRT! FREE SPORTS SHOES whenever you buy a new 7 tonnes truck.

C. **Amphiboly**

Amphiboly gets its meaning from the creature amphibian, which is capable of living in two entirely different environments. This fallacy occurs when the use of grammar or sentence structure is ambiguous. Unlike the fallacy of equivocation, which happens due to ambiguous words or phrases, amphiboly occurs due to syntactic deficiency such as a grammatical error or mistake, that is, the ambiguity of the sentence structure or grammatical construction leads to the fallacy of amphiboly. For example:

a. Dr. K gave a talk on suicide in lecture room 8. I gather that a lot of people have committed suicide in that room.
b. Dr. K. donated along his wife, various traditional artefacts.
c. I have been driving for years when I fell asleep at the wheel and had an accident.

In essence, there is no logical connection between the premises and the conclusion.

D. **Composition**

The fallacy comprises two dimensions, that is, an invalid inference from the nature of the parts to the nature of the whole or an invalid inference from attributes of members of a group to attributes of the group itself. This is to say that it occurs when one infers what is true of the parts or whole of something applies to the whole of the thing. The fallacy occurs when the fact that is true of the members or parts of something is taken to mean it will be true of the whole.

For example;
a) Each part of this car is light. Therefore, the car is light.
b) Each player of rugby is poor. Therefore, the team is poor.

E. **Division**

The fallacy of division is the opposite of composition. This fallacy occurs when an invalid inference is made from the nature of the whole to the nature of the parts. For example;
a) The car is heavy. Therefore, each of its parts is heavy.
b) The national economy has grown. Therefore, Kenyans have become rich.

F. **Hypostatization**

Accordingly, "the fallacy of hypostatization occurs when an abstract word or phrase is used as it were a concrete thing with a set of characteristics we could experience or empirically verify."[24] Freedom, truth, democracy, rights are often used as if they are concrete. Here are some examples of hypostatisation:
 a) Dr. K: Jesus is the truth!
 b) Water is life.
 c) Love is blind.

5.6 Conclusion

The chapter has explained the meaning and nature of fallacies. Fallacies are arguments that might sound reasonable or true but are actually flawed or dishonest and contrary to the truth. It is viable to assert that they have false premises, incorrect, invalid, unsound and at best bad argumentation. Generally, it is clear from the discussion of fallacies that they are "non sequitur" a Latin phrase which means "does not follow." Fallacies are "non sequitur" arguments in which the conclusions simply do not follow from the premises. Thus every fallacy is, in that general sense, also a non sequitur.

Specifically, we discussed the types of informal fallacies namely, the fallacies of relevance, presumption and ambiguity giving relevant examples. The fallacies of relevance entail the fact that the given premises are irrelevant to the given premises. The fallacies of presumption occur due to unwarranted assumption while fallacies of ambiguity occur when there is unclear or incorrect use of language or sentence structure.

We have constantly emphasized that critical thinking is normative in character, that it entails good argumentation and good reasons. Fallacies contravene these aspects of the nature of critical thinking. Fallacies are not based on good thinking, good reasons or reasoning. Fallacies do not provide putative or probative forces of reason to support the given conclusion. As demonstrated, fallacies are based on bad reasons such as grammatical constructs, threats, emotions, wrong authority, and false cause among others.

In addition, the nature of critical thinking entails critical attitude or critical spirit, the dispositions, character traits, tendencies or habits of mind, the willingness to conform or follow the dictates of reasons. This moral/ethical component abhors fallacious reasoning since the latter embraces intellectual dishonesty as a means to its end. A critical thinker ought to treat others with respect, care about how reason is used and its point. Such valuing of good reasoning, that is respect for reasons, is incompatible with fallacious reasoning. This critical attitude, or critical spirit, entails demanding justification, investigating unsubstantiated claims, assumptions, and not accepting any claim *prima facie*. Ideally, a critical thinker is inclined to seek reasons and evidence. In essence, critical attitude, or critical spirit, guards a critical thinker from falling prey to fallacious reasoning.

Such a discussion is vital so that a critical thinker is intellectually alert or aware, and hence guards herself against committing or being a victim of fallacies. Critical thinkers ought to detect fallacies, avoid them in one's own arguments, and be able to spot them in others' arguments. As a critical thinker, one should not be a victim of, or manipulated or fooled by fallacious or erroneous reasoning. One becomes critically alert to identify such fallacious or erroneous reasoning in media, advertisements, in politics, and in religious domains such but to mention a few. This knowledge is vital in our everyday activities.

It is plausible to conclude that the central role of critical thinkers is to identify, expose, and avoid fallacies. Such an ability/skill and disposition to do so, makes analysis of arguments easier and more so facilitates the recognition of good patterns of reasoning. On the contrary, if we allow ourselves to be manipulated by fallacious or erroneous reasoning, then we fall short as critical thinkers.

Finally, the chapter has underscored the fact that informal logic is relevant to critical thinking. ideally, critical thinkers or rational persons should be able to analyze the 'because' or 'for the reason that' in order to determine if the reason(s) offered or provided by the premise(s) do or do not in fact support the claim it is offered in support of. Informal logic is key component to be understood by a critical thinker for it facilities evaluation or justification of reasons given determining if they are good or bad.

5.7   End Notes

1. Harvey Siegel, *Rationality Redeemed? Further Dialogues on an Educational Ideal,* (New York: Routledge, 1997), 16.
2. Copi, I. M. and Cohen, C., *Introduction to Logic* **(9th Ed)**. (New York: Macmillan, 1994), 114.
3. Barker, S. *Elements of Logic* **(5th Ed)**. (New York: Macmillan, 1984), 154.
4. Harvey Siegel, *Rationality Redeemed? Further Dialogues on an Educational Ideal*, op. cit., 14.
5. Harvey Siegel, *Educating Reason: Rationality, Critical Thinking and Education,* (Routledge, 1988), 25.
6. Robert H. Ennis, *Critical Thinking* (Prentice–hall, Inc, 1996), XXI.
7. Sharon Bailin & Mark Battersby, *Reason in the Balance: An Inquiry Approach to Critical Thinking,* (Cambridge: Hackett publishing Company, Inc.2016), 79.
8. Ibid., 80.
9. Ibid.
10. Ibid., 267.
11. Ibid.
12. Ibid., 274.
13. Ibid., 281.
14. Brooke Noel Moore and Richard Parker, *Critical Thinking 6th Ed,* (Boston: McGraw-Hill publishes, 2001), 149.
15. Copi, I. M. and Cohen, C., *Introduction to Logic,* **op. cit.,** 109.
16. Ibid., 131.
17. Aristotle, *Nichomachean Ethics,* **Book V**. Vol. 9, 376b.

18. Ibid., 25-26
19. Harvey Siegel, *Rationality Redeemed? Further Dialogues on an Educational Ideal,* op. cit., 14.
20. Ibid., 15-16.
21. Sharon Bailin & Mark Battersby, *Reason in the Balance: An Inquiry Approach to Critical Thinking,* op. cit., 91.
22. Brooke Noel Moore and Richard Parker, *Critical Thinking* 6th Ed, op. cit., 150.
23. Sharon Bailin & Mark Battersby, *Reason in the Balance: An Inquiry Approach to Critical Thinking,* op. cit., 94.
24. Wanda Teays, **Second Thoughts:** *Critical Thinking from a Multicultural Perspective,* (California: Mayfield publishes Company, 1996), 214.

6 CHAPTER SIX
THE RELEVANCE OF CRITICAL THINKING

> The "old-time Enlightenment metanarrative" that I defend can be taken, narrowly, as the idea that rationality is an ideal appropriate to all education and students. More broadly, it can be taken to be wide-ranging set of theses concerning the role of reasons in human life, the importance of individual autonomy, the centrality of considerations of justice to the evaluation of actual and possible social arrangements and relationships, the value of knowledge, the importance of believing responsibly, i.e. in such a way that beliefs are informed by and based upon relevant evidence and so on.[1]

What is the best way to teach so as to foster critical thinking?[2]

6.1 Introduction

This chapter address the question: why think critically? We will look at the relevance of critical thinking as explicated by some of the philosophical theorists discussed in chapter one, focusing on education, democracy and religion. In addition, we will demonstrate that critical thinking literature and discussions are not limited to addressing complex, inconsistencies and controversies or 'in house disputes' as Siegel calls them, as reflected in chapter two, but it is valuable to educational, religious, social-political and even multicultural spheres. Consequently, critical thinking theorists have made their ideas applicable and relevant to different contexts. In this respect, critical thinking cannot be criticized or regarded as indifferent or not factoring social and political issues in its deliberations or desiderata.

6.2 Critical Thinking in Education

In this section, we discuss the relevance of critical thinking in terms of educational activities and more so, the importance of thinking critically for a student who attends any education programme. We will demonstrate that developing the ability to think critically is an important element for education as reflected in the ideas of the philosophical theorists discussed in this section. Hence, this section, exposes the relevance, essentiality and indispensability of critical thinking to education.

We begin with the views of Israel Scheffler.

Israel Scheffler's Reason in Teaching

In this sub-section, we will expose the relation between philosophy, critical thinking and education as understood by Scheffler.

Scheffler asserts that "critical thought is of first importance in the conception and organization of educational activities."[3] He views critical thinking as essential in the educational process or activities. Hence, it is helpful in organising and setting the objectives of educational enterprises or efforts. This, of course, reflects Scheffler's conviction that philosophical analysis provides critical scrutiny to educational matters. For Scheffler, rationality is a central aspect of critical thinking and the teaching thereof. He notes that critical thinking is vital for initiation "into the rational life, a life in which the critical quest for reasons is dominant and integrating motive."[4] That is to say that critical thinking draws from rationality and reasonableness as its fundamental concepts. This Schefflerian perspective of rationality uses specific reasons or evidence as its content, and refers to the capability to involve oneself in a critical and open assessment of rules and principles in all areas of life. In other words, rationality is "the free and critical quest for reasons."[5] It is clear that this Schefflerian perspective pays homage to free inquiry and rationality. Hence, rationality helps in the acquisition of truth constantly challenging the sufficiency of our understanding of the world.

On the basis of this, education for Scheffler ought to concern itself with teaching students to be critical thinkers. Scheffler views a teacher "as a philosopher in critical aspects of his role."[6] In other words, a teacher must embrace philosophy in order to be critical thinker. Scheffler is reacting to the conception that a teacher is characterized by subject-matter competency, the only knower, educator over against been a critical teacher. This conception of the ideal teacher, education and schooling is contrary to a dialectical and critical approach to learning. Scheffler's remarks are correct for it is clear that society follows this popular conception of education as schooling in which the common understanding of a teacher has been competence in a certain area and not embracing criticality. Unhappy with the status quo, Scheffler redefines "teaching" by characterising it as an instructive activity that engages the mind. The teacher and the concept of teaching must be based on the ideals of free inquiry and rationality.

We now turn attention to the Schefflerian notion of teaching. This notion of teaching must be philosophical in nature. The Schefflerian conception of teaching is the commitment to the ideals of free inquiry and rationality, and hence an initiation of, free rational discourse. This conception does not embrace conformism or acculturation or the banking concept of education but it is an initiation to free rational discourse. This is contrary to teaching which is based on non-rational methods such deception, propaganda, indoctrination, and conditioning among other ideologies. If teaching embraces these non-rational methods, then it fails to meet the standards of rationality and free inquiry spirit. Accordingly, the teacher must be ready to acknowledge the student's right to ask questions:

> To teach in the standard sense, is at some points at least to submit oneself to the understanding and independent judgement of the pupil, to his demand for reasons, to his sense of what constitutes an adequate explanation. To teach someone that such and such is the case is not merely to try to get him to be believe it: deception, for example, is not a method or a mode of teaching. Teaching involves further that, if we try to get the student to believe that such and such, is the case, we try also to get him to believe it for reasons that, within the limits of his capacity to grasps, are our reasons. Teaching, in this way, requires us to reveal our reasons to the students and, by so doing, to submit them to his evaluation and criticism.[7]

Teaching as conceived by Scheffler is an attitude aimed at making students critical thinkers and is not about deception, preconceived ideas, skills, methods or acquiring new techniques as such. Scheffler asserts that:

> This educational course precludes taking schooling as an instrument for shaping [students] minds to a preconceived idea. For if they seek reasons, it is their evaluation of such reasons that will determine what ideas they eventually accept.[8]

Such as an educational course for students "encourage them to ask questions, to look for evidence, to seek and scrutinise alternatives, to be critical of their own ideas as well those of others."[9] This conception of teaching helps students to be critical and not just perceive or docile recipients of information. From the above quotations, it is plausible to infer that teaching is necessarily related to rational explanation, critical dialogue and it is a critical process.

Teaching is done by teachers and hence Scheffler addresses the question of the ideal teacher. He regards teachers as "free men and women with a special dedication to the values of the intellect and the enhancement of the critical powers of the young."[10] The ideal teacher, for Scheffler, must be critical thinker, that is, able to be creative, cultivate curiosity and skepticism. Furthermore, in the context of teaching, critical thinking is reinforced by a teacher's critical spirit, considered a principal obligation. Besides being a rational person or a critical thinker, the ideal teacher must have the virtues of humility, open mindedness, courage, impartiality, and objectivity among others.

Scheffler is open and in favour to teaching that promotes critical thinking. For him, this would enable children to judge their beliefs, desires, actions, and their cognitive and non-cognitive emotions based on appropriate criteria or standards and good reason, and engage them "in the critical dialogues that relate to every area of civilization."[11] Scheffler is not in favour with orthodoxy teaching but seeks to advocate for an approach which embraces critical dialogue.

Scheffler then seeks to justify why the ideal teacher must embrace the ideal conception of teaching. We have given an account of the Schefflerian emphasis on the ideal conception of teaching. Such a conception of teaching by Scheffler is against the authoritarian conception of teaching because authoritarianism negates the principle of respect for the students and fallibility of knowledge. Critical thinking crosses a threshold between teaching criticality, authoritarian and indoctrinating. Teaching students to think critically must include allowing them to come to their own conclusions. Critical thinking, for him, as an approach to teaching welcomes questioning and reciprocates by giving the student honest reasons. Further he sees this as a gradual process.

It would be unfair to the Schefflerian view if we do not expose his alleged deadly educational sins or vices. These sins or vices are: ignorance, negativity, forgetting, guesswork, irrelevance, procrastination, and idleness. He seeks to demystify and convert these vices into virtues. Again it is important to note his perspective on educational slogans, metaphors and definitions in education. Educators must critically seek their meaning and value.

Scheffler views learning as a process. He points out that "learning takes place not just by computing solutions to problems, nor even just exchanging words, but by emulation, observation, identification, wonder, supposition, dream, imitation, doubt, action, conflict, ambition, participation, regret."[12] This is a broad conception of learning which involves all the above aspects as well as skills/abilities, dispositions, appreciation and understanding. Scheffler is also concerned with the ideal curriculum for education. The ideal educational curriculum is not limited to the basics but must also question the status quo.

In conclusion, Scheffler's ideal education must be informed by critical thinking. The teacher must be a critical thinker and not the absolute knower while the students must be initiated into an education which gives room for asking questions.

In the following section, we examine Harvey Siegel's perspective of critical thinking as an educational ideal.

Siegel and Critical Thinking as an Educational Ideal

Harvey Siegel, in *Educating Reason*, and his other works advocates and endorses critical thinking as an educational ideal. Hence our objective here is to spell at length the Siegelian view of critical thinking (reasons conception) as an educational ideal. According to him:

> A striking feature of critical thinking (understood, from now on, as the reasons conception) is its imperative generality and wider-ranging relevance to education. Critical thinking is relevant to, and has implications for, the ethics of education as well as the epistemology of education. It touches the manner as well as the content of education.[13]

From this quotation, it is clear that Siegel identifies four relevant aspects of critical thinking to education namely; ethics, epistemology, content and the manner of education. These aspects for him account or demonstrate critical thinking as an educational ideal.

He further gives four reasons to justify critical thinking as an educational ideal, which we will systematically examine.

A starting point is Siegel's assertion that:

> Critical thinking is best conceived, consequently, as the *educational cognate* of rationality: critical thinking involves bringing to bear all matters relevant to the rationality of belief and action; and education aimed at the promulgation of critical thinking is nothing less than education aimed at fostering of rationality and the development of rational persons.[14]

Siegel views critical thinking as an ideal because of its nature of rationality. Critical thinking coexists with rationality, with reasons such that it is impossible to separate the two. Education must seek to foster rationality/critical thinking. Hence it is necessary to recap what Siegel understands as critical thinking in order to see how he relates it to education.

The nature of the ideal critical thinking which he refers to as the *reasons conception account of critical thinking*, that is, to be appropriately moved by reason, entails two important but distinct aspects that contribute to good reasoning. One, to be *appropriately* moved by reason, the reason assessment component entails the skills/abilities to reason. Two, to be appropriately *moved* by reason, is the critical attitude or critical spirit component that entails the dispositions to be moved by reason, to follow the dictates of reason. The reason assessment component deals with the rules, principles of thinking while the critical attitude or critical spirit component entails certain mental dispositions, attitude or character traits or habits of mind. This understanding of the ideal critical thinking for Siegel is vital for the ideal education.

Again, it is vital to understand what the ideal education for Siegel is. This is important since it will facilitate in comprehending how Siegel relates it to the ideal critical thinking. Critical thinking which is rationality coexisting with reason is the prime facie of education. Hence for Siegel, the primary obligation of education is to instil critical thinking. Education hence entails teaching or fostering reasons conception account of critical thinking, that is, the reasons assessment component as well as the critical attitude or critical spirit. He confirms this when he writes that "fostering these skills, abilities, attitudes, and dispositions amounts to helping students to become critical thinkers; that is, helping them to become rational or reasonable persons."[15] Education should foster skills/abilities and dispositions of critical thinking. For a student to be rational or a critical thinker, that student must grasp and evaluate the role of reasons in actions, beliefs and judgments. Siegel writes that:

> Critical thinking, we have seen, recognizes the importance of getting students to understand and appreciate the role of reasons in rational endeavor, and of fostering in students those traits, attitudes, dispositions which encourage the seeking of reasons for grounding judgment, belief and action.[16]

He then asserts that critical thinking is paramount in educational matters:

> To regard critical thinking as a fundamental educational aim is to hold that educational activities ought to be designed and conducted in such a way that the construction and evaluation of reasons (in accordance with relevant criteria) are paramount throughout the curriculum.[17]

There is, therefore, an indispensability of critical thinking and education for Siegel. Educational activities must be modelled and guided by critical thinking.

By connoting *critical thinking as imperative generality,* Siegel sees this feature as a significant aspect in relation to the ethics, epistemology, content and manner of education. Siegel emphasizes that efforts to foster critical thinking skills/abilities and dispositions have relevant and wide implication for these four areas which he has spelled at length in his book, *Educating Reason.* We summarize them below.

According to Siegel, critical thinking is relevant in two ways namely; it calls for ethical input in education by the educators in respect to the manner of teaching and fostering ethicality to the recipients of education. In addition, critical thinking informs or has implications to the epistemology of education. This implies that the knowledge dimension of education or the "know how" ought to be dictated by rationality and not simply by memorisation or repetitions. Further still for Siegel, there is the need to interrogate the manner and content of education. He asserts that "we can usefully divide the realm of education into two distinct parts: the *content* of education, which includes all that educators seek to impact to their students, and the *manner* of education, which includes the ways in which educators try to impact that content."[18] By this, he intends to demonstrate the generality of critical thinking. What he refers to as the critical manner serves as the connection between critical thought and the manner of teaching. He explains that "the critical manner is that manner of teaching that reinforces the critical spirit."[19] This means that the educator must be open minded, critical and questioning the ordinary things and willing to be challenged by students. Siegel captures this when he asserts that "teaching in the critical manner is thus teaching so as to develop in the students skills and attitudes consonant with critical thinking."[20] This entails the combination of reasons and the manner of teaching. He goes on to assert that "teaching in the critical manner is thus perhaps the clearest way in which the ideal of critical thinking appropriately guides education practice."[21]

Critical thinking is helpful to the second realm that is, content of education, according to Siegel. Education entails training of knowledge how, that is skills/abilities and knowledge that, that is, propositional information.

This means that education must foster knowledge how and also critical thinking as the reasons conception in its two dimensions that is, as reason assessment as well as a critical spirit or critical attitude.

He then concludes by affirming that "this, we have seen, is part of the way in which critical thinking in an important part of the content of education, touching both the "knowledge how" and "knowledge that" portions of that content."[22]

We quote Siegel at length to illustrate his point that critical thinking must and ought to be conceived as an educational ideal:

> We should, we think, conceive of it as an educational *ideal*. Critical thinking, at least in the way it has been conceptualized in the present chapter, speaks to virtually all of our educational endeavors. It provides both important goals for our educational efforts, and direction for the achievement of those goals. It is highly relevant to the determination of what we should teach, how we should teach, how we should organize educational activities, what the points of the many activities are, how we should treat students and others in the educational setting, and so on. Perhaps most importantly, it provides a conception of the sort of person we are trying, through our educational efforts, to create, and the sort of character to be fostered in such a person. Critical thinking provides an underlying rationale for educational activities, a criterion for evaluating those activities, and a guiding principle for the organization and conduct of those activities. Surely such a broad–gauged notion is properly thought of as an ideal.[23]

According to him, critical thinking is relevant to virtually all of our educational endeavors or activities such the manner and content of teaching among others.

Another reason why he conceives critical thinking as an educational ideal is its regulative nature. Siegel puts the point as follows:

> In fact, I should like to suggest, critical thinking is best thought of as a *regulative ideal*. It defines regulative standards of excellence which can be used to adjudicate between rival educational methods, policies and practices.[24]

Critical thinking should be used evaluate or adjudicate the various features of education such as; the practices, qualities and attitudes of the teacher; the policies, methods, practices, testing of the content of the curriculum; and context and organisation of educational activities. The features of critical thinking as reasons conception and its constituent components that is, skills/abilities and dispositions or character traits or habits of mind should facilitate this regulative role.

It is clear that for him then, critical thinking is the yardstick or basis from which to adjudicate, evaluate and justify various educational activities or enterprises. Siegel observes that:

> In general our guiding question in assessing educational activities should be: does this manifest, and foster, critical thinking? To the extent that we take this as our guiding evaluative question, we take critical thinking to be a fundamental ideal.[25]

Essentially, the features of critical thinking as reasons conception purpose the regulative educational ideal, which provides the basis for adjudicating, evaluating, determining and cross examining educational activities or enterprises.

Having exposed Siegel understanding of education and critical thinking, this leads to exploration of the reasons he gives as to why critical thinking is justifiable as an educational ideal. Siegel raises a fundamental question: "why does the ideal need to be justified?"[26] He still raises the following questions: "What is the basis of our conviction? How do we justify educational interventions aimed at the development of critical thinking in students?"[27] These questions arise because "it should be clear that taking critical thinking to be an educational ideal is a highly significant move, with potentially far-reaching, even revolutionary, consequences. Hence it is far from clear that we should take it as such."[28] Siegel's point is that there is the need to demonstrate the desirability or worthiness of critical thinking is an educational ideal. Basically for this ideal there is, like any other philosophical theory, the need to offer its justification. Siegel's task is to provide reasons which would justify granting critical thinking the prestige, the force and the power to guide educational activities or enterprises. Such a task, for Siegel, is inevitable and cannot be wished away.

In addition, Siegel observes that the ideal needs justification due to the prevailing various forms of skepticism. The forms of skepticism range from scientific creationism to fundamentalism by both parents and preachers to general members of the public including school boards and administrators who are against all forms of liberalism; Marxism to academic/intellectual community including educational theorists, feminists, deconstructionist (Derrida), some Marxist, epistemologists and philosophers of science (Feyerabend), and in literary domains (Dostoevsky).[29] Siegel articulates and captures this point when he writes:

> Finally, I wish simply to point out that the simple assumption that critical thinking is a worthy educational goal is contentious, and masks enormous allied assumptions concerning the nature of education and the educated person. Many educational theorists have denied and would deny not only that critical thinking is a fundamental educational ideal, but that it is a worthwhile ideal at all. For many such theorists have favoured ideals which are not only alternatives to, but are incompatible with, ideal of critical thinking. Such alternatives include the production of docile citizens or good workers; the maximization of individual happiness; the fostering of ideological purity and commitment; and so on. In short, the aims of education are controversial and contentious. It is not *obvious* that the fostering of critical thinking is a good thing or a worthy aim of our educational endeavors.[30]

This necessarily leads to the need for critical thinking as an educational ideal to be justified and inevitably reflects the concerns of philosophy of education. There is fundamental importance to justify critical thinking as an educational ideal and to demonstrate that fostering of critical thinking skills/abilities and dispositions, is a good thing or a worthy aim of our educational endeavors. In addition, such efforts of fostering the educational aim are justifiable.

Clearly, Siegel seeks to provide a positive account of the desirability and worthiness, that is, the justification of critical thinking as an educational ideal. Before embarking on justifying critical thinking as an educational ideal, Siegel addresses a key question; "what sort of "justification" is wanted?"[31] Siegel answer is clear and eloquent:

> What I am after, rather, is a "philosophical" justification of critical thinking: production of reasons for regarding critical thinking as a fundamental educational ideal which are rationally persuasive to a rational, objective (perhaps ideal) inquirer into the question of the proper aims of education.[32]

What can be inferred from this quotation is that Siegel seeks to provide a philosophical justification of critical thinking as an educational ideal or aim. In addition, he seeks to demonstrate that critical thinking is a justified ideal, that there are philosophical reasons that constitute its merits, interests or desirability or worthiness as a focus for educational activities or endeavours or efforts. For Siegel, there are philosophical reasons that establish or support critical thinking as an educational ideal. While pragmatic considerations are important as justification for critical thinking in education, Siegel transcends such concerns to offer philosophical justifications or reasons. Hence, the term justification for him connotes philosophical argumentation. He asserts that:

> If education for critical thinking is rationally preferable to education for ideological purity, maintenance of the political and social *status quo*, maintenance of a docile and unquestioning citizenry, the transmission of fundamental religious commitments, or any other "uncritical" educational aim, that rational preferability must be established by means of substantive philosophical argument concerning educational ideals and the aims of education.[33]

From these quotations, it is clear that the justification of the ideal is necessarily a rational justification, a rational evaluation, a philosophical grounding or argumentation in nature. The aim is to provide philosophical reasons or rationale for justifying critical thinking as an educational ideal.

Siegel then proceeds to assert that to accept critical thinking, as an educational ideal is to appreciate the autonomous and self-sufficiency of people: "If we accept critical thinking as a fundamental educational ideal, we explicitly acknowledge the desirability of the attainment by students of self-sufficiency and autonomy."[34] Critical thinkers guided by skills/abilities and dispositions or character traits or habits of mind, must be autonomous and self-sufficient. In light of this, he asks:

> How can the educational ideal of critical thinking–which promulgates the development in students of autonomy, self-sufficiency, the skills of reason assessment, and the attitudes, dispositions, habits of mind, and character traits of the critical spirit, and erects those features of persons as the fundamental guidelines for the evaluation and transformation of society–be justified? [35]

He then seeks to provide reasons which would justify critical thinking as an educational ideal guided by the questions: *"in what sense is critical thinking an educational ideal? What sort of ideal is it?* It is "the ideal of critical thinking" that Siegel seeks to justify "as an educational ideal." In other words, he wants to give reasons, to justify, and demonstrate why critical thinking is vital for education. In Siegel's words "it is of fundamental importance to justify critical thinking as an educational ideal, and so to establish the fostering of critical thinking as a justifiable educational aim and efforts at such fostering as justifiable activities."[36] Hence guided by these questions and by his understanding of the nature of the ideal critical thinking and the nature of the ideal education, we explore Siegel's understanding of critical thinking as an educational ideal.

Siegel's observation that critical thinking is an educational ideal implies that the notion of critical thinking, its constituent components, can and should be used as a basis from which to evaluate their desirability or worthiness of various features of or proposals for the educational enterprise or efforts or activities. He asserts that:

> To justify critical thinking as an educational ideal is to offer a positive account of the desirability and worthiness of educational efforts which have as their aim the fostering of critical thinking in students; it is also to show that the sorts of challenges to the ideal just viewed can be met, that the ideal can survive criticisms made against it.[37]

He, then, provides four reasons for justifying critical thinking as an educational ideal.

First, critical thinking entails an ethical obligation of administrators and teachers to treat students and others persons with respect, essentially, conducting education in the critical manner. He writes that "this first consideration is simply that we are morally obliged to treat students (and everyone else) with respect."[38] This means that teaching in the critical manner is to teach in such a way as to treat students with respect and more generally to respect everyone else.

Second, the educational endeavours must serve as a preparation for adult life. He observes that:

> The second reason for taking critical thinking to be a worthy educational ideal has to do with education's generally recognized task of preparing students to become competent with respect to those abilities necessary for the successful management of adult life. We educate, at least in part, in order to prepare for adulthood.[39]

It is evident that education ought to prepare students with various competencies for prosperous participation in society as adults. This, for Siegel, does not imply training students with preconceived careers, that is, 'to know their best suited place' as Plato advocated in his theory of education but developing the student to become self-sufficient and autonomous to be able to make rational choices in determining or managing one's adult life. He corroborates this when he writes that:

> If we accept critical thinking as a fundamental educational ideal, we explicitly acknowledge the desirability of the attainment by students of self-sufficiency and autonomy...The critical thinker must be autonomous-that is, free to act and judge independently of external constraint, on the

basis of her own reasoned appraisal of the matter at hand.[40]

This entails that critical thinking as an educational ideal seeks to ensure that a student become autonomous and self-sufficient person. He or she acts and judge according to his or her own reasoned assessment.

Initiation into rational traditions is the third reason for taking critical thinking to be a worthy educational ideal. This is because these traditions foster critical thinking skills/abilities and dispositions. Since critical thinking is rationality simpliciter and that a critical thinker needs to be familiar with proper evaluation of reasons, then initiation into rational traditions helps foster in students critical thinking. He writes that:

> These traditions–science, literature, history, the arts, mathematics and so on–have evolved, over the long history of their development, guidelines concerning the role and the nature of reasons in their respective domains. Thus, for example, a science student must learn, among other things, what counts as a good reason for or against some hypotheses, theory, or procedure; how much weight the reason has; and how it compares with other relevant reasons.[41]

These rational traditions facilitate students to learn how to evaluate reasons properly and to appreciate the evolving nature of the standards of rationality governing reason assessments in each tradition. Therefore, educational endeavours should gear towards initiating students into these rational traditions. For him, therefore, these rational traditions foster critical thinking skills/abilities and dispositions to students:

> If education involves initiation into rational traditions, then we should take critical thinking to be an educational ideal because so taking it involves fostering in students those traits, dispositions, attitudes and skills which are conducive to the successful initiation of students into rational traditions.[42]

In regarding education as initiation into rational traditions provides the third reason for taking critical thinking to be an educational ideal. Since critical thinking/ rationality seeks to foster skills/abilities and dispositions, it follows that initiation of students into rational traditions is initiating them to appreciate the proper evaluation of reasons since rationality plays a vital role in these domains. Understanding, accepting, appreciating the criteria of rationality and the role of reasons in each traditions is the path way to becoming a critical thinker.

Finally, a fourth reason for taking critical thinking to be a worthy educational ideal has to do with democracy. He writes that "finally, consider the relation between critical thinking and democracy. It is truism that the properly functioning democracy requires an educated citizenry. What sort of education does such a citizenry require?"[43] For Siegel, the answer is clear that education that entails critical thinking skills/abilities and dispositions as its ideal is indispensable for democratic living.

This implies that critical thinking is vital to the democratic processes. In addition to offering a defensible conception of critical thinking as a democratic ideal, Siegel's account is tailored in such a way that if citizenry are more enlightened, critical thinkers, they fully embrace, participate and are well informed in politics in a democratic manner. This educational ideal is relevant in that there is an urgent need to foster critical thinking to our students in order to help them to reason well regarding issues of politics, public policy, societal issues, champion for justice among other matters, as autonomous critical thinkers. Critical thinking and democracy is developed in details in the next section.

In the light of these discussions, it is clear that Siegel has established, defended and endorsed, with four philosophical reasons or qualifications or justifications, that critical thinking is an educational ideal.

In accordance with Siegel, critical thinking as an educational ideal has been subject to criticisms. What follows is an examination of the issues which have been raised regarding the ideal. The first criticism is the ideology objection which "...denies that educational ideals such as critical thinking do in fact admit of rational justification. Such ideals and values, rather, are determined by prior ideological commitment; a "justified" educational ideal is simply an ideal which is sanctioned by one's ideology."[44] This challenges the Siegelian goal of justifying critical thinking rationally or philosophically as an educational ideal. In other words, there is no need for a rational evaluation or rational justification for any educational ideology because virtually all educational ideals are sanctioned by an ideology and critical thinking is not exceptional and any attempts would amount to question-begging. This charge has two dimensions:

> The first challenge to the enterprise of justifying critical thinking (or anything else) as an educational ideal hinges on the idea that everything

educational is fundamentally political. The second is based on a strong thesis of the ideological determination of thought.[45]

For Siegel, while it is the case that all educational ideals have political ramifications (including critical thinking), it is not necessarily the case that all educational ideals are politically or ideologically biased. Further, it is not the case that an educational ideology cannot be independent of any political or ideological inclinations. For example, critical thinking has political ramifications but it is distinct and independent from political or ideological perspectives. In affirming that educational ideals such as critical thinking have political ramifications is not affirming that they are politically or ideologically inclined. They can be intellectually neutral even if they are not politically or ideological neutral. This ensures that the justification of critical thinking as an educational ideal is not a question-begging endeavour since it is not the case that educational ideology such as critical thinking is prior determined by another ideology. On the *"ideological determination of thought"* brings to bear the issue of the relationship between ideology and rationality. The issue has been: which determines the other? Rationality and not ideology is basic because of its putative force of reason. Rationality and indeed, critical thinking evaluates ideologies.

Indoctrination is another charge brought against critical thinking as an educational ideal. The challenge lies on the premise that if indoctrination cannot be avoided, then critical thinking as an educational ideology collapses. For Siegel, the danger is that, if critical thinking becomes a doctrine that can be indoctrinative, then it loses its value for persons would not embrace it for good reasons. If Critical thinking is indoctrinative then it is no longer rationally justifiable and the persons indoctrinated are no longer critical thinkers. If Critical thinking as reasons conception, which entails the reason assessment component as well as the critical attitude or critical spirit component, can be indoctrinated, then it is no longer an ideal. According to Siegel and rightly so, indoctrination is uncritical and must be avoided. If one fails to overcome indoctrination then one is harmed, his or her autonomy compromised, embraces impartiality, becomes a prisoner of her own convictions and set of beliefs hence sees no other alternatives, lacks dispositions to seek reasons, fails to seek evidence, life becomes limited, fails to determine one's future, adopts docility rather questioning attitude, simply one becomes a slave of uncritical convictions.[46] These malaises can only be subdued when one embraces critical thinking as an ideal. It is clear from the argument presented here by Siegel that not all cases of justification are indoctrinative. He then calls for the adoption of non-indoctrinative belief-inculcation (which enhance rationality) rather than indoctrination in the educational activities. Such a move fosters not indoctrination but enhancement of critical thinking/rationality and the quest for seeking evidence or reasons for belief and action. Siegel asserts that "if we inculcate beliefs *sans* reasons, but encourage the development of rationality and an evidential style of belief–that, if we encourage the development of critical thinking–we are not indoctrinating."[47] This ensures that there is room for the development of critical thinking/rationality. In conclusion Siegel confidently and rightly so asserts that "...we can non-indocrinatively educate for critical thinking..."[48] given the fact that rationality is cognate of critical thinking.

In addition, there are two other areas where Siegel grounds the relevance of critical thinking as an educational ideal namely; in science education and the minimum competence testing in educational policy and practice. We begin with the relevance of critical thinking to science education.

Siegel addresses the role or relevance of critical thinking as an educational ideal in the domain of science. His aim is to demonstrate that science education can be shaped by the ideal of critical thinking. This is because science has been taught in a narrow, rigid, dogmatic, indoctrinative and hence in an uncritical or anti-critical manner. Such an approach for Siegel, abhors the ideal of critical thinking. Accordingly, the goal of critical thinking is to shape science education in overcoming these negative tenets. This entails embracing skills/abilities and dispositions such as; open-mindedness, encourage questioning, look for evidence, seek an evaluate alternatives and in essence embrace criticality on matters of science. In this respect, Siegel points out that:

> In helping a student, by way of pluralistic science education, to become a critical thinker with respect to science, one is helping the student to develop a respect for reasons; an inclination to seek reasons and take them seriously as guides to belief and action; an appreciation of objectivity, impartiality, and honesty in the consideration of evidence and argument; and a general commitment to the ideal of rationality as guide to life.[49]

This noble enterprise of fostering skills/abilities and dispositions of critical thinking should not only be limited to science education but it ought to be fostered to all aspects of life or contexts. The ideal of rationality must guide or shape both science education and life. This goal is to be strengthened by teaching philosophy of science:

> One way is to focus on the *philosophy* of science in teaching science. Philosophy of science takes as its subject matter a variety of issues and questions relevant to the nature, role, and assessment of reasons in science. The nature of evidence, the relation between evidence and theory, the evaluation of the strength of evidence, the role of evidence and reason in testing and in theory choice–these are all matters which bear directly on the nature of reasons in science, and which philosophy of science takes as central to its concerns. A science student studying philosophy of science would in so doing, be attuned to issues involving scientific reasoning, and to the nature and proper understanding of such reasoning.[50]

This will facilitate the acquisition of a more detailed understanding of some particular debates in science and the development of the ability to think independently about philosophical problems by critically assessing arguments in these areas.

He further observes that "another way to utilize philosophy of science so as to impact to the science student a solid understanding of the nature and role of reasons in science is to contrast genuine science and pseudo-science."[51] This according to Siegel will facilitate in in highlighting the nature and role of reasons in scientific enterprise or activities. The alternative theoretical perspectives help students in grasping the role of reasons in scientific endeavours. Critical thinking becomes the handmaiden of science education according to Siegel.

We now turn attention to the relevance of critical thinking to educational policy and practice focusing on minimum competence testing (hence forth MCT). For Siegel MCT is has not been addressed from a philosophical perspective in relation to educational goals or aims. From a philosophical dimension, critical thinking is the educational ideal. This ideal is incompatible with MCT. Siegel captures this when he writes that:

> My aim is two-fold: first, to argue that MCT is foe, and not a friend, of critical thinking; second, to argue that the first result is of fundamental importance for the assessment of MCT, and, more generally, that it is a folly to neglect philosophical considerations concerning the aims of education in considering the desirability of educational policies and practices.[52]

Accordingly, MCT with its failures such as arbitrariness is a folly because it lacks a defensible philosophical ideal such as critical thinking and more so its incompatibility with the ideal. Again MCT lacks philosophical inputs and hence for Siegel philosophical considerations must be factored in educational policies and practices assessment.

The aims of MCT is success in tackling exams, improved performances, increased scores, good test marks, which are a foe to critical thinking skills/abilities and dispositions. Such a practice for Siegel calls for memorisation, 'banking' concept of knowledge, schooling as the way of learning from one level to the next, passing exams and acquisition of grades as the mode of education. His point been that the aim of education is not just limited to 'testing and passing' but fostering critical thinking skills/abilities and dispositions which have wide ramifications beyond MCT.

In addition to the above, Siegel, like Scheffler, seeks to understand the ideal teacher and the ideal teaching when he asks:

> What is it to teach? Which characteristics of teaching episodes should we applaud; which should we condemn? What should teachers strive to achieve? What should they strive to be? Should teaching be conceived primarily as a matter of modelling? Much teaching be didactic? Socratic? Should it inspire by example? There is no shortage of answers to such questions. Many answers, however, are bad ones."[53]

The best answer for Siegel is the rationality theory of teaching. He writes that "I wish to recommend a conception of teaching in which rationality is central; this conception is known in the philosophy of education literature as the "rationality theory of teaching,"[54] which is opposed to the automaton conception of a teacher. He puts it that:

> According to the "teacher as automaton" conception of teaching, the teacher is not thought of as an intellectual engager of the student, who encourages and honors the students developing critical awareness or engages the student's intellect with her own. Rather, the teacher is thought of as a quasi-programmed technician, capable of exemplifying certain standard behaviour but not utilising judgement.[55]

This teacher as automaton conception is problematic and has various difficulties. These include; that the teacher is mindless automata, uncritical, programmed, through training and conditioned to behave in certain ways. This conception fails to understand students and educational aims as envisioned by Siegel as discussed above. The teacher automaton conception does not instil or foster in students, critical thinking skills/abilities and dispositions making students automata. This is contrary with critical thinking as an educational ideal whose aim is to treat students with respect and not as objects; to prepare them for adulthood life; to initiate them into rational traditions and into democratic living.

Therefore, this teacher automaton conception is to be replaced with rationality theory of teaching which is compatible with critical thinking as an educational ideal. From this perspective, then the rationality theory of teaching entails:

> Taking seriously the idea that students ought to be helped to foster the abilities, dispositions and character traits associated with the critical thinker requires a conception of the teacher which places her independent judgement and rationality at the centre of her activities as a teacher. The critical abilities and propensities of the teacher and students, and their stature as educational desiderata and centrality as elements of educational content, doom any conception of teachers which portrays them as mindless automata, technicians, or preprogrammed performers.[56]

The teacher must embrace the ideal of critical thinking, that is, the skills/abilities and dispositions and more so, be autonomous thinkers. The rationality theory facilitates the belief-inculcation earlier discussed which is opposed to other forms of teaching such as indoctrination, falsehood, conditioning, peer pressure, propaganda, force etc. This rationality theory of teaching, its acts of belief inculcation to be eligible or deemed as acts of teaching must embrace critical thinking skills/abilities as well as the critical attitude or critical spirit enhance ensuring that students can raise questions and demand answers.

As a pedagogical strategy, the teacher should reject epistemological relativism and as such should teach that critical thinking is not relativism as Siegel advices:

> In examining issues and arguments, be honest with students. Tell them what you think of reasons offered, and why. Make claims, and give reasons and evidence for your claims. Take stands, and defend them. Perhaps most important of all, give them up when appropriate- that is when reasons opposed to your view are more powerful than your own. In demonstrating to students that it is the convicting force of reasons to which you are committed, you help make clear to them the regard you have for critical thinking, i.e. for belief and action based on the proper evaluation of reasons, and for the disposition to be moved by reasons.[57]

Such a pedagogical approach fosters, in students, critical thinking skills/abilities and dispositions.

Finally, Siegel calls for inclusion of felt reason into the rationality theory to teaching. He notes that "for felt reasons, I want to argue, have particular important role to play in education, especially in education which aims at the fostering of rational dispositions, attitudes and abilities in students."[58] Felt reasons is the appeal to ordinary reasons of particular event which are more visceral impact or forceful kind of reason. Felt reasons is instinctive quality of some reason.

In conclusion, one; Siegel has justified that critical thinking is an educational ideal worthy guiding educational activities by giving four philosophical reasons namely; respect for students as persons, self-sufficiency and preparation for adulthood, initiation into rational traditions and requirements of democratic living. Second; classical goal of empowering and liberating students is not excluded in Siegel account of critical thinking as an educational ideal. His account is also a liberationist ideology in that it empowers students and people in general not to be docile citizenry but critical thinkers. Third; he focused on the relevance of the ideal on educational practices and policies and on testing practices concluding that critical thinking and philosophical considerations are indispensable from these educational activities. Fourth, he argues for the rationality theory of teaching which entails criticality of both the teacher and the student. It also entails incorporating felt reason as mode of belief inculcation. Finally, in justifying critical thinking as an educational ideal, Siegel re-introduces the philosophical cum normative aspects of education. Again he re-opens the need for pure philosophical interest in matters of education beyond the pragmatic interests. In other words, he sees the fundamental need to link philosophy and education.

While there so many educational ideals such creativity, citizenship, happiness among others, Siegel regards his view as *"primus inter pares,"* that is, "...the proposition that critical thinking is, at minimum, "first among equals" in the pantheon of educational ideals."[59]

Finally, "all of this suggests that education aimed at the development of critical thinking is a complex business, which must seek to foster a host of attitudes, emotions, dispositions, habits and character traits as well as a wide variety of reasoning skills."[60] In addition:

> In such education our aim is to help students develop the ability to evaluate arguments and the probative force which putative reasons have,

and to encourage students to believe and act on the basis of reasons–to be *appropriately moved by reasons*.[61]

This calls for students to be educated in critical thinking skills/abilities and dispositions. This is the Siegelian view of critical thinking as an educational ideal.

In the following section, we explore Sharon Bailin's contributions regarding the relevance of critical thinking to education.

Bailin and Education

According to Sharon Bailin:

> A central goal of contemporary education is to improve the thinking skills of students, and the notions of critical thinking and of creative thinking provide focusses for this effort. As educators we would like our students to be better critical thinkers. This implies thinking more effectively within curricular subject areas understanding the reasoning employed, assessing independently and appropriately, and solving problems effectively. It involves, as well, improved thinking skills in dealing with real life problems–in assessing information and arguments in social contexts and making life decisions. We also want students to be more creative–not simply to reproduce old patterns but to respond productively to new situations, to generate new and better solutions to problems, and to produce original works.[62]

Hence for her, critical and creative thinking is vital or central to education. The objective of educators is foster thinking skills to students in order to make them critical thinkers. This implies the application of critical and creative skills in order to foster criticality. This cannot be realized when critical and creative thinking are separated. Such a separation becomes problematic to educational efforts:

> ...outcomes such as a basic curriculum in the schools which is static and encourages appeal to authority, a consequent picture of knowledge in general as authoritarian, the notion of critical thinking as a set of isolatable add–on techniques, and a downplaying of skills and knowledge in favour of intuition and irrationality in the name of creativity.[63]

It is clear for her that the separation of critical and creative thinking has detrimental effects to education. Further this radical separation of critical and creative thinking leads to the various subject areas to be perceived and defined as fixed bodies of knowledge which are static collections of facts to be memorised and remembered.

The end product according to her is that "students are thus left with a sense that knowledge is complete, definite, and fixed, and that it is based on an appeal to authority–be it of the text, of the teacher, of the unnamed 'they' who say that it is so."[64] This radical separationist view of thinking and the picture of knowledge as definite and fixed, inhibit students from enhancing critical thinking skills and stultifying creativity. Such a conception negates the fundamental principles of critical and creative thinking. In particular, it stultifies and kills criticality and creativity in students. Hence, she sees the value of critical and creative thinking as indispensable to educational efforts or activities.

However, for her, merely incorporating the two into the educational curriculum does not address the issue of conceptualizing knowledge as fixed, static, complete, definite and authoritarian. This is opposed to the real nature of knowledge which is critical and creative. She captures this by asserting that "disciplines are not merely static collections of information but are modes of inquiry, containing open questions, areas of controversy, and ongoing debates."[65] This is to say that criticality which is by nature found in the disciplines must help students to counteract the authoritarian conceptualization of knowledge. Furthermore, appreciation of the mode of inquiry which entails criticality and creativity as inbuilt nature of disciplines leads to a dynamic conceptualization of knowledge.

She also views critical and creative thinking as indispensable to education and that it is also subject domain. She asserts that "this implies thinking more effectively within curricular subject are..."[66] Creativity is advancement through an in-depth understanding of specific discipline via critical judgment. She observes that "thus I am advocating that we really emphasize mastery of disciplinary knowledge and skills as a precondition for any creative achievement."[67] This is problematic since critical thinking is both subject specific and subject neutral as we pointed out in chapter two.

This leads to the question; what is the best educational ideal according to her? From this discussion so far, it is plausible to infer that she has a distaste with an education system which is static, fixed and not based on inquiry. This conceptualization of knowledge as earlier noted inhibits criticality and creativity. She then envisions knowledge or education which is based on critical and creative thinking. She captures this when she writes that:

> Knowledge must be understood not as an authoritative body of facts, but as something made by people who are thinking well about problems. This type of picture of knowledge as dynamic, non-authoritarian and creative

would, I think, give rise to a more critical attitude on the part of students with respect to thinking in all areas.[68]

In essence educational ideal must embrace knowledge as dynamic hence it grows and develops over against been rigid within fixed frameworks. Such an educational ideal does not entail reproduction of old patterns, memorisation, and appeal to authority where the teachers knows it all. Rather it is a dynamic educationality which appreciates fluidity, non-authoritarianism, dynamic curriculum, and most of all creates a critical and creative attitude.

A vital issue for her then becomes how to teach this critical and creative thinking as indispensable aspects of the educational ideal. The two dimensions must be taken into account in the teaching. Further in impacting critical and creative thinking, the context must be factored for they do not occur in vacuum. Thus:

> This points to the necessity to present critical thinking skills within real and dynamic contexts, and to encourage the ability to reconstruct opposing arguments and to develop an independent line of reasoning. The dialectical aspect of critical thinking is thus emphasized by the recognition of the creativeness of critical thinking.[69]

She concludes by asserting that "thus I would advocate the encouragement of critical thinking and of creative thinking as joint and inseparable goals in education."[70] This is Bailin perspective on the relevance of critical and creative thinking to education. One aspect that I clarified in chapter two is the fundamental relationship between critical and creative thinking affirming that the two are intertwined. However, Bailin here uses the two terms as distinct.

Besides demonstrating the relevance of critical and creative thinking to education, Bailin and Battersby, in their book, "Reason in the Balance," elucidate the values or significance of critical inquiry approach to critical thinking. Due to the fact that knowledge is fallible, critical inquiry helps one to discern the truth with a degree of certainty: "the point is that inquiry allows us to come up with the best judgment we can, given the information which is currently available. We can try to base our beliefs and actions on the very best reasons possible (this is called **justification**).[71] This is epistemologically important. They further support this position when they observe that "despite its uncertainties inquiry is still the most reliable method (some would say the only method) for seeking the truth–even though we can't ever be completely certain that we've found it."[72] Accordingly, critical inquiry facilitates the acquisition of truth with great degree of certainty. Truth is one aim or goal or objective of inquiry:

> A central goal of inquiry is to have a better understanding of the world– an understanding that should enable us live richer and more effective lives. We wish to understand not only the nature of the phenomena but also how scholars, artists, scientists make sense of the world. We need to know how inquirers establish their theories and claims and how they weave what they are learning into great tapestry of knowledge.[73]

Hence besides the desire for truth, inquiry facilitates the understanding of the world which is indeed helps us to live better and effective lives. It leads us to appreciate what others have understood the world to be. In addition,

> Inquiry also provides a means for being more **autonomous** and self-directed. As thoughtful citizen as well as responsible individuals, we need a means for thinking critically about the complex issues which we face. Otherwise, we are in danger of falling into prey to the manipulation of marketers, the rhetoric of politicians, or the innumerable bad arguments which barrage us daily. The ability to make judgments on the basis of reason is central to our notion of what it means to be a mature, independent, and responsible human being.[74]

Inquiry facilitates autonomy and self-directedness, problem and decision making. It also guards one from fallacious thinking and ensures that judgments are made on the basis of reason.

Communication or dialogue is an important aspect of a mature, independent and responsible person hence in:

> Engaging in a dialogue focused on inquiry is also a way of "civilizing the discourse." An inquiry dialogue is a particular way of conducting a conversation which focuses on reasoning, is respectful of the views of the other participants, and gives these views serious and careful considerations.[75]

In a dialogue one is not seeking to win an argument or to score points but to understand the other person's viewpoint guided by the notion that the other person could be right hence civilising the discourse. This entails serious and careful consideration of the other participants in the dialogue as Socrates would do. Above all, treat your dialogue partner with respect. This is a basic principle of dialogue.

Finally, Inquiry is important for the democratic process according to Bailin and Battersby. We will revisit this aspect in the next section.

From the above we may summarize the values of inquiry approach to critical thinking as including reasoned judgement, justification or reasons for our beliefs, acquisition of truth and comprehension of the world; further it makes us autonomous, responsible, and facilitates dialogue with others respectfully as critical thinkers and all this is indispensable for a democratic living or life.

Richard Paul and Elder Linda's Strong Sense Critical Thinking for Education

Richard Paul and Linda Elder acknowledge, and indeed emphasize, the importance of including critical thinking in education. This acknowledgement is based on Paul-Elder distinction between weak sense and strong sense critical thinking. For them, education has to be modelled on the strong sense critical thinking.

In chapter one, we discussed their understanding of the two senses, hence in this section the task is to spell out how they relate the two to education. For them, they argue that students cultivate and unwilling to challenge deep-seated uncritical, egocentric and sociocentric habits of thought. Accordingly, students do not what to get out of their comfort zone so to speak. They use newly acquired skills and techniques to protect their accustomed worldview. This is the result of teaching critical thinking in the weak-sense. This we have seen in chapter one is the sophistry or atomistic weak-sense of critical thinking. This is wrong manner of teaching critical thinking since it is unhelpful to students for they end being uncritical.

The goal of this atomistic approach to critical thinking is to impact certain skills or techniques or proficiencies for purposes such as avoiding violating the very skills or techniques or questioning one's accustomed 'world view.'

If critical thinking is to be of any relevance to students, it must transcend from been atomistic in character or approach to teaching it in the strong sense. Paul and Elder assert that educators must embrace the Socratic criticality of seriously questioning previously held beliefs and assumptions. Teaching critical thinking in the strong sense must enhance the student's ability to question and cross-examine positions, seek clarity and precision and more so be skeptical. In essence they advocate that teaching critical thinking ought to be based on Socrates as the model for critical thinking. For Paul and Elder, and rightly so, failure to implement this teaching approach to critical thinking in the strong sense in education leads to constant frustrations and disappointment.

Paul and Elder's contention is that critical thinking must be taught focusing on those areas where egocentric, sociocentric biases, identity and vested interests are most deep seated in bid to counteract them. Such an approach is vital pedagogically and also practically, since egocentrism and sociocentrism reasoning, acting in bad faith and self-deceptions are vices which must be eradicated through teaching critical thinking in the strong sense.

Besides the above benefits accrued to teaching critical thinking, they also advocate the dialectical/dialogical approach to education. Accordingly, students should not be encouraged to the craft of winning arguments or sophistry but on the contrary, they ought to be motivated to the inclination of mutual dialogue or dialectic aimed at arriving at understanding either of an issue, argument or each other. This is a good ideal for teaching critical thinking, for Paul and Elder, since students embrace the give-and-take approach over against competing with each other in arguments or issues as was the mode of the sophists.

This is the ideal critical thinking to education according to Paul and Elder which also has ramifications for general life. The critical thinkers should sufficiently analyze the reasons by which they live, examine the assumptions, commitments, and logic of daily life. Strong sense critical thinking is indispensable in corporate and organizational life. According to Paul and Elder, a critical thinker should understand in corporate and organizational life, obstacles to critical thinking such as; the covert struggle for power; group definitions of reality; problem of bureaucracy; the problem of misleading success; unhealthy competition and success; irrational thinking in organizational life and should question organizational realities. As Paul and Elder put it, the basic problem is irrational, illogical, and unexamined living. In their book, *"Critical Thinking: Tools for Taking Charge of Your Professional and Personal Life,"* describe the relevance of critical thinking in everyday life. In summary, Paul and Elder assert that:

> Critical Thinking is about becoming a better thinker in every aspect of your life: in your career, and as a consumer, citizen, friend, parent, and lover. Discover the core skills of effective thinking; then analyze your own thought processes, identify weaknesses, and overcome them. Learn how to translate more effective thinking into better decisions, less frustration, more wealth, and above all, greater confidence to pursue and achieve your most important goals in life.

For Paul and Elder, in order to survive in a hard cruel world that is constantly changing, dangerous, and complicated, strong sense critical thinking is essential and indispensable. Accordingly, strong sense:

> Critical thinking helps us to see with new eyes. It does not require us to endanger ourselves or act against our best interest. We must integrate three dimensions of thought. We must be idealistic (and thus capable of imagining a better world). We must be realistic (and thus see things as they are). And we must be pragmatic (and thus adopt effective measures for moving toward our ideals).

Education should facilitate in designing one's life. Through the processing of learning, a critical thinker is able to model or design his or her life:

> In the life of a critical thinker, active learning is a tool for continually bridging the gap between what is and what could be. We then recognize the role that learning plays in our lives: establishing habits of continual improvement, of always reaching for the next level of skill, ability, and insight. Critical thinkers are lifelong learners and take charge of their experience, their learning, and the patterned behavior that defines their lives. They, in essence, "design" how they think and feel, and hence lay the foundation for how they live. They recognize that their thinking will shape their emotions and that their emotions impact their thinking. They use this recognition as a tool in self-deliberation.

Such critical thinkers are autonomous, design their goals, objectives, and critically evaluate logic of experiences, social forces, and new mass media such as the internet, issues or problem or decisions. In particular, the new mass media influence our thinking hence as critical thinkers we need to counteract the biasness or prejudices, misconceptions, half-truths, propaganda, stereotypes, over-simplification conceptualization of the world such as the third world or developing world, and media-engineered experiences or 'created meanings:'

> One of the most powerful ways to open our minds to alternative experiences, and thus to counteract the influence of social conditioning and the mass media, is to read "backward." That is, to read books printed in the past: 10 years ago, 20 years ago, 50 years ago, 100 years ago, 200 years ago, 300 years ago, 400 years ago, 500 years ago, 700 years ago, 800 years ago, even 2000 years ago, and more. This provides us with a unique perspective and the ability to step outside of the presuppositions and ideologies of the present day. When we read only in the present, no matter how widely, we are apt to absorb widely shared misconceptions taught and believed today as the truth.

While Siegel advocates for philosophy of science as the most vital way to foster critical thinking, Paul and Elder champion for reading backwards in order to to-think the present. Further, Paul and Elder justify the role of reading backwards by observing that:

> ...reading widely in the past creates multiple perspectives in the mind that enable one to better understand the complexities of the present. Critical reading creates a lens through which we come to better understand the role in history in our lives, even the role in history of critical thinking itself.

These are vital insights which were incorporated in the chapter three.

In conclusion, Paul and Elder lament and condemn the manner in which critical thinking is taught:

> To the present, critical thinking is being taught only to a minority of citizens, and even then usually in a one-sided way. Critical thinking tends to be taken no further than the skill of attacking and defending ideas, or more usually, the skill of attacking ideas inconsistent with the status quo and defending it in turn. Very often, critical thinking has been indistinguishable from "sophistry," the ability to manipulate people into thinking that the reigning ideology was always "correct and complete." Typically, only a small minority learns and uses critical thinking to question a ruling ideology. We can see this if we scan the history of critical thought.

Accordingly, and rightly so, critical thinking is not taught to everyone and as an indispensable social value. This is the perspective of Paul and Elder of the ideal critical thinking in education.

In the next section, we analyze John McPeck's critical thinking and education.

John McPeck: Critical Thinking and Education

In his book, *Critical Thinking and Education*, John McPeck, focuses on the place of critical thinking in education. McPeck writes that:

> What I shall argue is not only that it would be a good thing if our educational institutions could get students to be critical thinkers, but also that, insofar as the purpose of schools is to educate, this task logically cannot be accomplished without critical thinking. In short, critical thinking is a necessary condition for education.[76]

For him, the aim of education is to guide or make students to be critical thinkers and therefore, critical thinking is a necessary condition that is indispensable in the educational enterprise. In this respect for McPeck, "critical thinking must, therefore, command a place in any institution committed to the pursuit of education because critical thinking is a necessary condition of it."[77] This is the link between critical thinking and education.

However critical thinking as presented, for him, does not foster in students' critical thought. He argues that this is the case because critical thinking is taught as general skills. Hence his book, *Critical Thinking and Education* seek to assert the "proper" conceptualization of critical thinking and its role in education and how it should be taught.

For him, the conceptualizing and teaching critical thinking as general skills is wrong. McPeck articulates that to the claim teach students to think is false and at best misleading. Critical thinking for him cannot be taught. This is the case because to think is to think about something as discussed in chapter one and two. His main thesis then is it impossible to teach critical thinking as an independent subject. For him a general "critical thinking" course is a mistake because it cannot develop skills/abilities and dispositions that are applicable in any of a range of fields such as history, politics, physics, and chemistry among other disciplines. He denies and rejects critical thinking as subject that can be taught in its own and more so that it is a general skill. He further contentiously and unacceptable writes that:

> The real problem with uncritical students is not a deficiency in a general skill, such as logical ability but rather a more general lack of education in the traditional sense...I shall attempt to show why courses in logic fail to accomplish the goal of developing critical thinkers and how the epistemology of various subjects would be the most reasonable route to the end...there is both a conceptual and a pedagogical link between epistemology, critical thinking, and education, but the study of logic or critical thinking as such has no part in this linkage.[78]

As discussed in chapter one and as reflected in this quotation, McPeck argues that critical thinking can only and effectively be taught from as myriads of epistemologies. He then blames the traditional teaching of logic and critical thinking as the main reason for the nature of uncritical students and calls for a replacement of both with subject oriented epistemologies:

> The standard approach for developing critical thinking ... has been to teach logic and various kinds of reasoning skills. Presumably, the rationale for this is that since logic plays a role in every subject, and logic is intimately related to reasoning, the study of logic should improve one's ability to assess arguments and statements in any subject area. What I wish to argue is that the plausibility of this reasoning can be sustained only seriously underestimating the complexity of the different kinds of information used in arguments and by overestimating the role

of logic in these assessments of some statement or argument, the major requirements for such assessment are epistemological, not logical in character.[79]

McPeck then seeks to describe how conceptual and a pedagogical link between epistemology and critical thinking can be infused in education. He argues that critical thinking can and must be taught as domain-specific or subject-specific or content-specific, that is, particular epistemologies. That it is only meaningful to have critical thinking inbuilt in particular or specific disciplines. For McPeck, critical thinking can and must be explained by, or reduced to, specialized knowledge or domain-specific skills. This leads him to conclude that critical thinking associate "conceptually with particular activities and special fields of knowledge."[80] The implication is that critical thinking is specific to a range of fields such as physics, chemistry, history, and politics among other disciplines. Thinking is thinking in a specific category or domain or subject area.

This is McPeck's model of critical thinking and education hence it is "muddled nonsense" to conceptualize general and taught critical thinking skills/abilities and dispositions as a distinct subject on its own.

There are many reactions to McPeck's position due to his contentious position as discussed in chapter two. As a recap, philosophical theorists such as Siegel, Ennis and Paul advocate for the incorporation of both general and specific critical thinking skills/abilities and dispositions in educationality. It follows from this that it makes sense to talk about critical thinking as a distinct subject and that it therefore can profitably be taught as such. The statement 'I teach critical thinking,' simpliciter, is not vacuous because there are both subject and generalized skill/abilities and dispositions properly called critical thinking that can be taught. In essence and contrary to McPeck, critical thinking should be reified into a curriculum subject and the teaching of it an area of expertise of its own. In addition, to the extent that critical thinking entails specific subject X and also general skills/abilities and dispositions it is both conceptually and practically viable.

Finally, McPeck misses the point when indeed he rejects the role of logic in critical thinking. Logic is central to critical thinking as vital tool for the determining good argumentation from bad ones. Again McPeck must realize that indeed the proper conceptualizations of epistemology and rationality are the handmaiden of critical thinking and indispensable in educationality as discussed in chapter two. Siegel regards McPeck's perspective as an "unsuccessful effort." Accordingly, McPeck does not both to justify critical thinking as educational ideal. McPeck opts to go along the line of thought of "general lack of education in the traditional sense" as cause of lack of critical thought. For Siegel "…McPeck's view of the relation between education and critical thinking–that one entails the other…"[81] is unsuccessful attempt to justify critical thinking as an education ideal.

Next we discuss "thinking in education" according to Mathew Lipman.

Lipman and "Thinking in Education"

Lipman asserts that "the two principal aims of education have been the transmission of knowledge and the cultivation of wisdom."[82] He then explores a number of worthwhile concerns regarding the first aim of education. He observes that there are some issues in the first principal aim: "knowledge, conceived in such societies as a stockpile of truths, is transmitted from the older to the younger generations. It is thought of as a body of eternal verities, perennially applicable to an unchanging world."[83] Such perspective is indifferent to the notions of alterability, fallibilism and critical thinking. Of significant concern for Lipman is that such a conception does not entail critical thinking but a banking conception of knowledge.

This conception becomes obsolete, irrelevant and hence the need to rethink afresh of such a conception. He points out the contemporary conception of education as inquiry combines the transmission of knowledge as well as the cultivation of wisdom:

> Our contemporary conception of education as inquiry combines both of these aims. Its emphasis is on the process as well as on the product- -on thinking as well as on knowledge, on inquiry as well as on truth. It grants each discipline a slowly changing, ever-accumulating fund of knowledge representing the precipitated experience in that discipline. Nevertheless, students are nowadays expected to think critically, and not merely to learn what is already known.[84]

Inquiry approach emphasis thinking, acquisition of knowledge ad truth. Inquiry underscores thinking critically, and not only learning. He proceeds to stress that "critical thinking, then, is a cultivation of that strand of traditional education which stressed the cultivation of wisdom and its application to practice and to life."[85] Critical thinking entails fostering wisdom and applying it to practice and to life.

Lipman pays attention to "critical thinking" which he regards as poorly understood and conceptualized. He then seeks look for a more viable conceptualization, which will be relevant to education. Lipman asks and makes the observation:

> But what is critical thinking? If we are to foster and strengthen critical thinking in the schools and colleges, we need a clear conception of what it is and of what it can be. We need to know its defining features, its characteristic outcomes, and the underlying conditions that make it.[86]

Lipman seeks to develop a conceptualization, outline the features, characteristics and conditions of critical thinking. As we expounded in chapter one, he defines critical thinking as "skilful, responsible thinking that facilitates judgements because it relies on criteria, is self-correcting and is sensitive to context."[87] According to him, educators must understand this definition "if schools are to succeed in teaching critical thinking."[88] For him, critical thinking is a skill, whose outcome is judgement based on criteria, is self-correcting and takes into consideration its context. He asserts that the criteria of reason facilitates good thinking:

> The improvement of student thinking--from ordinary thinking to good thinking--depends heavily upon the ability of such students to identify and cite good reasons for the opinions they utter. Students can be brought to realize that, for a reason to be called good, it must be relevant to the opinion in question and *stronger* (in the sense of being more readily accepted, or assumed to be the case) than the opinion in question.[89]

What is he offering is that educationality that is based in a functional brand of rationality to which the promotion and practice of reason is employed, foster reasonableness and hence critical thinking to students. Lipman advocates that the criteria used when thinking critically is of rationality, which operate dynamically and critically. His definition further emphasizes that valuable instruments of rational procedure are criteria and standards that are vital for education.

Lipman uses the term "community of inquiry" when speaking of the ideal classroom. The community of inquiry fosters inquisitiveness and dispositions to learn and think:

> One of the most important advantages of converting the classroom into a community of inquiry (in addition to the undoubted improvement of moral climate it brings about) is that the members of the community begin looking for and correcting each other's methods and procedures.

Consequently, insofar as each participant is able to internalize the methodology of the community as a whole, each participant is able to become self-correcting in his or her own thinking.[90]

Community of inquiry methodology analyzes the problems and the questions interrogated facilitate learning, self-correcting and correcting of others. The end product of such an activity, is critical thinking. More so, the concept of judgment is enriched in the Lipmanian ideal community of inquiry. Further, Lipman points out that critical thinking is reliable when it is able to be assessed by self and others. This is to imply that critical thinkers must evaluate their own thought processes and those of the others. This critical reflection of one's own thought processes and those of others progresses critical thinking processes via the process of self-correction. In the community of inquiry, critical thinking occurs when participants have to examine their own arguments and the arguments of others in the dialogue. Since the inquiry operates on participants being reflective, this method naturally adopts critical thinking as its practice.

Lipman then seeks to justify critical thinking as an ideal for education when he raises the following questions: "What, then, is the relevance of critical thinking to the enhancement of elementary school, secondary school and college education? Why are so many educators convinced that critical thinking is the key to educational reform?"[91] These questions lay the foundations for him to demonstrate that critical thinking is vital for students because it facilitates thinking and judgement.

He writes that "part of the answer lies in the gradual shift that is occurring in the focus of education–the shift from *learning* to *thinking*. We want students to think for themselves, and not merely to learn what other people have thought."[92] Lipmanian perspective condemns without reservation the concept of learning without thinking as completely opposed to everything education ought to be. This is because it destroys and abhors criticality. Education, for him, must foster independent thinking and good judgement among those being educated. He further observes that:

> But another part of the answer lies in the fact that we want students who can do more than merely think: it is equally important that they exercise good Judgment. It is good judgment that characterized the sound interpretation of a written text, the well-balance, coherent composition, the lucid comprehension of what one listens to, and the persuasive argument. It is good judgment that enables one to weigh and grasp what a

statement or passage states, assumes, implies or suggests. And this good judgment cannot be operative unless it rests upon proficient reasoning skills that can assure competency in inference, as well as upon proficient inquiry, concept-formation and translation skills. If critical thinking can produce an improvement in education, it will be because it increases the quantity and quality of meaning that students derive from what they read and perceive and that they express in what they write and say.[93]

Education ought to foster not only good thinking or thinking critically but also nurture the practice of good judgment. The benefits accrued by good judgment whose foundation is critical thinking, are numerous as he indicates in the above quoted passage.

This is to be realized if the curriculum is to incorporate critical thinking. He asserts that "the infusion of critical thinking into the curriculum carries with it the promise of the academic empowerment of the student."[94] The educational curriculum as part of its desiderata should incorporate critical thinking. On acknowledging this, then it will be necessary to interrogate the best way to blend the two.

Lipman warns and cautions that "in the meantime, it will be well to keep in mind that students who are not taught to use criteria in a way that is both sensitive to context and self-corrective are not being taught to think critically."[95] Students must be educated properly on the role of criteria, its sensitivity to context and on self-correcting for effective fostering of critical thinking.

Using the analogy of an orchestra, he argues that:

> Critical thinking, as we know, is skillful thinking, and skills are proficient performances that satisfy relevant criteria. When we think critically, we are required to orchestrate a vast variety of cognitive skills, grouped in families such as reasoning skills, concept formation skills, inquiry skills and translation skills. Without these skills, we would be unable to draw meaning from a written text or from a conversation. Nor could we impart meaning to a conversation or to what we write. But just as, in an orchestra, there are such families as the woodwinds, the brasses and the strings, so there are these different families of cognitive skills. And just as, within each orchestral family, there are individual instruments--oboes and violas and French horns, each with its own standards of proficient performance, so there are individual cognitive skills, like deductive inference or classification that represent particular kinds of proficient performances in accordance with relevant criteria. We are all familiar with the fact that an otherwise splendid musical performance can be ruined if so much as a single instrumentalist performs below acceptable standards. Likewise, the mobilization and perfection of the cognitive skills that go to make up critical thinking cannot neglect any of these skills without jeopardizing the process as a whole. This is why

> we cannot be content to give students practice in a handful of cognitive skills while neglecting all the others that are needed for the competency in inquiry, in language and in thought that is the hallmark of proficient critical thinkers. Instead of selecting and polishing a few skills that we think will do the trick, we must begin with the raw subject matter of communication and inquiry--with reading, listening, speaking, writing and reasoning--and we must cultivate whatever skills the mastery of such processes entails. It is only when we do this that we realize that only logic, epistemology and other philosophical disciplines can provide both the skills and the criteria that are presently lacking in the curriculum.[96]

What he stresses is that critical thinking should not work in insolation but it should be 'orchestrated' with other skills such as reading, listening, speaking, writing, cognitive skills such as reasoning skills derived from logic, epistemology and other philosophical disciplines to derive meaning from judgment. This is the ideal of critical thinking to education, according to Lipman.

In the next section, we briefly explore Ken Robinson perspective.

Ken Robinson on "Do Schools Kill Creativity?"

Ken Robinson in his books; *The Element: How Finding Your Passion Changes Everything (2009), Out of Our Minds: Learning to be Creative* (2011), and *Finding Your Element: How to Discover Your Talents and Passions and Transform Your Life,* (2013) focuses on the question: *"do schools kill creativity?*

Ken Robinson argues that the current education system is *"educating people out of their creativity."* Accordingly, the conventional system of schooling is "killing" of creativity.

His argument then as remedy to problem is that creativity now is as important in education as literacy, and we should treat it with the same status. In other words, schooling must promote creativity, in essence critical thinking.

Learners need to be helped in the systems of education to be creative and essentially to acquires critical thinking skills/abilities and dispositions. The systems of education are among the institutions that foster and reinforce such critical and creative skills but this is not the case, according to Ken Robinson. He calls for the recognition that teaching content and skills is of minor import if learners do not also develop critical thinking skills and dispositions. His perspective is a reaction to institutionalized functions of educations that stifle criticality.

6.3 Critical Thinking and Democracy

One theme that kept coming up in the discussions of educational aims or ideals is the relevance of critical thinking to democracy. The importance and practical aims of critical thinking as educational ideal by some of its philosophical theorists also led to its consideration as an ideal for democratic living or life. In this respect, this section focuses on the important contributions to democracy from a critical thinking perspective. For the purposes and intentions of demonstrating the relevance of critical thinking to democracy, it will suffice to discuss the views of Harvey Siegel, Israel Scheffler, Robert Ennis, Bailin and Battersby. We begin with the views of Harvey Siegel.

Harvey Siegel in his various works has argued for the relevance or fundamentality of critical thinking skills/abilities and dispositions to democracy. We have illustrated that for Siegel, democracy is one of the aims and reasons for justifying critical thinking as an educational ideal. He writes that:

> ... I have offered four reasons for thinking that critical thinking, as just conceptualized, constitutes a fundamental educational ideal: respect for students as persons; self-sufficiency and preparation for adulthood; initiation into rational traditions; and democratic living.[97]

In this section, we wish to spell at length this fourth reason, that is, the link between democratic living or life and critical thinking. Siegel observes that:

> The democratic citizen requires a wide variety of the many things which education can provide. She needs to be well-informed with respect to all sorts of matters of fact; to grasp fully the nature of democratic institutions and embrace fully their responsibilities; to treat her fellow democrats as equal partners in political life, etc. She also needs to be able to examine public policy concerns: to judge intelligently the many issues facing her society; to challenge and seek reasons for proposed changes (and continuations) of policy; to assess such reasons fairly and impartially, and to put aside self-interest when it is appropriate to do so; and so on. If the democratic citizen is not a critical thinker, she is significantly hampered in her ability to contribute helpfully to public life. Democracies rely for their health and well-being on the intelligence of their citizens. My point is simply that such intelligence, if it is truly to be of benefit, must consist in part of the skills, attitudes, abilities and traits of the critical thinker. It is not simply an intelligent citizenry, but a critical one, which democracy wants.[98]

From the above quotation, Siegel asserts that education must provide to citizenry eight ideals: intelligence, information, facilitate understanding of nature of democratic institutions and embrace fully their responsibilities, duties and obligations, respectful treatment of others, ability to examine public policies, ability to judge impartially societal issues, ability to question change of policies, and to be impartial.

Clearly, he conceptualizes critical thinking as an educational aim or goal that ought to promote democracy. What should be the aim of education? What is the nature of democratic states? What is the proper education for citizens? Siegel responds that "one common answer, which we endorse, is that it should aim at fostering in students, the skills and abilities, and the attitudes and dispositions, needed to participate in decision making and more generally, in democratic life."[99] Accordingly, the nature of democratic society requires educated critical citizenry. Critical thinking as an educational ideal must and ought to foster these skills/abilities, and the attitudes or dispositions or traits of mind or habits of mind which lead to empowering students to be critical citizens. For him intelligent citizenry is important but not sufficient for both intelligent and critical citizenry is necessary and sufficient for democratic governance, life or living. He observes that:

> What is need is, I submit, is a critical citizenry; that is, citizens who are able, and disposed, to settle matters of public policy and concerns by appeal to relevant reasons. For democratic states to flourish, their citizens must be able to conceive, consider, and properly evaluate reasons for and against alternative policies and practices concerning the many, varied matters that require public deliberation and decision. Citizens must be able to construct arguments imaginatively, and to assess their own arguments and those of others in accordance with the epistemic principles governing the assessment reasons and arguments, in order to determine wisely the course of social policies and institutions. Without a critical citizenry, the state itself is threatened.[100]

For Siegel, Epistemology, a crucial component of critical thinking skills/abilities, is vital for enabling critical citizenry in conceiving, considering, evaluating reasons for and against public policy. Education ought to empower citizenry in order that they can raise good arguments regarding public matters. Any state, according to Siegel, which does not facilitate an education that fosters critical thinking skills/abilities and dispositions, is threatened.

In this respect, public policies and decisions are subjected to critical appraisal by critical citizenry due to the critical thinking skills/ abilities and dispositions hence promoting a vibrate democracy.

Critical citizenry employs the use of reasons assessment and in particular the epistemic principles to consider and evaluate public matters. Siegel captures this when he writes that:

> Still, if democratic social organisation and change can be independently justified, as we think, then critical thinking and skilled argumentation will be of fundamental importance for participants engaged in the contemplation and actualisation of social change. For they promise to contribute importantly to the quality of democratic discussion of social policy and social change, precisely because critical thinkers can make better–epistemologically better–judgement and decisions concerning the desirability of potential social changes. These judgements and decisions will be better precisely because they will be based on fair evaluation of relevant evidence and argument, and in this way reflective of the standards of reason assessment which rightly guide and inform critical thinking.[101]

Critical thinking is fundamental to democracy for it helps citizenry participate and contribute critically to social and political matters. This is due to the fact that they support their arguments epistemologically, that is, on basis of reasons and justifications. For Siegel, uncritical citizenry in democratic states do harm to themselves and the state because:

> Such a citizen has no adequate way to contribute to public discussion, to voice her concerns, to protect her and her community's interests, or to work for constructive political change. She is marginalised, left on the side, unable to participate meaningfully in democratic life. Her lack of critical abilities and dispositions renders her unable to enjoy the fruits of that life.[102]

Accordingly, we must deplore uncritical and marginalised citizenry since it leads to poor quality of life. It is to be stated that democratic society needs people to think critically if they are to participate, be heard, promote common good, human and political rights. Voicing concerns, that is, ability to question is vital for social, political and constructive change in society. Hence the link between critical thinking and democracy is of fundamental importance. For Siegel then, critical thinking is of fundamentality to democratic living or life since it provides good thinking, careful analysis and reasoned deliberation ensuring critical citizenry and flourishing of democracy.

Israel Scheffler also weighs on the relevance of critical thinking as skills/abilities and dispositions to democracy when he writes that:

> We talk of "citizenship" as if it were a set of skills, whereas our educational aim is, in fact, not merely to teach people how to be good citizens but, in particular, to be good citizens, not merely how to go voting, but to vote.

> We talk about giving "the skills required for democratic living," when actually we are concerned that they acquire democratic habits, norms propensities.[103]

Scheffler's argues that skills/abilities and habits, norms, propensities, or dispositions are essential for proper democratic living. He offers a fundamental link between critical thinking and democracy.

Robert Ennis stresses the significant role of critical thinking to democracy when he asserts that:

> Critical thinking is also important to the survival of a democratic way of life. If the people in a democracy do not make reasonable decisions in voting and the conduct of their everyday public lives, then the democracy in which they live is threaten. Given the current conditions, once democracy is lost, it will be very difficult to recover. This is because modern technology (TVs, computers, etc) makes available superbly efficient techniques for monitoring and controlling people's activities and thoughts. Unfortunately, these techniques are readily available for use by any totalitarian government. So the reestablishment of democracy, if lost throughout the world, would, I fear be unlikely. Assuming that democracy should be encouraged and preserved, we then have additional responsibility. We have a public responsibility to try to make reasonable civic decisions–that is, to try, to think critically in civic matters, and to help others do so as well.[104]

From this quotation, it is clear that critical thinking is vital for citizenry in making informed critical decision in matters of voting, evaluating public policies and decisions. This is important for if society comprises of uncritical citizenry, then it is under threat. The modern day mass media and its new platforms such as the internet with its various aspects can be used for controlling and manipulating the masses when it comes to political matters if they are controlled by totalitarian regimes. To establish or re-establish democracy under such circumstances is not an easy task. To do so, we need rationality, reasonableness, that is, critical thinking. This will provide participation in democratic processes institutions and procedures in a reasoned discourse and deliberations, which according to him, is the citizenry public responsibility. This is possible through an education, which fosters critical thinking skills/abilities and dispositions to students and the masses at large to enable them participate in civic matters. Consequently, if the citizenry is uncritical, then the uncritical masses and democracy itself is under threat. The democratic way of living becomes an illusion. Hence there is the need to prepare the citizenry to participate in democratic processes and institutions by fostering critical thinking skills/abilities and dispositions. This ensures that citizenry make mature, independent and informed political decisions hence responsible politically in their choices.

Bailin and Battersby contribute to the complex issue of democracy when they assert that:

> Inquiry allows us to interact in a more civil and respectful manner, even when we disagree. Treating the views of others with respectful consideration does not mean that we necessarily agree with these views, perhaps even disagree passionately. Yet respect for others is a basic moral principle, and the freedom to hold one's belief is a central norm of a democratic society.[105]

Accordingly, critical inquiry is viable to the aspects of democratic life such as liberties or freedoms, responsible participation and pluralistic dialogue, mutual respectful understanding of individuals, and the fulfillment of a common civil life, and reasonable dialogue.

In conclusion, this section has focused on enhancing critical thinking as a crucial component for students as well as citizens who need it to participate in political society. The ideal of critical thinking is of indispensable value to pluralistic and democratic society. Embracing critical thinking as a democratic ideal entails commitment to equal political institutional and procedural participation. No one will feel left out or marginalised or side lined in such a democratic ideal informed by critical thinking. Such an ideal manifest a reasoned deliberation, which characterize democratic state. Again, critical thinking makes citizenry to make informed decisions when voting, evaluate policies and institutions. Essentially, lack of critical thinking skills/abilities and dispositions leads to bad governance and poor democracy. Therefore, critical thinking is critical for any democratic society, living or life.

6.4 Critical Thinking and Religion

In this section, we will focus on the relevance of critical thinking to religion. My venture into religions focuses on the difficulties that are germane to them and how critical thinking is helpful in shedding some light. This task is not without reservations. It is completely impossible to cover all religions and their aspects within the scope of this book. We will therefore be very general in addressing the relevance of critical thinking to religions. It therefore suffices to mention some of the major religions in the world such as Judaism, Buddhism, Hinduism, Sikhism, Christianity, African religion(s) among others. In what follows, we will attempt to demonstrate how critical thinking as skills/abilities and dispositions, is relevant to religions.

Unfortunately, 'critical thinking' has a negative connotation within religious circles because it is associated with assessing or even criticizing God, religious scriptures, doctrines, experiences, language, miracles, faith, dogmas, signs and symbols. On the basis of this, critical thinking is stifled. On the contrary, critical thinking requires that a person base her beliefs on reason, facts and evidence. A critical thinker assesses the reasons and justifications of one's beliefs. She must be able to distinguish if the given answers to questions such as – who is God? What is the nature of God? What is the origin of the universe? Was the universe created or can it be explained otherwise? What is faith and what is its relation to reason? What are miracles, religious experiences, signs and symbols? How is language used in religion? Is evidence or verification necessary for religions? – are good reasons.

Siegel, in addressing teaching and reasoning issues in the philosophical novel, *The Brothers Karamazov*, written by Fyodor Dostoyevsky points out that this novel highlights:

> ...fundamental issues such the existence of God, the problem of evil, the relation between religion and morality, the nature of morality, the relation between psychology and philosophy, the relations between motivation, explanation and justification, the conflict between reason and faith, the nature and power of rationality, and the role of reason in human life."[106]

The novel deals with issues of atheism, atheists, the notions of belief and unbelief, goodness, faith, fideism, freewill, the meaning of human life and the reasons for justifying each of these issues. In particular, the problem of evil and suffering raises fundamental philosophical concerns and critical questions:

> ...how can a loving god permit the horrible and seemingly senseless suffering of which he cannot help but be aware ... [Suffering] ... a vivid type of evil most difficult to reconcile with the existence of god. [107]

The world is full of unspeakable, horrific and terrifying suffering which "explaining it does not explain it away."[108] The novel depicts the "conflict between belief and unbelief, but also the more general conflict between faith and reason,"[109] and how reason and rationality is used to address these issues. This highlights that the content of religion must be subjected to critical thinking. In treating the contents of this great novel, Siegel inevitably brings to attention the role of philosophy and in particular, critical thinking in religion. Though his intention is to demonstrate that fiction can be used to foster and enhance critical thinking skills/abilities and dispositions to students, however, in the process, this goal is extended to matters to do with religion and philosophy of religion.

In short, there is no blanket acceptance without questioning religious matters when one embraces critical thinking. Bailin and Battersby capture this when they advise that "believing something because I have good reasons for the belief is vastly preferable to believing something uncritically, just because someone with power has told me to believe it or because that's what the people around me believe."[110] The problem of identification with our beliefs or religion uncritically is a major problem today. Any religion we identify ourselves with, it becomes a sign of weakness to question it hence we fail to "subject those views to critical scrutiny."[111]

Bailin and Battersby caution that "even some modes of reasoning such as appeal to sacred texts as source of truth about the word, are culturally based approaches that are often problematic.[112] Siegel calls for appraisal of belief while Ennis definition of critical thinking as *"a process, the goal of which is to make reasonable decisions about what to believe and what to do,"* has implication to religious matters.

In conclusion, fostering of critical thinking skills/abilities and dispositions encourages a questioning attitude towards religions. In this respect, people are encouraged to question, decide for themselves what they believe and in so doing, they protect themselves from religious indoctrinations, extremisms are able to discern the truth from falsehood and are able to evaluate what constitutes good and bad reasons in religions.

6.5   Conclusion

This chapter has focused on the relevance of critical thinking to education, democracy, religion and general life. In so doing, it has served the purposes of watering down the view that critical thinking focuses on internal or inner house matters as exposed in chapter two, paying little attention to social matters.

What follows from these discussions is that critical thinking theorists have emphasized the idea that critical thinking skills/abilities and dispositions have indispensable value to education.

Essentially, for them, the aim of education generally is to foster critical thinking skills/abilities and dispositions that can, should and ought to be factored in educational desiderata. They have deliberated appropriately on critical thinking as an educational ideal to be factored in curricula content, its implementation, the manner of teaching and learning. Education system as a set of strict hierarchical structure loathes critical thinking as an educational aim since the teacher is no longer "the knower" and the students would not be the docile receipts of their knowledge. Such an order of strict hierarchical structure does not promote students' criticality, treat students with respect or encourage them to raise questions, at the best docility is the perking order. It was noted that such an order of educational activity does not introduce students to rational traditions of knowledge and how such traditions have benefited from critical thinking nor do they initiate or prepare students for adult life. This status quo is to be rejected and replaced with critical thinking as an educational ideal.

For the theorists the term "critical" is a valued educational aim. They urge educators to help students become more skeptical toward commonly accepted truisms. Again, they agree about the need for more critically oriented classrooms. What emerged is that education ought to challenge students to be critical thinkers; not merely indoctrinative or homogeneity in nature. For education is not about indoctrination or mere acquisition of knowledge but fosters critical thinking. Again, it is important to note, following Siegel, that there are no dogmatic or orthodoxy solutions for the educational problems but a critical and more so philosophical considerations or evaluation. Specifically, philosophy and in particular, critical thinking was seen as indispensable in evaluating the standardised tests or minimum competency test (MCT), as an educational practice and how such practices abhor critical thinking as an educational ideal. Such educational practices, it was argued stifle critical thinking skills/abilities and dispositions. Clearly, it was argued that educational policies, practices and directive must have critical thinking and in general, philosophical considerations or in puts. Essentially, therefore, the application of critical thinking skills/abilities and dispositions as educational ideal, enrich and deepen educational activities as reflected in the ideas of Israel Scheffler, Harvey Siegel, Mathew Lipman, Richard Paul and Linda Elder, Robert Ennis, Ken Robinson and Sharon

Bailin and Mark Battersby.

In line with their ideas of the relevance of critical thinking to educational activities, we also examined their views on the fundamentality of critical thinking to democracy. It emerged that fostering critical thinking is important for democracy to flourish. It was pointed out that critical thinking skills/abilities and dispositions are core aspects for a critical citizenry to participate in a democratic society or life or living. The acquisition of these critical thinking skills/abilities and dispositions facilitates active, critical, competent participation in policies, public matters, institutions and political discussions. Education was argued as the means to this ideal, that is, it must and ought to foster these skills/abilities and dispositions essential for a democratic living or life.

In addition, the chapter focused on the significance of critical thinking to religion. We argued that critical thinking is of fundamentality to religions in order to discern the truth and to be able to raise questions about religions. In essence, the beliefs of a critical thinker are to be justified by reason, that is, they are to be based on good reasons or rational justification.

From the discussions in this chapter, it has become clear that critical thinking is fundamental for understanding our "everydayness" in society. Critical thinking skills/abilities and dispositions are applicable to general life. Thinking that is productive, purposeful and intentional is at the centre of our lives. In this respect, critical thinking transcends the specialized and technical activity and becomes a way of life. By applying critical thinking skills/abilities and dispositions, people develop an understanding of the processes they can employ whenever they encounter problems, unfamiliar information, decision making and new ideas. Critical thinking leads to a philosophy of life implying the quality of life of a free critical thinking individual in all domains of life. Critical thinking skills/abilities and dispositions are indispensable tools to suitably react to the new challenges of an ever changing world and the quest to understand it. It is plausible to note that the problematic and complex aspects of life, education, democratic life or living and religious aspects are yet to be resolved and certainly need to be frequently revisited and reviewed from a critical thinking dimension. Hence, this is not last word on these matters and much more is needed to be spelled out in length and therefore, the need for further research.

6.6 End Notes

1. Harvey Siegel, *Rationality Redeemed? Further Dialogues on an Educational Ideal*, (New York: Routledge, 1997), 2.
2. Ibid., 65.
3. Israel Scheffler, *Reason and Teaching* (New York: Bobbs-Merill, 1973), 1.
4. Israel Scheffler, *Conditions of Knowledge,* (Chicago: Scott Foresman and Company, 1965), 107.
5. Ibid., 63.
6. Israel Scheffler, "Philosophy and the Curriculum," in *Reason and Teaching,* (New York: Bobbs-Merill ,1973), 32.
7. Israel Scheffler, *The Language of Education,* Springfield, III.: Charles C. Thomas, 1960, 57.
8. Israel Scheffler, *Reason and Teaching,* op.cit., 143.
9. Ibid.,
10. Israel Scheffler, "University Scholarship and the Education of Teachers," in *Reason and Teaching,* op. cit., 92.
11. Israel Scheffler, (1991). "*In Praise of the Cognitive Emotions.*" In Praise of the Cognitive Emotions, Israel Scheffler (New York: Routledge), 64.
12. Ibid., 90.
13. Harvey Siegel, *Educating Reason: Rationality, Critical Thinking and Education,* (Routledge, 1988), 42.
14. Ibid., 32.
15. Harvey Siegel, *Education's Epistemology: Rationality, Diversity and Critical Thinking,* (New York: Oxford University Press, 2017), 280.
16. Harvey Siegel, *Educating Reason: Rationality, Critical Thinking and Education,* **op. cit.,** 60.
17. Harvey Siegel, *Education's Epistemology: Rationality, Diversity and Critical Thinking ,* op.cit., 5.
18. Harvey Siegel, *Critical Thinking as an Educational Ideal.* The Educational Forum 1980; 10, November.
19. Ibid., 11.
20. Ibid.
21. Ibid.,
22. Ibid., 12.
23. Harvey Siegel, *Educating Reason: Rationality, Critical Thinking and Education,* op. cit., 46.
24. Ibid.
25. Ibid., 47.
26. Ibid., 48

27. Ibid.
28. Ibid., 47.
29. See ibid., 48-51.
30. Ibid., 50.
31. Ibid., 51.
32. Ibid.
33. Ibid., 54.
34. Ibid.
35. Ibid., 55.
36. Ibid., 54.
37. Ibid., 50.
38. Ibid., 56.
39. Ibid., 57.
40. Ibid., 54.
41. Ibid., 59.
42. Ibid., 60.
43. Harvey Siegel, *Educating Reason: Rationality, Critical Thinking and Education,* op. cit., 60.
44. Ibid., 62.
45. Ibid., 69.
46. See. Ibid., 88
47. Ibid., 89.
48. Ibid., 90.
49. Ibid., 110.
50. Ibid., 112.
51. Ibid., 113.
52. Ibid., 116.
53. Harvey Siegel, *Rationality Redeemed? Further Dialogues on an Educational Ideal,* op. cit., 44.
54. Ibid.
55. Ibid.,
56. Ibid., 46.
57. Ibid., 22.
58. Ibid., 49.
59. Harvey Siegel, *Educating Reason: Rationality, Critical Thinking and Education,* op. cit., 137.
60. Ibid., 41.
61. Harvey Siegel, *Rationality Redeemed? Further Dialogues on an Educational Ideal,* op cit., 20.
62. Sharon Bailin, *Critical and Creative Thinking, Informal Logic* Vol. IX.1, Winter 1987, 23.

63. Ibid., 24
64. Ibid., 27.
65. Ibid., 28.
66. Ibid., 23.
67. Ibid., 28.
68. Ibid., 29.
69. Ibid.
70. Ibid.
71. Sharon Bailin & Mark Battersby, *Reason in the Balance: An Inquiry Approach to Critical Thinking,* op. cit., 18.
72. Ibid.
73. Ibid.
74. Ibid.
75. Ibid., 18-19
76. McPeck, J. E. *Critical Thinking and Education,* (Oxford: Martin Robertson, 1981), 34.
77. Ibid., 37.
78. Ibid., 22.
79. Ibid., 23.
80. Ibid., 56.
81. Harvey Siegel, *Educating Reason: Rationality, Critical Thinking and Education,* op. cit., 54.
82. Matthew Lipman, "*Critical Thinking: What Can It Be?*" *Inquiry, Series 1,* No.1. 1988, 4.
83. Ibid.
84. Ibid.
85. Ibid.
86. Ibid.
87. Mathew Lipman, *Thinking in Education,* (New York Cambridge University Press, 2003), 212
88. Matthew Lipman, "*Critical Thinking: What Can It Be?*" op.cit., 38.
89. Ibid., 7-8
90. Ibid., 11.
91. Ibid., 13.
92. Ibid.,
93. Ibid.,
94. Ibid.,
95. Ibid., 10-11
96. Ibid., 14.
97. Harvey Siegel, *Rationality Redeemed? Further Dialogues on an Educational Ideal,* op. cit., 4.

98. rationality 60.
99. Harvey Siegel, *Education's Epistemology: Rationality, Diversity and Critical Thinking,* op. cit., 280.
100. Ibid., 281
101. Harvey Siegel, *Rationality Redeemed? Further Dialogues on an Educational Ideal,* op. cit., 97.
102. Harvey Siegel, *Education's Epistemology: Rationality, Diversity and Critical Thinking,* op. cit., 281.
103. Israel Scheffler, *The Language of Education,* Springfield, Ill.: Charles C. Thomas, 1960, 98-9.
104. Robert H. Ennis, *Critical Thinking,* (Prentice–hall, Inc, 1996), xvii.
105. Sharon Bailin & Mark Battersby, *Reason in the Balance: An Inquiry Approach to Critical Thinking* (Cambridge: Hackett publishing Company, Inc.2016), 19.
106. Harvey Siegel, *Rationality Redeemed? Further Dialogues on an Educational Ideal* op. cit., 39.
107. Ibid., 40-41.
108. Ibid., 42.
109. Ibid., 43.
110. Sharon Bailin & Mark Battersby, *Reason in the Balance: An Inquiry Approach to Critical Thinking,* op. cit., 18.
111. Ibid., 269.
112. Ibid., 270.

CHAPTER SEVEN
CONCLUSION

In this chapter, we wish to summarize and recapitulate this book and use it as a way to indicate the next steps and implications that we suggest.

In chapter one, it was stated, that the aim of this book was to expose, assess and spell out in details the nature of critical thinking. The subsequent chapters have shown that there is no easy answer to that question. Hence in chapter one, we elaborated the definitions, theories and nature of critical thinking with intentions to identify its underpinning foundations, methodological, characteristics, scope, goals and its processes. Clearly, what is important was not the definition of critical thinking which of course is of fundamental need but the key point is to initiate students to become critical thinkers. In view of this, various models of critical thinking were considered for the purposes mentioned above. In understanding of all these critical thinking models, one appreciates their unique aspects, their commons views as well as their divergent perspectives. The examination and review of critical thinking models reinforce the rationale for further research. The convolution in reaching an agreed understanding of the nature of critical thinking, creative thinking, decision making, problem solving and higher order of thinking is acknowledged. It has been suggested that there is the need to harness all these aspects as instances of critical thinking.

In chapter two, a comprehensive review was also conducted on the various issues such as skills, dispositions, virtues, logic, epistemology, rationality, context, philosophy among others that emerged from the nature of critical thinking. We showed how critical thinking entails both skills/abilities and dispositions, that is, the reason assessment component and as well as the critical attitude or critical spirit. It was demonstrated that critical thinking involves thinking about epistemology, the study of how we know what we know, and even the study of whether we can know certain kinds of things. We pointed out that critical thinking also involves reasoning carefully about reason and rationality and generally philosophising about reason or reasoning. This was essential since these issues under debate were considered in order to fully understand critical thinking. Further, we identified and observed that these issues are key areas for further research. These observations and identifications of areas of research gaps we hope will open the way for new contributions and to further progress in the domain of critical thinking.

In chapter three, an overview of critical thinking, its origin, its deep roots coming from ancient, mediaeval, modern philosophers and its development in the 21st century was developed. Such a detailed treatment of the history of critical thinking highlights its necessity and importance.

In chapter four, we exposed and discussed in length the role of logic in critical thinking. We argued and demonstrated that critical thinking needs to involve not just the logic of arguments, the importance of distinguishing valid and invalid arguments; sound or unsound arguments; cogent or uncogent arguments or one's ability to analyze accurately empirical evidence. It also needs to be able to assess presuppositions and usage of language. Such a treatment was necessary for in understanding argument analysis one is a position to evaluate issues in all domains of knowledge.

A central role of critical thinking is the identification, exposure and avoidance of fallacies, a task undertaken in chapter five. The chapter explained what fallacies are and how to protect oneself from them. Fallacies are worth knowing and it is important to avoid them for these are types of arguments that appear convincing but are actually misleading and erroneous.

In chapter six, we explored various critical thinking theorists and their perspective on education. We were able to demonstrate that critical thinking is an educational ideal. Further, we argued and demonstrated the importance of critical thinking to students. In addition, we contended that critical thinking is a democratic ideal. Critical thinking is an important or even a legitimate, area of democracy. Especially noteworthy is the place of criticality in characterisation of democracy as a crucial component of the competence of citizens in order to participate in political society. We also demonstrated the crucial role of critical thinking in religion. In our view, there are three crucial reasons why critical thinking is essential to religions: 1) defending faith, 2) facilitates reasonable and rational talk about it to skeptics and antagonists, and most importantly 3) it enables identification and rejection of the many falsehoods and plenty of inaccuracies espoused in religions.

In summarizing this book, permit us to recapture some salient points of our expose.

First, we believe that there must be a solid understanding of what critical thinking means. The research we have done and as capture in this book, for instance, is by no means conclusive. However, we have begun to better understand what it means to become a critical thinker and we are certain that this will improve our practice of encouraging critical thinking to our students and other readers of this work. Ideally, there is the need to understand the nature of critical thinking that is, critical thinking instructors should recognize the conceptual importance of the critical thinking.

Second, educators must be critical thinkers themselves and must model students to be critical thinkers. Clearly, such a task is noble for critical thinking helps nurture rationality. This further means the movement to think and to express ideas, to an enriched freedom based of critical thinking skills/abilities and dispositions. In promoting critical thinking, increase the chances that our students will believe in their need to be critical thinkers, and thus strive to become contributors to the building of our collective critical society.

Third, if critical thinking is to be successfully implemented, it must be of a greater focus within the educational curriculum than it is presently. In our view, there is little regard or adequate concern for an effective superintendence of the primacy of critical thinking in educational curriculum.

Fourth, Critical thinking is a *conditio sine quo non* or at best *primus inter pares* for the definitive attainment of rational life. Critical thinking is ineluctability in every instantiation of education, politics, religion, multiculturalism and at best in all social arrangements. Clearly no society can survive meaningfully in the absence of fostering critical thinking skills/abilities and dispositions to its members.

The four points we have raised in this concluding chapter are important in creating an environment where critical thinking can be developed and nurtured in our students. The points are likely incomplete, but certainly they are a move towards the recognition of the importance and indispensability critical thinking and the need to foster the same.

SELECTED BIBLIOGRAPHY

Bailin, S & Battersby, M. (2016): *Reason in the Balance: An Inquiry Approach to Critical Thinking*, Cambridge: Hackett publishing Company, Inc.

Bailin, S., Case, R., Coombs, J., & Daniels, L. (1993): *A Conception of Critical Thinking for Curriculum, Instruction and Assessment.* Ministry of Education, Province of British Columbia.

Baron J.B. and Sternberg R.J. (Eds.) (1978): *Teaching thinking skills: Theory and practice.*

Barker, S. *Elements of Logic (5th Ed).* (1984), New York: Macmillan.

Beyer, B. (1987): *Practical Strategies for the Teaching of Thinking*, Boston: Allyn & Bacon.

Burbules, Nicholas C. (1993): *Dialogue in Teaching: Theory and Practice,* (New York: Teachers College).

Copi, I. M. and Cohen, C., (1994), *Introduction to Logic (9th Ed).* New York: Macmillan.

Descartes, René, *The Philosophical Writings of Descartes,* Vol. I, (1985), Trans. John Cottingham, Robert Stoothoff, Dugald Murdoch, and Antony Kenny (Cambridge: Cambridge University Press.

Ennis Robert (1996): *Critical Thinking,* Upper Saddle River, NJ: Prentice Hall.

Groarke, L. A. & Tindale, C. W. (2008): Good Reasoning Matters! A constructive approach to critical thinking. London: Oxford University Press.

Lawhead, William F., (2011), The Philosophical Journey: An Interactive Approach (5th Ed), New York: McGraw-Hill.

Layman, Stephen C. (2002): *The Power of Logic,* Boston: McGraw Hill Companies, Inc.

Lipman, M. (1991): Thinking in Education, New York: Cambridge University Press,

Mbiti, John S. *African Philosophy and Religions,* (1969). London: Heinemann Publishes.

Selected Bibliography

McPeck, J. E. 1981: Critical Thinking and Education. Oxford: Martin Robertson.

_____ 1990: Teaching Critical Thinking. Great Britain: Routledge.

Munson Ronald (1996): In Intervention and Reflection: Basic Issues in Medical Ethics (5th Ed), Belmont: Wadsworth Publishing Company.

Moore Brooke Noel and Parker Richard: Critical Thinking, 6th Ed. (2001). Boston: McGraw-Hill publishes.

Nigel Blake, Paul Smeyers, Richard Smith and Paul Standish (Eds) (2003): *The Blackwell Guide to the philosophy of Education*: Oxford: Blackwell Publishing

Norris, Stephen P. (1992): *The Generalizability of Critical Thinking*, New York: Teachers College Press.

Ochieng'-Odhiambo, F., *African Philosophy: An Introduction* (2002): Nairobi: Consolata Institute of Philosophy.

Paul, Richard (1990): *Critical Thinking: What Every Person Needs to Survive in a Rapidly Changing World* (Rohnert Park, CA: Center for Critical Thinking and Moral Critique.

Paul, R. & Elder, L. (2008), Critical *Thinking: Tools for Taking Charge of Your Learning and Your Life.* Pearson/Prentice Hall.

_____ (2010): *The Miniature Guide to Critical Thinking Concepts and Tools.* Dillon Beach: Foundation for Critical Thinking.

Rescher, Nicholas (1988): *Rationality: A Philosophical Inquiry into the Nature and Rationale of Reason,* Oxford: Clarendon Press of University Press.

Scheffler, Israel, (1960): | *The Language of Education,* Springfield, Ill.: Charles C. Thomas.

_____ (1965): *Conditions of Knowledge,* Chicago: Scott Foresman and Company.

_____ (1973): *Reason and Teaching,* New York: Bobbs-Merill.

_____ (1991): *In Praise of the Cognitive Emotions,* New York: Routledge.

Scott-Kakures, Dion and Castagnetto, Susan et al, *History of Philosophy*, (1993): New York: Harper Perennial publishers Inc.

Somerville John and Santoni Ronald E., (1963). *Social and Political Philosophy: Readings from Plato to Gandhi*, New York: Double Day.

Stumpf, Samuel E. *Socrates to Sartre: A History of Philosophy*, (1999). Boston: McGraw-Hill College.

Siegel, Harvey (1988): *Educating Reason: Rationality, Critical Thinking, and Education*, New York: Routledge.

_____(1997): *Rationality Redeemed? Further Dialogues on an Educational Ideal*, New York: Routledge.

_____(2017): *Education's Epistemology: Rationality, Diversity and Critical Thinking*, New York: Oxford University Press.

Talaska, Richard A. (1992): *Critical Reasoning in Contemporary Culture*, Albany: SUNY Press.

Teays Wanda (1996): *Second Thoughts: Critical Thinking from A Multicultural Perspective*. California: Mayfield publishes Company

Wiredu Kwasi (1980): Philosophy and African Culture, Cambridge: Cambridge University Press.

INDEX

A

abusive ad hominem 197
African philosophy 136, 137
African Philosophy 142, 191, 271, 272
allegory of the cave 103, 104, 116
Allegory of the Cave 104
ambiguity 74
  fallacies of 197
Ambiguity
  definition 1, 2, 3, 33, 40, 50, 56, 61, 62
  Definition 2
  fallacies of 153, 197, 205, 215, 216
  Fallacies of 197, 212
  in language 213, 253
Ancient Period 97
appeal to authority 19, 42, 239, 241
Appeal to authority 112
Appeal to Authority 201
appropriately 2, 225, 239, 261
appropriately be moved by reasons 14
appropriately moved by reason 2, 224
appropriately moved by reasons 2, 6, 11, 14, 70, 71, 80, 239
Appropriately moved by reasons 14
Aquinas 107, 108
arguments x, 1, 4, 5, 6, 21, 22, 37, 38, 40, 41, 43, 44, 45, 47, 51, 54, 60, 70, 77, 80, 83, 97, 98, 99, 100, 122, 143, 144, 146, 148, 149, 150, 151, 158, 159, 160, 162, 163, 165, 166, 172, 173, 183, 186, 187, 189, 190, 193, 195, 206, 207, 215, 216, 235, 237, 238, 239, 241, 242, 244, 247, 251, 255, 256, 268
  arguments forms 159, 165
Arguments 122, 144, 145, 146, 148, 149, 150, 158
Argumentum ad Hominem 197
  circumstantial ad hominem 197
  Circumstantial ad Hominem 198
  Tu quoque 197, 199
  Tu Quoque 199
argumentum ad ignorantiam 204
Argumentum ad Ignorantiam 203
Argumentum ad Misericordiam 202

argumentum ad populum
  Bandwagon 200
Argumentum ad Populum 200
Aristotelian logic 177, 183
Aristotelian Logic 182
Aristotle 105, 106, 107, 108, 109, 110, 111, 113, 114, 117, 118
assumptions 26, 28, 30, 31, 32, 33, 40, 48, 52, 104, 105, 119, 134, 197, 205, 207, 216, 228, 243, 244
Assumptions 205
Augustine, St 107

B

Bailin Sharon 73
begging the question 85, 86, 205, 206
  circular reasoning 36, 85, 205
Begging the question 207
Begging the Question 205
belief vii, 8, 9, 12, 14, 24, 25, 27, 70, 79, 80, 81, 82, 122, 194, 223, 224, 234, 237, 238, 258, 259, 260
Belief 79
bias 59, 60
  prejudices 16, 22, 23, 54, 61, 89, 116, 117, 134, 136, 139, 245
  race 134, 197, 198

C

categorical logic
  categorical syllogism 188, 189
Categorical logic 173
  categorical logic 276
  categorical proposition 167, 179
  categorical syllogism 173, 175, 182, 183, 184, 185, 187, 188, 189
  Categorical Syllogism 173, 182, 186
  Rules and Fallacies 187
  standard form 173, 175, 178, 182, 184, 185
  Standard Form 173
  Venn diagrams 175, 176, 179, 180, 184, 185
  Venn Diagrams 175
character traits 2, 4, 5, 10, 11, 13, 15, 62, 72, 83, 85, 87, 88, 97, 106, 216, 224, 227, 229, 237, 238
cogent 77, 149, 150, 190, 268
  inductive arguments 150, 151, 190
  Inductive arguments 149
  Inductive Arguments 148, 149
  uncogent arguments 77, 268

Uncogent Arguments 150
Cogent 150
Complex Question 207
Conclusion 145, 182, 190
Connie Missimer 71, 72, 89, 93, 96, 139, 140
context and critical thinking 87
creative and critical thinking 50
credibility of sources 19, 20, 28, 40, 61, 71, 112, 113
Credibility of sources 19
criterion 8, 11, 33, 112, 138, 207, 226
critical attitude 10, 12, 13, 71, 241, 269
  critical citizenry 255, 256, 262
  Critical citizenry 256
  democratic citizen 254
Critical Inquiry 39, 40
critical spirit 10
Customs 129, 130

D

decision making ix, 27, 40, 41, 53, 54, 55, 56, 57, 58, 62, 63, 69, 88, 89, 92, 242, 255, 262, 267
deductive arguments 148, 150, 151, 173
Deductive arguments 148
Deductive Arguments 148
definitions 156, 157
Definitions 156, 157
definitions of critical thinking 1, 69, 91
Definitions of Critical Thinking 2
democracy x, 57, 131, 136, 138, 215, 219, 232, 254, 255, 256, 257, 258, 260, 262, 268
  critical thinking and democracy 232, 256, 257
  Critical thinking and democracy 232
  Critical Thinking and Democracy 254
Democracy 208, 254
Dichotomy or Bifurcation 207
dilemma 167, 168, 169
  constructive 170, 171
  Constructive 167, 170
  destructive 170, 171
  Destructive 167, 171
disjunctive syllogism 166
Disjunctive Syllogism 166
dispositions 143, 145, 201, 216, 223, 224, 225, 227, 228, 229, 231, 232,

233, 234, 236, 237, 238, 239, 247, 248, 250, 253, 254, 255, 256, 257, 258, 259, 260, 261, 262
  of critical thinking 219, 220, 223, 224, 225, 226, 227, 228, 229, 230, 232, 233, 234, 235, 237, 238, 239, 241, 243, 244, 246, 247, 248, 249, 250, 251, 252, 253, 254, 255, 256, 257, 258, 260, 261, 262
  of democracy 136, 138, 256, 257, 258, 268
  of education 220, 221, 223, 224, 225, 226, 227, 228, 229, 230, 232, 235, 236, 238, 246, 247, 249, 251, 253, 255, 261
  of Education 263, 266
doctrine 1, 233
doctrine of 116
Dostoevsky 228
dream arguments 122
Dream Arguments 122

E

eccentricity 132, 133, 138
Eccentricity 132
education 97, 103, 113, 114, 117, 131, 136
  aims of education vii, 228, 229, 235, 249
  critical thinking and education 220, 225, 246, 248
  Critical Thinking and Education 246, 247, 263, 264, 265
  epistemic 8, 9, 79
  ideals 220, 221, 232, 233, 238
  relevance of critical thinking to education 235, 239, 260, 262
elements of thought 22, 26, 30
  elements of reasoning 22, 31
  Elements of Wellbeing 128
Elements of Thought 26
Ennis Robert 271
epistemology and critical thinking 82, 91, 248
equivocation 158
Equivocation 153, 158
ethics vii, 41, 99, 108, 110, 116, 201, 223, 225
  morals 133
eurocentricism
  Afrocentricism 136, 137
  equivocation 213, 214
  Equivocation 213
Eurocentricism 136

F

fair-mindedness 20, 21, 22, 23, 33, 43, 44, 61
Fair-mindedness 22, 23, 43

fallacies 153, 188, 190, 193, 194, 195, 196, 197, 212, 215, 216
  informal fallacies 196, 197, 215
  Informal Fallacies 196
  irrelevant premises 197
  Irrelevant Premises 197
  meaning 193
  Meaning 193
  of ambiguity 74, 153, 212, 216
  of Ambiguity 212
  of presumption 197, 205, 215
  of Presumption 205
Fallacies 187, 195, 196, 215, 216
FALLACIES 193
fallacious reasoning 193, 194, 195, 201, 216
Fallacious reasoning 194
fallacy
  red herring 212
Fallacy
  biased statistics 212
  Biased Statistics 212
  false analogy 207
  False Analogy 207
  False Dilemma 208
  Red herring 211
  straw man 211
  Straw Man 211
fallacy of accident 210
fallacy of amphiboly 214
fallacy of division 215
fallacy of equivocation 213, 214
fallacy of false cause 208
  Non causa pro causa 208
  Oversimplified cause 208, 209
  Post hoc, ergo propter hoc 208
Fallacy of False Cause 208
fallacy of hasty generalization 209, 210
fallacy of irrelevant conclusion 204
Fallacy of misleading vividness 212
fallibilism 9, 41, 42, 80, 82, 99, 105, 111, 112, 249
Fallibilism 99
false analogy 207

felt reasons   14, 86, 238
Felt reasons   238
Francis bacon   113
Francis Bacon   96, 110, 113
Frisco   19
FRISCO   15, 16, 19, 20, 57
Fyodor Dostoyevsky   259

G

Galileo Galilei   110, 112, 118
generalist   73, 74, 75
Generalist   73
  specifist   73, 74, 75
  Specifist   73
  specifists   75
genius   123, 131, 132, 133
Genius   131
geocentric   110, 111, 201
  heliocentric   110, 111, 201

H

habits of mind   2, 4, 5, 10, 11, 13, 15, 23, 43, 58, 61, 62, 196, 216, 224, 227, 229, 255
  character traits   4, 10, 11, 13, 15, 62, 83, 88
  dispositions   vii, ix, 2, 4, 5, 10, 11, 12, 13, 14, 15, 17, 18, 19, 21, 22, 32, 33, 35, 36, 37, 38, 39, 44, 45, 56, 58, 61, 62
  Dispositions   4
Habits of mind
  tendencies   4, 10, 14, 17, 33, 36, 54, 58, 59, 61, 62, 76, 114
harm principle   125
  self-protection   125, 126
Harvey Siegel   2, 5, 38, 78, 254
high order thinking   53, 58, 62, 69, 88, 89
hypostatisation   215
Hypothetical syllogism   166

I

ideals   233
Ignoratio Elenchi   204
immediate inferences   178
  Contraposition   181
  Conversion   181
  Obversion   181
Immediate Inferences   181
indoctrination   136, 221, 233, 234, 237, 261

Indoctrination 28, 233
inductive arguments 150, 151, 190
Inductive arguments 149
Inductive Arguments 148, 149
informal fallacies 196, 197
Informal Fallacies 196
informal fallacy
  Argumentum ad Baculum 199
inquiry 3, 34, 40, 41, 42, 43, 44, 49, 50, 51, 58, 60, 63
Inquiry 39, 41, 42, 43, 57
intellectual traits 22, 23
  intellectual virtues 13, 22, 23, 32, 45, 75, 76
  Intellectual virtues 76
  Intellectual Virtues 22, 75
Intellectual Traits 22
Israel Scheffler 219, 220, 254, 256, 261, 263

J

John McPeck 1, 3, 35, 71, 73, 246
John S. Mbiti 136, 138, 142
John Stuart Mill 95, 125, 134
justification of rationality 85, 86

K

Ken Robinson 253, 261
Kwasi Wiredu 95, 136, 137, 142

L

language 29, 40, 42, 103, 108, 116, 117, 119, 136, 151, 153, 154, 156, 157, 159, 173, 194, 196, 210, 211, 213, 216, 259, 268
  ambiguity 151, 152, 153, 156, 157, 170
  Ambiguity 151, 152, 153
  and logic vii, 19, 37, 77, 244, 247
  Cognitive and Emotive Functions 151
  euphemism 153, 154
  loaded 21, 28, 151, 153, 211
  Loaded 155
  vagueness 74, 135, 151, 152, 153, 156, 157
  Vagueness 151
Language 151
liberty 125, 126, 127, 128, 129, 131, 133, 134
Liberty 125
  civil or social liberty 125
  of thought and discussion 127
logic 245, 247, 248, 253

basic concepts 144, 150
Basic Concepts 144
logic and critical thinking iii, 104, 143, 247
relevance of critical thinking 219, 234, 244, 251, 254, 256, 258
RELEVANCE OF CRITICAL THINKING 219
Logic 248

M

Mathew Lipman 1, 3, 33, 63, 66, 67, 71, 249, 261, 265
Matthew Lipman 265
medieval period 108, 116, 117
Medieval Period 107
minimum competence testing 234, 235
Missing the point (ignoratio elenchi)
    ignoratio elenchi 204, 205
Missing the Point (Ignoratio Elenchi) 204
modern period 107, 108, 117
modus ponens 172
Modus Ponens 165
modus tollens 171, 172
Modus Tollens 166

N

necessary and sufficient conditions 10
Necessary and sufficient conditions 160
Necessary and Sufficient Conditions 160
Nicolaus Copernicus 109, 110, 112, 118
normative conceptualization 1, 2
Normative Conceptualization 1

O

observation 19, 20, 99, 109, 110, 114, 116, 130, 222, 230, 250
Observation 20
obstacles to critical thinking 59, 62, 115, 116, 244
Obstacles to Critical Thinking 58
Ochieng'-Odhiambo 137, 142, 272

P

petitio principii 205
Petitio principii 205
Petitio Principii 205
philosophy 17, 41, 78, 87, 89, 90, 91, 92
Philosophy 63, 64, 66, 67, 90, 92, 94
Plato 99, 100, 103, 104, 105, 107, 108, 114, 135
Plato's dialogues 156

Plato's Dialogues 100, 103
  Apology 100, 101, 103, 202
  Crito 100, 103, 170
  Euthyphro 100, 158, 169
  Meno 100, 101, 103
Post Aristotelian Thought 106
prejudice 59, 89, 136
premise 20, 144, 145, 146, 148, 149, 165, 182, 183, 188, 189, 233
Premise 145
pre-socratic philosophers 98, 99
probative force 143
probative forces 7, 22, 40, 193, 216
problem of evil 107, 171, 259
problem solving ix, 27, 40, 41, 53, 54, 55, 58, 62, 63, 69, 88, 89, 92, 123, 267
proposition 36, 146, 167, 183, 211, 238
Proposition 146
  statement 35, 146, 248
  Statement 146
Ptolemy 41, 110
  Ptolemaic system 110
putative forces 144, 145, 190

R

rationality theory of teaching 236, 237, 238
rational passions 13
reason assessment component 6, 7, 8, 9, 10, 11, 12, 13, 14, 61, 74, 75, 76, 77, 224, 233, 267
reasoned judgement 3, 40, 42, 44, 242
Reasoned judgement 42
reasons conception 2, 5, 9, 13, 14, 47, 75
Reasons Conception 5, 62
relevance of critical thinking 219, 234, 235, 239, 244, 251, 254, 256, 258, 260
  relevance of critical thinking to democracy 254
  relevance of critical thinking to education 235, 239, 260, 262
  relevance of critical thinking to religion 258
RELEVANCE OF CRITICAL THINKING 219
renaissance 108, 113, 117
Renaissance 107, 108, 109, 113
Rene Descartes 27
Richard Paul and Elder Linda 55, 243
Robert Ennis 1, 2, 15, 18, 51, 56

S

Scepticism 36, 99
Sharon Bailin and Mark Battersby 3, 261
skills 95, 96, 99, 104, 105, 106, 108, 112, 113, 119, 124, 130, 134, 137, 139
skills/abilities and dispositions 95, 96, 99, 106, 112, 113, 119, 124, 134, 139
skill view 72
Skill View 72, 97
society 220, 229, 230, 254, 255, 256, 257, 258, 262, 268, 269
Socrates 17, 25, 99, 100, 101, 102, 103
Sound and Unsound Arguments 148
spirit of inquiry 40, 43, 44, 60, 61, 195
Spirit of Inquiry 39, 43, 59
square of opposition 177, 178, 179, 180
  modern square of opposition 179
Square of Opposition 177
standards of reasoning 30, 31
  intellectual standards 22, 30
  standards of thought 1
Standards of Reasoning 30
strong sense critical thinking 20, 21, 55
Strong sense critical thinking 21
subject-neutral principles 6, 9, 77
subject-specific principles 6, 7

T

teachings 108, 109, 114
  Bailin and Education 239
  conceptions of 70
  manner of teaching 72, 225, 243, 261
  Robinson on "Do Schools Kill Creativity?" 253
  Scheffler's Reason in Teaching 220
  Siegel and Critical Thinking as an Educational Ideal 223
  Strong Sense Critical Thinking for Education 243
  thinking in education 53, 228, 243, 246, 249, 269
  Thinking in Education 63, 66, 67, 219, 249, 271
tendencies 4, 10, 54, 216
  character traits 4, 5, 10
  dispositions 56, 58, 61, 62
  habits of mind 2, 4, 62
the nature of critical thinking 1, 35, 39, 42, 62
  as inquiry 53, 78, 249

as Inquiry 54
  as skills 17, 72, 75, 76, 96, 134, 223, 256, 259
  as Skills 70
  as skills view 96
  community of inquiry 34, 51, 250, 251
  Community of inquiry 251
  Community of Inquiry 51
  definition ix, 69, 70, 72, 91, 100, 157, 158, 250, 260, 267
  Definition 157, 158
  definitions 1, 69, 91, 156, 157, 158, 159, 162, 222, 244, 267
  Definitions 156, 157, 158
  domain-specific 35, 36, 39, 73, 75, 248
  Domain-Specific 35
  FRISCO 15, 16, 17, 19, 20, 57
  reasons conception account 5, 11, 12, 14, 47, 58, 74, 76, 81, 91, 224
  Reasons Conception account 62
  strong sense critical thinker 22, 32, 99
  strong sense critical thinking 3, 20, 21, 22, 23, 55, 59, 243, 244
  Strong sense critical thinking 21, 244
  Strong Sense Critical Thinking 20, 243
  Tripartite View 33
THE NATURE OF CRITICAL THINKING 1
  truth 8, 21, 27, 36, 40, 41, 42, 44, 79, 80, 81
  Truth 80
    U
universalism 89
    V
v
  Contraposition 182
valid argument forms
  deductive arguments 148, 151
  Deductive arguments 148
  Deductive Arguments 148
Valid Argument Forms 165
value of inquiry 42
variety 2, 4, 13, 23, 29, 34, 38, 39, 59, 235, 238, 252, 254
    W
weak sense critical 21, 32, 59, 99

www.ingramcontent.com/pod-product-compliance
Lightning Source LLC
Chambersburg PA
CBHW030821230426
43667CB00008B/1319